A DOVE TO THE LAND OF WAR

Peter van 't Riet

A Dove to
the Land of War

*The Book of Jonah
Translated Word for Word and Explained*

FOLIANTI – KAMPEN

Since the days of the *esprit critique* we are stuck with a twofold rationalistic approach of the Bible which rejects (the) *haggadah* just like that:

- The historic-critical approach – a continuation of the *esprit critique* at the verge of the 17th and 18th century – all the time dividing the sources while seeking the historic facts, and in doing so robbing the biblical documents of their haggadic elements, as if they were a kind of non-historic ballast, and going right against it;
- The biblicistic-fundamentalistic approach, frenetically attempting to prove, that all what is in fact *haggadah*, is not 'fictitious', but 'historically true', 'it's really happened'.

In both approaches a rationalistic blindness is revealed to the meaning of the *haggadah* in the message of the Bible.

Dr. Rudolf Boon, in: *Hebreeuws Reveil*. (English: *Hebrew Revival*).

Original title in Dutch: Als een duif naar het land van de oorlog
© Folianti, Zwolle, The Netherlands 2009 (2nd revised printed edition)

© Folianti, Kampen, The Netherlands 2018 (paperback edition)
Translated into English by Dick Broeren Sr

ISBN/EAN: 978-90-76783-47-5
NUR-code: 703 (Bible Sciences)

All rights reserved. Nothing in this publication is allowed to be multiplied, stored in an automated database and/or published, in any form, or in any way, neither electronically, nor mechanically, by press, photocopies, microfilm, records or in what way ever, without preliminary and written permission given by the publisher.

Content

Content 5

Preface 7

1   Was this not my word? 9
A word for word translation of the Book of Jonah 9
    1.1   Introduction to the translation 9
    1.2   Translation of the Book of Jonah 12

2   The second time, saying 21
The literary character of the Book of Jonah 21
    2.1   A remarkable book 21
    2.2   The use of word stems 23
    2.3   Linguistic usage 25
    2.4   Style and narrative technique 28
    2.5   Structures in the text 30
    2.6   The composition of the Book of Jonah 34
    2.7   The character of the Book of Jonah 34

3   Tell us 38
The Book of Jonah as Midrash 38
    3.1   Jonah in canon and liturgy 38
    3.2   The Book of Jonah and the Torah (Genesis in particular) .. 41
    3.3   Jonah and the prophets (especially Elijah) 45
    3.4   The Book of Jonah as midrash 49
    3.5   Nineveh, that big city 50
    3.6   Jonah, the dove 62
    3.7   Summary and preview 65

4   And call against her 66
The ethics of the Book of Jonah 66
    4.1   Jonah, Tanakh and the nations of the world 66
    4.2   Jonah, Ezra-Nehemiah and the Persian Empire 70
    4.3   Jonah, the rabbis and proselytism 74

Content

    4.4   From seer to prophet 77
    4.5   Jonah and the Jewish-biblical feasts 82

5 By the decree of the king and his big ones 92
The Book of Jonah in its time 92
    5.1   The time of the origin of the Book of Jonah 92
    5.2   From Assyria to Persia: the Babylonian Exile 97
    5.3   The political situation in the Persian age 106
    5.4   The Book of Jonah and the Persian empire 117
    5.5   Summary and conclusions 123

6 And he goes down 125
Annotations to Jonah 1:1-16 125

7 Out of the belly of Sheol 159
Annotations to Jonah 2:1-11 (1:17-2:10) 159

8 Who knows He turns around 176
Annotations to Jonah 3:1-10 176

9 And I, wouldn´t I have pity on Nineveh? 188
Annotations to Jonah 4:1-11 188

10 What shall we do to you? 202
Updating the Book of Jonah 202

Appendix 1 – Word stems and their translation 207
Appendix 2 – Literary relationship between the chapters 210

Notes 213
Literature 223

Preface

When in 1986 the first edition of this book was published with the title *A dove to the land of Assur* it wasn't immediately obvious to all readers that with *Assur* the 'land of war' was meant. That was the reason why I have chosen the title *A dove to the land of war* for the republication in 2015.

The first 1986 edition was published under the names of Will J. Barnard and the present writer. Will J. Barnard had become my teacher and friend since my wife and I attended his house of study from halfway through the seventies of the 20th century in Bussum (The Netherlands). In 1979 he got a cerebral hemorraghe and couldn't write any longer. But what I wrote he was able – more or less – to read and to provide with some comments for better or worse. Out of respect for this and because I was allowed to use his notes and library, I published my books in the eighties under both our names. Will Barnard died in 1993. When, almost thirty years later, in 2015, the revised edition appeared, I published the book under my own name to indicate that I'm entirely responsible for the present text.

In fact this book consists of two parts. The first five chapters deal with a general introduction to the Book of Jonah, and are followed by four chapters with a verse by verse commentary which regularly refers to the introducing chapters. And finally there is a short chapter in which I have written down some thoughts on the question how a book of the Bible as Jonah could and/or couldn't be actualized today.

With this book I'd like to explain the Book of Jonah both from the Tanakh (the Old Testament) and from the rabbinic tradition, and this from the context of the days when the Book of Jonah was written. In doing so, I won't read the text in a historicizing way, but in a literal and cultural-historical way. Because I think that only on the basis of such an approach we could discuss the meaning of Jonah.

I do not intend to write an extensive, scientific commentary on the Book of Jonah. Only some scientific issues which, to my mind, are important for the understanding of the Book of Jonah, I dealt with within the text or in the notes and glosses. For example I mention the question whether the prayer of Jonah in Jonah 2 has ever belonged to the original text of the book, or has only been added later. Besides

Preface

there are the questions of the historical context of the book and of the widespread notion that the Book of Jonah was supposed to go contrary to the alleged narrow religious nationalism of Ezra and Nehemiah. However, comprehensiveness in the representation of the scientific discussion of these and other questions has not been my intention and I have only added a limited amount of literature for this republication.

I'd like to make some remarks of a technical character. Though the translator and I have made an own translation in English of the Book of Jonah, one could regularly sense the influence of the (R)KJV in the discussion of the Jonah story. In general we have also used this translation to quote from other books of the Bible. But now and then we did modernize and/or adapt the English of the (R)KJV to modern theological views.

In addition I'd like to observe that there exist two different divisions into verses in Jonah 2. In some translations Jonah 1 has seventeen verses and Jonah 2 ten. In the Hebrew however Jonah ends with verse 16 and Jonah 2 has eleven verses. In this book I use the Hebrew division, but now and then I'll add the other division in brackets.

Finally I'd like to express my gratitude for the help I'd had in making the first edition of the late Will J. Barnard of blessed memory (see above), of the late Thomas Snijders MA of blessed memory, with his many instructions about the translation of the Hebrew text of the Book of Jonah into Dutch, and of the late dr. Willem H. Zuidema of blessed memory, with his corrections and critical remarks about the first three chapters of this book.

My special thanks for this English edition are for Dick Broeren Sr who analysed the text and translated it into English. We discussed a great deal about parts of the text – a very agreeable experience – which contributed to the clarification of yet indistinct passages in the original. With this translation we hope to contribute to a wider spread of knowledge about and a better understanding of the Book of Jonah.

Autumn 2018   Peter van 't Riet

1 Was this not my word?

A word for word translation of the Book of Jonah

1.1 Introduction to the translation

If you want to look at a Book of the Bible, especially so if you're after a serious exegesis, the text of the book itself will be the first issue. And when it's a small and condensed book like the Book of Jonah, careful research of the text is imperative. And then you'll have to face the problem of anyone who uses another language than the language of the source text, Hebrew. Thus this text should be translated before we'll be able to speak and write sensibly in English about Jonah. That's why I begin my discussion of the book with a chapter dealing with the translation.

In the next section I present a translation of Jonah of my own hand. Perhaps you'll wonder why. After all, there are many English translations available of this small book of the Bible, aren't there? That is correct. And yet I thought to tackle the the job myself because most translations show clearly that many characteristics of the Hebrew text are, indeed, lost in translation! The sentence structure, the wording, the metaphors of Hebrew, all this and a lot more is usually lost when the source text is rendered into modern English. Sometimes translations can even be misleading for those who want to try to understand the original text. I'll give some examples to illustrate the above claim.

In the Hebrew-English Tanakh[1] (= Hebrew Bible) we find in Jonah 1:3: "He **went down** to Joppa and found a ship … and he **went aboard**." The words in bold type are two different translations of one and the same Hebrew verb form *wajéired*, which means "and he goes down."[a] In this way the image of someone or something "going down" gets lost completely in the translation. One wonders why it isn't translated with: "And he **went down** to Joppa and found a ship … and he **went down** in it." A clear example of how the characteristic imagery of the Bible story is violated in the translation.

---

[a] See for the use of the present tense in my translation the explanation below in this section.

Not only the metaphorical language gets often lost in translations. The Hebrew sentence structure too, can hardly ever be reproduced in properly running, modern English. For instance in Hebrew the verb is usually put before the subject and the direct object. The Hebrew sentence usually begins with the verb, contrary to an English sentence which, in general, begins with a subject. Consequently the Hebrew text looses a lot of its dynamics, as can be seen in the next two translations of Jonah 1:1.

Current translation	Word for word translation
Now the word of the LORD came unto Jonah, the son of Amittai:	And (it) occurs a word of Adonai to Jonah, son of Amitai

The common English translation changes the Hebrew word for 'and' into 'now' and gives the subject 'the word of the LORD' next. The action that is going to be performed is still to come. Therefore the word of Adonai is introduced as a static subject. When next the verbal form is mentioned, the subject begins to move, starting from a situation of rest. Thus this movement starts slowly. Because of the close link with 'occurs', the word 'to' hardly contributes to the continuation of this movement. As soon as we end up at 'Jonah, son of Amitai', the movement comes to a halt. Which action the word to Jonah is going to perform ("to say"), isn't mentioned in the translation at all.

This is different in the word for word translation in the next section, which follows the word order of Hebrew, which produces 'strange' English, but may be read as a poem. Yet before we realize, who or what we're dealing with, the action begins: "And it occurs." As soon as the subject "a word of Adonai" is introduced, the action is there, in abundance. Consequently the word of Adonai is experienced immediately as a dynamically active force. The preposition 'to' in the part "to Jonah, son of Amitai" causes the movement not to stall, but to go on harmonically with the action proper "saying." By keeping this word order in the translation, we get a story with a lot of dynamics, a tension and a tempo which prosaical English won't be able to lend. That's why I've tried to maintain the Hebrew word order in my translation of the Book of Jonah as much as possible, even of it goes counter to English grammar.

Finally a third example which shows that we have to be cautious with some translations of the Book of Jonah. Not only many distinctive features of the original text are translated 'away'. From time to time unwished-for elements are added to the story in the translation, which influence reading it. That is for instance the case in the NET Bible in Jonah 1:7, where the men of the ship in the storm say to one another: "… to find out whose fault it is that this disaster has overtaken us." In Jonah 1:8 and 12, also in the NET Bible we find the word 'fault' as well. So the reader may get the impression that a fault has been made, but the Hebrew text doesn't have this word 'fault'. The text says something like 'by whom' or better even 'concerning whom'. Not only the question of someone's fault is left aside, but also the question *whose* fault it was is not answered. The usual translation too easily takes for granted that it is Jonah's 'fault'. But very probably the ship's crew sooner thought about a god who'd sent them a storm, for whatever reason!²

So there are reasons enough to make an own translation of the Book of Jonah before giving a further explanation. In the translation of the next section I have tried to fit in as much as possible with the original in this way: in the first place the words have been reproduced in the same order as in Hebrew, apart from a single exception. In the second place I added some words now and then which have no equivalent in de Hebrew text. Sometimes words like that can't be avoided to get a reasonable English sentence, more or less, even though that sentence could look more like poetry than prose. These added word are put between round brackets: (…). And of course, I have tried to avoid inaccurate interpretations. In the third place I've translated Hebrew words and words derived from a selfsame Hebrew stem as much as possible with an identical English word or with one of its conjugations. For instance, I've always translated the Hebrew word *ra'ah* with 'evil' and not as is the case, in many English translations with 'fury', or 'calamity', or other words. Therefore it is possible to examine and compare, by means of the translation, the specific use of words in de various chapters of the Book of Jonah. However, I couldn't be completely consistent, as I wanted to avoid deviating too much from a translation that can be understood without too many problems. In Appendix 1 at the end of this book a list is printed of those Hebrew stems which occur twice or more in Jonah, together with the translated English words, chosen by me.

Nevertheless, many features of the Hebrew text couldn't be mirrored back, even in my translation. In the verse for verse commentary in the chapters 6 to 9 I'll give more information occasionally about the Hebrew words and about the translation chosen by me. In that case too, the original Hebrew text is referred to regularly. By trying to fit in as closely as possible with the original text, I wanted to make the references to the Hebrew language as accessible as possible.

At the end of this section I'd like to go into a not unimportant issue with regards to the translation. For the Hebrew language doesn't know tenses like our modern Western European languages do. The Hebrew verb has two kinds of conjugation: the prefix conjugation with prefixes added to the front (I'll call them the "imperfect tenses") and the suffix conjugation with suffixes added to the back (the so-called "perfect tenses"). In general the imperfect tense indicates a continuing process. By contrast the perfect tense usually indicates a completed action or a more or less permanent situation. This means that the Book of Jonah should not necessarily be translated in the past tense, as is usually done. Therefore I have chosen the present tense for my translation, not suggesting this to could be a better translation, but to show – as a contrast to the usual translation – that it doesn't matter at all, perfect tense or not. So I have not systematically made a distinction between Hebrew verb forms in the perfect or imperfect tense, but have chosen the English verb forms dependent on the context of the story.

1.2   Translation of the Book of Jonah

You'll find the text of the Book of Jonah below. The Hebrew text is on the left, and on the right the word for word translation.

JONAH 1:1-16

א וַיְהִי, דְּבַר-יְהוָה, אֶל-יוֹנָה בֶן-אֲמִתַּי, לֵאמֹר.   1 And (then) occurs a word of Adonai to Jonah, son of Amitai, to say:

WORD FOR WORD TRANSLATION

ב קוּם לֵךְ אֶל-נִינְוֵה, הָעִיר הַגְּדוֹלָה--וּקְרָא עָלֶיהָ: כִּי-עָלְתָה רָעָתָם, לְפָנָי.

2 "Rise up, go to Nineveh, that city, the big one, and call against her, for up comes their evil to my face."

ג וַיָּקָם יוֹנָה לִבְרֹחַ תַּרְשִׁישָׁה, מִלִּפְנֵי יְהוָה; וַיֵּרֶד יָפוֹ וַיִּמְצָא אֳנִיָּה בָּאָה תַרְשִׁישׁ, וַיִּתֵּן שְׂכָרָהּ וַיֵּרֶד בָּהּ לָבוֹא עִמָּהֶם תַּרְשִׁישָׁה, מִלִּפְנֵי, יְהוָה.

3 And up rises Jonah to flee towards Tarsis away from before the face of Adonai. And down he goes to Jaffo and he happens upon a ship (there), going to Tarsis. And he gives the fare thereof and down he goes into it, to go with them towards Tarsis away from before the face of Adonai.

ד וַיהוָה, הֵטִיל רוּחַ-גְּדוֹלָה אֶל-הַיָּם, וַיְהִי סַעַר-גָּדוֹל, בַּיָּם; וְהָאֳנִיָּה, חִשְּׁבָה לְהִשָּׁבֵר.

4 And Adonai throws a wind, a (very) big one, towards the sea. And (then) occurs a storm, a (very) big one, in the sea and the ship reckons to be wrecked.

ה וַיִּירְאוּ הַמַּלָּחִים, וַיִּזְעֲקוּ אִישׁ אֶל-אֱלֹהָיו, וַיָּטִלוּ אֶת-הַכֵּלִים אֲשֶׁר בָּאֳנִיָּה אֶל-הַיָּם, לְהָקֵל מֵעֲלֵיהֶם; וְיוֹנָה, יָרַד אֶל-יַרְכְּתֵי הַסְּפִינָה, וַיִּשְׁכַּב, וַיֵּרָדַם.

5 And afraid are the mariners and they cry out, (every) man to his god, and they throw the tools that (are) in the ship into the sea to lighten itself of them. And Jonah has gone down into the sides of the ship and he has lain down and is fast asleep.

ו וַיִּקְרַב אֵלָיו רַב הַחֹבֵל, וַיֹּאמֶר לוֹ מַה-לְּךָ נִרְדָּם; קוּם, קְרָא אֶל-אֱלֹהֶיךָ--אוּלַי יִתְעַשֵּׁת הָאֱלֹהִים לָנוּ, וְלֹא נֹאבֵד.

6 And (then) comes to him the master of the rigging and he says to him: "What('s the matter) with you, who is so fast asleep! Rise up, call to your god, perhaps he will change his mind – that god – about us and not we shall perish.

Word for Word Translation

ז וַיֹּאמְרוּ אִישׁ אֶל-רֵעֵהוּ, לְכוּ וְנַפִּילָה גוֹרָלוֹת, וְנֵדְעָה, בְּשֶׁלְּמִי הָרָעָה הַזֹּאת לָנוּ; וַיַּפִּלוּ, גּוֹרָלוֹת, וַיִּפֹּל הַגּוֹרָל, עַל-יוֹנָה.

7 And they say, (each) man to his fellow: "Let us go and let us cast lots and we may know for whose cause this evil, this one, (is) upon us." And they cast lots and (then) falls the lot on Jonah.

ח וַיֹּאמְרוּ אֵלָיו--הַגִּידָה-נָּא לָנוּ, בַּאֲשֶׁר לְמִי-הָרָעָה הַזֹּאת לָנוּ: מַה-מְּלַאכְתְּךָ, וּמֵאַיִן תָּבוֹא--מָה אַרְצֶךָ, וְאֵי-מִזֶּה עַם אָתָּה.

8 And they say to him: "Tell, we pray, to us for whose cause this evil (is) upon us. What (is) your mission and where are you going to? What is your country and of what people are you?"

ט וַיֹּאמֶר אֲלֵיהֶם, עִבְרִי אָנֹכִי; וְאֶת-יְהוָה אֱלֹהֵי הַשָּׁמַיִם, אֲנִי יָרֵא, אֲשֶׁר-עָשָׂה אֶת-הַיָּם, וְאֶת-הַיַּבָּשָׁה.

9 And he says to them: "A Hebrew (man) (am) I, and Adonai, God of the heavens, I fear (Him), who makes the sea and the dry land."

י וַיִּירְאוּ הָאֲנָשִׁים יִרְאָה גְדוֹלָה, וַיֹּאמְרוּ אֵלָיו מַה-זֹּאת עָשִׂיתָ: כִּי-יָדְעוּ הָאֲנָשִׁים, כִּי-מִלִּפְנֵי יְהוָה הוּא בֹרֵחַ--כִּי הִגִּיד, לָהֶם.

10 And (then) fear the men a fear (very) big and they say to him: "What (is) this (now that) you have made?" For (now) know the men that away from the face of Adonai he (is) fleeing, for he has told (it) to them.

יא וַיֹּאמְרוּ אֵלָיו מַה-נַּעֲשֶׂה לָּךְ, וְיִשְׁתֹּק הַיָּם מֵעָלֵינוּ: כִּי הַיָּם, הוֹלֵךְ וְסֹעֵר.

11 And they say to him: "What shall we do to you so that calm may be the sea unto us, for the sea (is) going and storming.

יב וַיֹּאמֶר אֲלֵיהֶם, שָׂאוּנִי וַהֲטִילֻנִי אֶל-הַיָּם, וְיִשְׁתֹּק הַיָּם, מֵעֲלֵיכֶם: כִּי, יוֹדֵעַ אָנִי, כִּי בְשֶׁלִּי, הַסַּעַר הַגָּדוֹל הַזֶּה עֲלֵיכֶם.

12 And he says to them: "Take me up and throw me into the sea, and calm will be the sea unto you, for knowing (am) I, that for my sake this storm, this big one, (is) upon you."

Word for Word Translation

יג וַיַּחְתְּרוּ הָאֲנָשִׁים, לְהָשִׁיב אֶל-הַיַּבָּשָׁה--וְלֹא יָכֹלוּ: כִּי הַיָּם, הוֹלֵךְ וְסֹעֵר עֲלֵיהֶם.

13 And hard row the men to turn around to the dry (land), and not (at all) they can (do it), for the sea (is) going and storming against them.

יד וַיִּקְרְאוּ אֶל-יְהוָה וַיֹּאמְרוּ, אָנָּה יְהוָה אַל-נָא נֹאבְדָה בְּנֶפֶשׁ הָאִישׁ הַזֶּה, וְאַל-תִּתֵּן עָלֵינוּ, דָּם נָקִיא: כִּי-אַתָּה יְהוָה, כַּאֲשֶׁר חָפַצְתָּ עָשִׂיתָ.

14 And (then) they call to Adonai and they say: "Oh, Adonai, not (at all) let us perish for the soul of this man (here), and not (at all) give upon us blood (that is) innocent, for You, Adonai, according to your wish You do."

טו וַיִּשְׂאוּ, אֶת-יוֹנָה, וַיְטִלֻהוּ, אֶל-הַיָּם; וַיַּעֲמֹד הַיָּם, מִזַּעְפּוֹ.

15 And up they take Jonah and they throw him towards the sea. And silent becomes the sea, from its raging.

טז וַיִּירְאוּ הָאֲנָשִׁים יִרְאָה גְדוֹלָה, אֶת-יְהוָה; וַיִּזְבְּחוּ-זֶבַח, לַיהוָה, וַיִּדְּרוּ, נְדָרִים.

16 And (then) fear the men a fear (very) big with regards to Adonai and they sacrifice a sacrifice to Adonai and they promise promises.

JONAH 2:1-11 (KJV 1:17 – 2:10)

א וַיְמַן יְהוָה דָּג גָּדוֹל, לִבְלֹעַ אֶת-יוֹנָה; וַיְהִי יוֹנָה בִּמְעֵי הַדָּג, שְׁלֹשָׁה יָמִים וּשְׁלֹשָׁה לֵילוֹת.

1 And (then) prepares Adonai a fish, a big (one), to swallow up Jonah. And it occurs: Jonah inside the fish, three days and three nights.

ב וַיִּתְפַּלֵּל יוֹנָה, אֶל-יְהוָה אֱלֹהָיו, מִמְּעֵי, הַדָּגָה.

2 And (then) prays Jonah to Adonai, his God, from inside the fish.

Word for Word Translation

ג וַיֹּאמֶר, קָרָאתִי מִצָּרָה לִי אֶל-יְהוָה--וַיַּעֲנֵנִי; מִבֶּטֶן שְׁאוֹל שִׁוַּעְתִּי, שָׁמַעְתָּ קוֹלִי.

3 And he says: "I call because of the affliction to me to Adonai and He answers me. Out of the belly of Sheol I shout for help, You hear my voice.

ד וַתַּשְׁלִיכֵנִי מְצוּלָה בִּלְבַב יַמִּים, וְנָהָר יְסֹבְבֵנִי; כָּל-מִשְׁבָּרֶיךָ וְגַלֶּיךָ, עָלַי עָבָרוּ.

4 And You cast me into the deep in the heart of the seas and the floods surround me. All Your wrecking billows and Your waves: over me they pass.

ה וַאֲנִי אָמַרְתִּי, נִגְרַשְׁתִּי מִנֶּגֶד עֵינֶיךָ; אַךְ אוֹסִיף לְהַבִּיט, אֶל-הֵיכַל קָדְשֶׁךָ.

5 And I, I say: "I am driven away from before Your eyes. Yet I will go on and look to the temple of Your holiness.

ו אֲפָפוּנִי מַיִם עַד-נֶפֶשׁ, תְּהוֹם יְסֹבְבֵנִי; סוּף, חָבוּשׁ לְרֹאשִׁי.

6 (They) encompass me, the waters, (even) to (my) soul, the depth surrounds me, the weeds are wrapped about my head.

ז לְקִצְבֵי הָרִים יָרַדְתִּי, הָאָרֶץ בְּרִחֶיהָ בַעֲדִי לְעוֹלָם; וַתַּעַל מִשַּׁחַת חַיַּי, יְהוָה אֱלֹהָי.

7 To the foundations of the mountains I go down, the earth with her bars blocking to me (access) to the world. And (then) You causes to go up from corruption my life, Adonai, my God.

ח בְּהִתְעַטֵּף עָלַי נַפְשִׁי, אֶת-יְהוָה זָכָרְתִּי; וַתָּבוֹא אֵלֶיךָ תְּפִלָּתִי, אֶל-הֵיכַל קָדְשֶׁךָ.

8 When faints in me my soul: Adonai I remember and (then) goes to You my prayer, to the temple of Your holiness.

ט מְשַׁמְּרִים, הַבְלֵי-שָׁוְא-- חַסְדָּם, יַעֲזֹבוּ.

9 They who observe worthless vanities: their kindness they forsake.

WORD FOR WORD TRANSLATION

• וַאֲנִי, בְּקוֹל תּוֹדָה אֶזְבְּחָה-לָּךְ, אֲשֶׁר נָדַרְתִּי אֲשַׁלֵּמָה: יְשׁוּעָתָה, לַיהוָה.	10 And I: with a voice of thanksgiving I will sacrifice to You. What I have promised I shall fulfil: salvation [is] of Adonai.
יא וַיֹּאמֶר יְהוָה, לַדָּג; וַיָּקֵא אֶת-יוֹנָה, אֶל-הַיַּבָּשָׁה.	11 And (then) says Adonai to the fish and it vomits (out) Jonah upon the dry land.

JONAH 3:1-10

א וַיְהִי דְבַר-יְהוָה אֶל-יוֹנָה, שֵׁנִית לֵאמֹר.	1 And it occurs – a word of Adonai – to Jonah the second time, to say:
ב קוּם לֵךְ אֶל-נִינְוֵה, הָעִיר הַגְּדוֹלָה; וּקְרָא אֵלֶיהָ אֶת-הַקְּרִיאָה, אֲשֶׁר אָנֹכִי דֹּבֵר אֵלֶיךָ.	2 "Rise up, go to Nineveh, that city, the big one, and call against her the calling that I word to you."
ג וַיָּקָם יוֹנָה, וַיֵּלֶךְ אֶל-נִינְוֵה-- כִּדְבַר יְהוָה; וְנִינְוֵה, הָיְתָה עִיר-גְּדוֹלָה לֵאלֹהִים--מַהֲלַךְ, שְׁלֹשֶׁת יָמִים.	3 And up rises Jonah, and he goes to Nineveh according to the word of Adonai. And Nineveh is a city, (very) big, before God with a going of three days.
ד וַיָּחֶל יוֹנָה לָבוֹא בָעִיר, מַהֲלַךְ יוֹם אֶחָד; וַיִּקְרָא, וַיֹּאמַר, עוֹד אַרְבָּעִים יוֹם, וְנִינְוֵה נֶהְפָּכֶת.	4 And (then) begins Jonah to go into the city by going a day, (only) one, and he calls and says: "Yet forty (times) a day and Nineveh shall be overthrown."
ה וַיַּאֲמִינוּ אַנְשֵׁי נִינְוֵה, בֵּאלֹהִים; וַיִּקְרְאוּ-צוֹם וַיִּלְבְּשׁוּ שַׂקִּים, מִגְּדוֹלָם וְעַד-קְטַנָּם.	5 And (then) trust the men of Nineveh in God. And they call a fast and put on sackcloth from their biggest (ones) and to their smallest (ones).

17

ו וַיִּגַּע הַדָּבָר, אֶל-מֶלֶךְ נִינְוֵה, וַיָּקָם מִכִּסְאוֹ, וַיַּעֲבֵר אַדַּרְתּוֹ מֵעָלָיו; וַיְכַס שַׂק, וַיֵּשֶׁב עַל-הָאֵפֶר.

6 And (then) comes the word to the king of Nineveh. And he rises up from his throne and he makes pass his robe from over him. And he covers (himself with) sackcloth, and he sits on the dust.

ז וַיַּזְעֵק וַיֹּאמֶר בְּנִינְוֵה, מִטַּעַם הַמֶּלֶךְ וּגְדֹלָיו, לֵאמֹר: הָאָדָם וְהַבְּהֵמָה הַבָּקָר וְהַצֹּאן, אַל-יִטְעֲמוּ מְאוּמָה--אַל-יִרְעוּ, וּמַיִם אַל-יִשְׁתּוּ.

7 And he causes (it) to be cried out, and to be said through Nineveh by the decree of the king and his big ones, saying: "The humans and the beasts, the cattle and the sheep, not (at all) they taste anything, not (at all) they feed, and the waters they shall not drink.

ח וְיִתְכַּסּוּ שַׂקִּים, הָאָדָם וְהַבְּהֵמָה, וְיִקְרְאוּ אֶל-אֱלֹהִים, בְּחָזְקָה; וְיָשֻׁבוּ, אִישׁ מִדַּרְכּוֹ הָרָעָה, וּמִן-הֶחָמָס, אֲשֶׁר בְּכַפֵּיהֶם.

8 And they cover themselves (with) sackcloth, the humans and the beasts, and they call to God with force. And they turn around, (each) man from his path of evil and from the violence that (is) in (the palm of) their hands.

ט מִי-יוֹדֵעַ יָשׁוּב, וְנִחַם הָאֱלֹהִים; וְשָׁב מֵחֲרוֹן אַפּוֹ, וְלֹא נֹאבֵד.

9 Who knows He turns around and He repents – this God – and (then) He turns around from the burning of his anger, and not we shall perish."

י וַיַּרְא הָאֱלֹהִים אֶת-מַעֲשֵׂיהֶם, כִּי-שָׁבוּ מִדַּרְכָּם הָרָעָה; וַיִּנָּחֶם הָאֱלֹהִים, עַל-הָרָעָה אֲשֶׁר-דִּבֶּר לַעֲשׂוֹת-לָהֶם--וְלֹא עָשָׂה.

10 And (then) sees this God their works, for they turn around from their path of evil. And (then) repents this God of the evil which He has worded to do to them and not (at all) He does (it).

WORD FOR WORD TRANSLATION

JONAH 4:1-11

א וַיֵּרַע אֶל-יוֹנָה, רָעָה גְדוֹלָה; וַיִּחַר, לוֹ.

1 And it causes evil to Jonah, an evil, (very) big, and it burns in him.

ב וַיִּתְפַּלֵּל אֶל-יְהוָה וַיֹּאמַר, אָנָּה יְהוָה הֲלוֹא-זֶה דְבָרִי עַד-הֱיוֹתִי עַל-אַדְמָתִי--עַל-כֵּן קִדַּמְתִּי, לִבְרֹחַ תַּרְשִׁישָׁה: כִּי יָדַעְתִּי, כִּי אַתָּה אֵל-חַנּוּן וְרַחוּם, אֶרֶךְ אַפַּיִם וְרַב-חֶסֶד, וְנִחָם עַל-הָרָעָה.

2 And he prays to Adonai and he says: "Oh, Adonai, was not this my word when I was on my soil? Because of that I hurried to flee towards Tarsis. For I know that You (are) a God, gracious and compassionate, slowly (becoming) angry and abundant in kindness, repenting of this evil.

ג וְעַתָּה יְהוָה, קַח-נָא אֶת-נַפְשִׁי מִמֶּנִּי: כִּי טוֹב מוֹתִי, מֵחַיָּי.

3 And now, Adonai, take please my soul from me, for good is my death over my life."

ד וַיֹּאמֶר יְהוָה, הַהֵיטֵב חָרָה לָךְ.

4 And (then) says Adonai: "Is it good (that) it burns to you?"

ה וַיֵּצֵא יוֹנָה מִן-הָעִיר, וַיֵּשֶׁב מִקֶּדֶם לָעִיר; וַיַּעַשׂ לוֹ שָׁם סֻכָּה, וַיֵּשֶׁב תַּחְתֶּיהָ בַּצֵּל, עַד אֲשֶׁר יִרְאֶה, מַה-יִּהְיֶה בָּעִיר.

5 And (then) leaves Jonah out of the city, and he sits down on the east side of the city and he makes for himself there a tabernacle. And he sits under it in the shadow till he sees what occurs to the city.

ו וַיְמַן יְהוָה-אֱלֹהִים קִיקָיוֹן וַיַּעַל מֵעַל לְיוֹנָה, לִהְיוֹת צֵל עַל-רֹאשׁוֹ, לְהַצִּיל לוֹ, מֵרָעָתוֹ; וַיִּשְׂמַח יוֹנָה עַל-הַקִּיקָיוֹן, שִׂמְחָה גְדוֹלָה.

6 And (then) prepares Adonai God a Kikayon and it comes up over Jonah to make it occur a shadow over his head to draw him away from his anger. And (then) rejoices Jonah about the Kikayon (with) a joy, (very) big.

Word for Word Translation

ז וַיְמַן הָאֱלֹהִים תּוֹלַעַת, בַּעֲלוֹת הַשַּׁחַר לַמָּחֳרָת; וַתַּךְ אֶת-הַקִּיקָיוֹן, וַיִּיבָשׁ.

7 And (then) prepares this God a worm when comes up the twilight the (next) morning. And it strikes the Kikayon and it withers.

ח וַיְהִי כִּזְרֹחַ הַשֶּׁמֶשׁ, וַיְמַן אֱלֹהִים רוּחַ קָדִים חֲרִישִׁית, וַתַּךְ הַשֶּׁמֶשׁ עַל-רֹאשׁ יוֹנָה, וַיִּתְעַלָּף; וַיִּשְׁאַל אֶת-נַפְשׁוֹ, לָמוּת, וַיֹּאמֶר, טוֹב מוֹתִי מֵחַיָּי.

8 And it occurs when up rises the sun. And (then) prepares God a wind from the east, a piercing (one). And (then) strikes the sun on the head of Jonah and he becomes faint and he requests his soul to die and he says: "Good (is) my death over my life."

ט וַיֹּאמֶר אֱלֹהִים אֶל-יוֹנָה, הַהֵיטֵב חָרָה-לְךָ עַל-הַקִּיקָיוֹן; וַיֹּאמֶר, הֵיטֵב חָרָה-לִי עַד-מָוֶת.

9 And (then) says God to Jonah: "Is it good that it burns to you because of the Kikayon?" And he says: "It is good that it burns to me towards my death."

י וַיֹּאמֶר יְהוָה--אַתָּה חַסְתָּ עַל-הַקִּיקָיוֹן, אֲשֶׁר לֹא-עָמַלְתָּ בּוֹ וְלֹא גִדַּלְתּוֹ: שֶׁבִּן-לַיְלָה הָיָה, וּבִן-לַיְלָה אָבָד.

10 And (then) says Adonai: "You, you have pity on the Kikayon for which not (at all) you have laboured, and (which) not (at all) you have caused to become big, which (like) a son of the night it has occured, and (like) a son of the night it has perished.

יא וַאֲנִי לֹא אָחוּס, עַל-נִינְוֵה הָעִיר הַגְּדוֹלָה--אֲשֶׁר יֶשׁ-בָּהּ הַרְבֵּה מִשְׁתֵּים-עֶשְׂרֵה רִבּוֹ אָדָם, אֲשֶׁר לֹא-יָדַע בֵּין-יְמִינוֹ לִשְׂמֹאלוֹ, וּבְהֵמָה, רַבָּה.

11 And I, (would)n't I have pity on Nineveh, that city, the big one, in which (there are) more than sixscore thousand humans that do not know (what is) between their right hand and their left hand, and (also) beasts, (very) many?"

2 The second time, saying

The literary character of the Book of Jonah

2.1 A remarkable book

Who reads the Book of Jonah for the first time, will inevitably get the impression of dealing with a curious and rather rambling story. Try to compare the main motives of the individual chapters and it is not immediately obvious how they relate:

- the storm at sea (Jonah 1);
- Jonah's staying in the belly of the fish (Jonah 2);
- the sudden turn-about of the entire population of a big city (Jonah 3);
- The squabble between Jonah and God, in which a tree, a worm and an easterly wind play such a peculiar part (Jonah 4).

They look like images sticking together like grains of sand, everyone of them.

Stranger yet becomes the story as soon as we're going to look at the details. Once the storm has broken with great violence, Jonah has apparently quietly gone to sleep, so the story tells (Jonah 1:5). At the beginning of the storm we read that the ship "reckons to be wrecked" (Jonah 1:4). How is it possible that after jettisoning the tools, after the conversations of the sailors among themselves and with Jonah, after casting the lots and after Jonah's "confession" there is, presumably, still enough time to row ashore (Jonah 1:13)? Why don't the men throw Jonah overboard immediately on his own advice (Jonah 1:12-13)?

In the prayer Jonah says in the belly of the fish (Jonah 2:3-10), not a single reference can be found to his stay on the ship, not even to him being in the fish! What does it mean that it's said in this prayer that Adonai threw Jonah into the sea (Jonah 2:4), and we know for sure that the crew did so (Jonah 1:15)? It's striking as well that Jonah already describes his salvation in this prayer and his journey to the temple afterwards, but at that moment he hasn't been saved yet

(Jonah 2:7b-8, 10)! Besides, in the second part of the book (Jonah 3 and 4) no attention at all is paid to what had happened in the storm and to his stay in the fish. God and Jonah could have talked about that, couldn't they (Jonah 4), they must have had ample opportunity! In spite of this, God doesn't enforce his arguments by referring to the storm and the fish. One could also wonder why the king of Nineveh needed to call a fast (Jonah 3:7). After all, the people of Nineveh had been fasting for some time now (Jonah 3:5). And why did God think it necessary to prepare a tree to overshadow Jonah's head, when Jonah had already built a tabernacle for the same end, shortly before that (Jonah 4:5-6)?

One gets the impression that the author of the Book of Jonah didn't deal too carefully with his material. These and other considerations made a lot of commentators doubt the literary unity of the Book of Jonah. Then they come up with a theory that the book could have been composed of different, originally independent stories.

On the other hand, various linguistic analyses show that the text of the Book of Jonah has been composed with great care. In spite of the great diversity of the motives used and the sometimes peculiar order of the events told, does the book show a great measure of literary unity. Only Jonah's prayer (Jonah 2:3-10) stands out as a text with a different character in many respects. That's why many commentators, who acknowledge the literary unity of Jonah 1, 3 and 4, keep seeing the prayer of Jonah as a later addition.[3] And indeed, at first sight the story runs on fluently when we leave out Jonah 2:3-10:

> "And (he) prays, Jonah, to Adonai, his God, from inside the fish. ... And (He) says, Adonai, to the fish and it vomits (out) Jonah upon the dry land."

In that case however, we could ask the question why Jonah should reach dry land again in this curious way. In other words: the contemplation taking place inside the fish in the form of a prayer, is highly suitable in the scope of the entire book and is psychologically seen the only right conclusion after the storm and its aftermath. After all, what would have been the meaning of Jonah's stay in the fish if this should not have ended in a searching contemplation of Jonah's on his own situation? If only on this ground, one could count the Psalm of Jonah to belong to the original text.

In the following sections I'll show something of the linguistic usage, the style, the narrative technique and the composition of the Book of Jonah. As it turns out, the deviating character of Jonah 2 can be explained from the fact that the prayer of Jonah is a song which especially describes feelings instead of actions and events. Finally I'd like to mention that if the Book of Jonah will be a well-considered book indeed – a view I adhere to – the thematic peculiarities should be explained by further study.

2.2 The use of word stems

Almost all words in Hebrew, whether they are nouns, adjectives, adverbs or verbforms have been derived from stems. These stems generally consist of three consonants and have verbal meanings, usually. So the original meaning, the etymon, of the stem *gimel-dalet-lamed* (G-D-L) is 'to be big'. By varying or changing the vowels between the consonants and sometimes adding one or more consonants before and/or after the stem or simply leaving them out, all sorts of different cognate words occur. For instance, *gadol* means 'big', whereas *jigdal* means 'he grows' or 'he becomes big'. Who studies the language of the Hebrew author, should not only pay attention to the use of the same words, but especially so to the use of the same stems. Already the Midrash of the first century CE draws our attention again and again to the fact that this form of repetition of cognate words within a certain part of the Bible is of great significance for the understanding of the text in question.[4]

Now, one of the most remarkable features of the Book of Jonah is that in this rather short text so many repetitions of stems occur. In the word for word translation in section 1.2 I have rendered the same or cognate Hebrew words as much as possible with an identical English word or English expression derived from an identical verb. The repetition of most of the words and stems in the Hebrew text could be checked (up) from the translation.[a] And then we'll find the following stems which occur six times or oftener in the text:

---

[a] See, in addition, the table in appendix 1.

- to say   22 tms
- to be big   15 tms
- to occur   10 tms
- to be evil   10 tms
- to call   9 tms
- to do/to make   8 tms
- to go   8 tms
- to word   7 tms
- to know   6 tms
- to fear   6 tms
- to rise up   6 tms

We're not talking here about normal numbers which can be shown by the stem 'to be big'. This happens only once in a verb form (Jonah 4:10) and fourteen times in the adjective 'big'. This can only be explained by the assumption that the author of the Book of Jonah wanted to provide the story with a certain tenor. Comparison with the texts of the other eleven minor prophets shows this clearly. Together they contain twenty times as much text as the Book of Jonah, but the adjective 'big' only happens twice as much, that is twenty-eight times. [5] So we could say that the author of the Book of Jonah has used the word 'big' ten times oftener than the authors of the other minor prophets together.

Besides the stems mentioned above many stems occur in the text of the Book of Jonah which are used less than six times, but which are, nevertheless, characteristic for the separate chapters. Examples are 'to throw' and 'to go down' in Jonah 1, 'to turn around' in Jonah 3 and 'to be good' in Jonah 4.

Moreover, with regard to the question of the literary unity of the Book of Jonah, it's important to consider in which way the various chapters tie in with their use of the same Hebrew stems. Observation shows that the Psalm of Jonah (2:3-10 in the Hebrew text) differs quite a lot, linguistically, from the other chapters. It uses its own specific language. In appendix 2 I mention a number of concerning arguments and facts. But we should consider that the Psalm differs from the other chapters in two ways:

1. The Psalm of Jonah does not consist of narrative prose, but is a prayer in the form of a poem;
2. The subject matter of this Psalm shows little or no connection with the themes in the other chapters.

With reference to this I'd like to mention that Jonah 1 and 4 also deviate quite a lot from one another as far as the use of stems is concerned.[a] And this is perhaps more peculiar than the differences with the Psalm of Jonah, for:

- Jonah 1 and 4 both show the literary form of narrative prose;
- Jonah 4:2 points back clearly to what has happened in 1:1-3;
- In both chapters some words are spent to Nineveh;
- God uses natural phenomena in both chapters.

Yet only a few people will, on this basis, doubt the fact that Jonah 1 and 4 both belonged to the original book. But this also implies that on the basis of the use of stems the Psalm of Jonah can't really be taken as something that doesn't belong in the Book of Jonah.

To sum up, my conclusion is that the use of stems points to the fact that in the Book of Jonah we're dealing with a literary composition in which word stems are used deliberately to give the story or parts of it a certain tendency. We can take it for granted that Jonah 1, 3 and 4 were written by one and the same author, but with regard to the second chapter further research will have to determine whether it should be reckoned to belong to the original book or not. And if so, which part the Psalm of Jonah plays in the frame of the whole story.

2.3 Linguistic usage

The linguistic usage of the Book of Jonah is not only characterized by the use of stems but also by frequent repetition(s) of the same or almost the same expressions. Many turns of phrases are used for different situations and sometimes for different persons, as is the case – for example – with the following phrases, repeated literally:

---

[a] See appendix 2 as well.

- away from before the face of Adonai (Jonah 1:3 (2x), 10;
- rise up, go to (Jonah 1:2;3:2);
- and not we shall perish (1:6; 3:9);
- that city, the big one (1:2; 3:2; 4:11);
- oh, Adonai (1:14; 4:2);
- to flee towards Tarsis (1:3; 4:2).

Other turns of phrases return in smaller or larger variations, like:

- rise up ... and call against (1:2; 3:2)/rise up, call to (1:6);
- a city (very) big (3:3)/that city, the big one (1:2; 3:2; 4:11);
- and afraid are the mariners (1:5)/and (then) fear the men a fear (very) big (1:10, 16);
- and (then) prepares Adonai (2:1)/ and (then) prepares Adonai God (4:6)/ and (then) prepares (this) God (4:7, 8);

Not only short turns of phrases are (being) repeated but also and regularly entire phrases, with some variations that is. In the next examples I only mention the variant from the first verse:

- for whose cause, this evil, this one, (is) upon us" (1:7, 8);
- for the sea (is) going and storming (1:11, 13);
- take me up and throw me into the sea and calm will be the sea unto you (1:12, 15);
- And they turn around (each) man from his path of evil (3:8, 10);
- for good is my death over my life (4:3, 8);
- is it good (that) it burns to you ... (4:4, 9).

The linguistic usage of the Book of Jonah is special in other respects as well. There is for instance the unusually frequent usage of the verbal infinitive[6] which even occurs twelve times in this short story:

- To say (1:1);
- To flee (1:3);
- To go towards (1:3);
- To lighten (1:5);
- To turn around (1:13);
- To swallow up (2:1);`

- To say (3:1);
- To go into (3:4);
- To do (3:10);
- To flee (4:2);
- To make (4:6);
- To draw away (4:6).

The described actions indicate a specific and continuous aim.

Another peculiarity is the regularly returning series of special Hebrew verb forms, the so-called consecutive imperfect. I translated them with expressions like "and ..." or "and (then) ...", the dots indicating the present tense of the English verb. Series like that produce enormous dynamics in the story:

- And up rises ... and down he goes ... and he happens upon ... and he gives ... and down he goes (1:3);
- And afraid are (they) ... and they cry out ... and they throw (1:5);
- And (then) comes to ... and he says (1:6);
- And up they take ... and they throw ... and silent becomes ... and (then) fear ... and they sacrifice ... and they promise ... (1:15, 16);
- And (then) trust ... and they call ... and put on (3:5);
- And (then) leaves ... and he sits down ... and he makes ... and he sits (4:5);
- And (then) prepares ... and it strikes ... and it withers (4:7);
- And it occurs ... and (then) prepares ... and (then) strikes ... and he becomes faint ... and he requests ... and he says (4:8).

The above mentioned examples are from Jona 1, 3 and 4 only. Jona 2 is not or much less characterized by repetition of specific choice of words, the use of the infinitive and consecutive imperfects. These three characteristics of linguistic usage are extremely functional when used in a rather short text which has to tell a lot. However, the Psalm of Jonah does not so much describe actions as states of mind (2:3-7a, 8-10) linked by some actions (2:7b). This psalm is a poem and not narrative prose. Therefore it's no surprise that we're dealing with different linguistic usage in Jonah 2.

Besides, other specific details can be mentioned of the linguistic usage of the Book of Jonah. For example, we come across different kinds of play on words in the Hebrew text.[7] It's also important to note that the book shows a number of words from Aramaic origin instead of Hebrew origin. These words play an important part in the discussion about the time the Book of Jonah was written in. I'll return to this in Chapter 5. Here it'll do to conclude that in Jonah 1, 3 and 4 we're dealing with a linguistic usage, characterized by intense concentration, purpose and dynamics.

2.4   Style and narrative technique

Jonah is also a special book from the point of view and narrative technique, characterized by frequent repetitions. In the narrative parts (Jonah 1, 3 and 4) we find a regular variety of events and conversations. A lot of questions occur in these conversations (Jonah1:6, 8, 10, 11; 4:4, 9, 11) and a lot of commands (Jonah 1:2, 6, 7, 8, 12; 3:2, 7-8). Hope and expectation on future events is expressed regularly (Jonah 1:6. 11, 12, 14; 3:4, 9; 4:2). It's remarkable as well that the same or similar words are used by different people (compare for instance Jonah 1:2 with 1:6; 1:6 and 14 with 3:9; 1:14 with 4:2 and 3).

Very often the details of the stories are told – characteristically – *after* the events, a kind of *information afterwards*. This narrative style – of *mentioning information afterwards* – is found in all narrative parts of the Book of Jonah. Jonah 1:4-5a tells us about the storm and the mariners' fear. And in verse 5b it's also told how Jonah went down into the ship's hold and allowed himself to fall asleep. Chronological order would lead to another order of the text: Jonah 1:3, 5b, 4, 5a, 6 (with some adaptions), 7 etc. The text of Jonah 1:10b points at something which Jonah must have told the men earlier. And once more we come across this narrative technique at the end of chapter 1. Once Jonah has been thrown overboard (Jonah 1:15), the story continues about the mariners (Jonah 1:16) and only later we hear that Jonah was swallowed by a fish (Jonah 2:1). In Jonah 3:6-9 the reaction of the king and his ministers can be taken as *information afterwards* with regard to verse 5. Chronologically Jonah 3:4, 6-9, 5, 10 should well be possible. In Jonah 4:2b it is told – again afterwards – what had motivated Jonah to run away from the word of Adonai. Also Jonah 4:5 tells something that – chronologically seen – could be placed before Jonah 4:1 or even before Jonah 3:5. In all these cases one could argue that the author of the Book of Jonah wants to first mention the decisive reactions of the persons and only afterwards the details.[8] In all those cases these decisive reactions are of a religious nature:[9] Thrice the mariners' fear; the conversion of the entire population of Nineveh; and Jonah's complaint against Adonai. The narrative technique of mentioning essential information afterwards, shows, just like the other literary characteristics I discussed above, the literary unity of Jonah 1, 3 and 4. And once again the Psalm of Jonah occupies a unique position.

This Psalm of Jonah, said in the fish's belly, has a very familiar style which shows large similarities with the other psalms in Tanakh.[10] For instance it often uses the so-called perfect form of the verb. And Jonah's prayer also shows the parallelism well-known in the psalms. That means that a specific thought is expressed twice or more after each other but always in a slightly different wording. The opening phrase of Jonah's Psalm is a beautiful example of this phenomenon:

Jonah 2:3a	Jonah 2:3b
I call because of the affliction to me to Adonai and He answers me.	Out of the belly of Sheol I shout for help, You hear my voice.

As regards content there are a lot of similarities with other psalms. Especially the similarities with Psalm 107 are striking indeed.[11]

On the basis of the foregoing it seems clear that linguistic usage and style show a remarkable difference between Jonah's prayer and the rest of the story. This once more raises the question of the literary unity of the book in its present form. In the literature on this subject we find two answers to this question. Some commentators consider this Psalm of Jonah's an integral part of the whole book and so they take it for granted that the author reproducing this psalm consciously deviated from his own linguistic usage and style, for any reason whatsoever. Whether they consider the fact that the author wrote the psalm himself,[12] or made it up with quotes from existing psalm-verses,[13] or copied an existing psalm in its entirety,[14] is of secondary importance. Other commentators think that Jonah's prayer is a later addition and should answer the question what exactly Jonah had prayed.[a, 15] Both views take the fact for granted that the story in Jonah 1, 3 and 4 makes up the proper contents of the Book of Jonah. But there is a third possibility I didn't find in the literature concerned: The story in Jonah 1, 3 and 4 could have been written as a further explanation of the Psalm of Jonah. In other words: To provide this psalm with a topical explanation – topical that is for the times of the author – he has composed the story of Jonah 1, 3 and 4 around it. In that case the story could be a *midrash* on the Psalm of Jonah and this psalm could be considered the heart of the book. I'll find some arguments indeed for this point of view,[16] and consequently this may put the question of the literary unity in a quite different light.

And finally I'd like to point at the strange, open end of the Book of Jonah. Jonah stuck to his anger and his wish to die (Jonah 4:9). God reacts with a question, after which the story stops. What could be the meaning of such an end?

2.5   Structures in the text

Characteristic for the literary character of the Book of Jonah are the pyramidical and concentric structures we see in the whole text. The first example, for one, we find in Jonah 1:3, the contents of which are arranged as follows:[17]

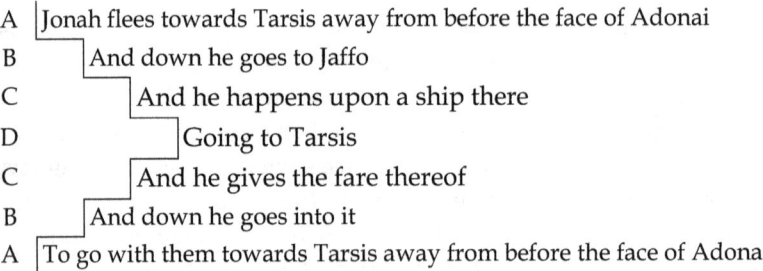

We find such pyramidical structures five more times in the Book of Jonah and, with the exception of Jonah 1:1-2 and 3:1-2, they take up the whole text. So Jonah 1:4-16 shows the following structure:

---

a   Jonah 2:2 may have belonged to the original story (see section 2.2 and end note).

```
A    4-5a   Throw to the sea - storm - afraid are the mariners
 B   5b      The mariners cry out to their god
  C  5c-6a    The mariners throw - Jonah asleep - master comes
   D 6b        And he says - words of the master
    E 7a        And they say - words of the mariners
     F 7b        The lot falls on Jonah
      G 8         They say - questions of mariners
       H 9-10a     Confession Jonah - men fear
      G 10b        They say - question of the men
     F 10c        Jonah has told that he is fleeing
    E 11         And they say - words of the men
   D 12        And he says - words of Jonah
  C  13       The men row
 B   14      The men call to Adonai
A    15-16  Throw Jonah to the sea - sea becomes silent - the men fear
```

Also Jonah 2:1-11 (Hebrew order) appears to be structured in the same way, which yields a powerful argument for the idea that the Psalm of Jonah must have belonged to the original text of the book:

```
A    1     Adonai prepares - fish swallows up Jonah
 B   2      Jonah prays to Adonai
  C  3       I call - He answers - I shout for help - You hear
   D 4        You cast me into the deep
    E 5        Driven away - go on and look - temple
     F 6        (my) soul encompassed
      G 7a       Go down to the foundations
     F 7b        You causes to go up my life
    E 8         Faint - remember - temple
   D 9        They forsake their kindness
  C  10a     Thanksgiving - sacrifice - promise - fulfil
 B   10b    Salvation of Adonai
A    11    Adonai says to - the fish vomits out Jonah
```

Next we come across a pattern like that in Jonah 3:3-4a:

```
A  Jonah rises up
B     He goes to Nineveh
C        according to the word of Adonai
B     a city, very big, before God
A  Jonah goes into the city
```

In addition to it we see an identical kind of structure in Jonah 3:4b-10:

```
A  4b   Jonah calls the judgement
B  5a      The men of Nineveh trust in God
C  5b         They call a fast
D  5c            They put on sackcloth
E  6a               The word comes to the king
F  6b                  He rises up – throne – robe
G  6c                     Sackcloth – sits on the dust
F  7a                  Cried out – the king – his big ones
E  7b               Words of the king – not taste, feed, drink
D  8a            They cover themselves (with) sackcloth
C  8b         They turn around
B  9       Who knows God turns around
A  10   And not (at all) He does (it)
```

Jonah 4 has also been structured pyramidically with one significant exception only:

```
A    1       Jonah is angry
B    2a         He wanted to prevent the salvation of Nineveh
C    2b            Adonai is compassionate about the evil
D    3-4              Jonah wants to die – question of Adonai
E    5                  On the east side of the city – shadow
F    6a                    Adonai prepares a Kikayon
G    6b                       Jonah rejoices
F    7                     Adonai prepares a worm
E    8a                 Wind from the east – sun strikes Jonah
D    8b-9             Jonah wants to die – question Adonai
C    10            Jonah has pity on the Kikayon
B    11        Adonai has pity on Nineve
A    ....    ........................
```

Considering all this, it attracts the attention that the central phrase of all six pyramidical structures indeed puts forward something "central". In Jonah 1:3 it seems less the case with "going to Tarsis", but this city is, at the beginning and the end of the text, linked up with "away from before the face of Adonai." In Jonah 4:2 Tarsis also expresses the opposite of following up the word of Adonai. In Jonah 3:3-4a the central expression is "according to the word of Adonai." Both texts – Jonah 1:3 and 3:3-4a – are opposites, both compositional and concerning content.

In Jonah 1:4-16 the central sentence (verses 9-10a) includes Jonah's confession of faith which makes up the core of the story of the storm at sea. In Jonah 2:1:11 the centre consists of the nadir of Jonah's descent into Sheol (verse 7a). From this absolute low the ascent can begin. It's remarkable that in Jonah 3:4b-10 the centre of the story is reached at the moment the king is covered with sackcloth and ashes. Here too an absolute low, from which the story can move upwards. In Jonah 4:1-11 Jonah's joy is in the centre of the story, a joy in sharp contrast to his subsequent attitude in this chapter.

Remarkable to the last structure in Jonah 4 is, that Jonah's anger is at the beginning, his joy is in the centre and the story breaks off when – according to the structure – it's Jonah's turn to react with a temper.

And in doing so it becomes crystal-clear that the author has wanted to leave Jonah's final decision to the reader. He or she will be obliged to define his or her position at the end of the book with regards to the difference of opinion between Adonai and Jonah. So everyone is asked the question: "What would you have done at the end of the story if you'd been Jonah?" The incomplete pyramidical structure in Jonah 4 once more underscores the book's open end and presents its function as a learning story, and challenges the reader to take up an own point of view. Taking up such a point of view should also be based on a further, intrinsic analysis of the Book of Jonah. The next chapters will be devoted to that analysis accordingly.

2.6   The composition of the Book of Jonah

In the previous section I showed some six pyramid structures in the text, demonstrating a clear, compositional order of the Book of Jonah. Initially the book consists of two parallel parts structured as follows:

Jonah 1:1-2	Jonah 3:1-2	Call of Adonai to Jonah
Jonah 1:3	Jonah 3:3-4a	Jonah's reaction
Jonah 1:4-16	Jonah 3:4b-10	Consequences of Jonah's reaction
Jonah 2:1-11	Jonah 4:1-11	Reflection/Discussion/Commentary

Comparing next the four chapters mutually, it is also conspicuous that thematically they are more or less equal in structure, as shown in table 2.1. Considering this strong composition of the Book of Jonah, it's no longer possible to maintain the idea that this small book should have ever existed without the Psalm of Jonah being part of it. Without Jonah's prayer the book won't stand up. And that would be in flat contradiction with the literary mastery it's written with, a mastery we met above time and again.

2.7   The character of the Book of Jonah

After everything I showed about the Book of Jonah in the previous sections the conclusion is obvious that this book of the Bible does not want to describe historical events, but is a literary creation written

Table 2.1

The thematic structure of the Book of Jonah. Clearly to be seen is the parallelism between the four parts with a small variation in Chapter 4.

Part 1 : The ship and the sea		Part 2: The town and the plain	
Subdivision 1a: Story	Subdivision 1b: Commentary	Subdivision 2a: Story	Subdivision 2b: Commentary
1:1-3 Circumstances	2:1 Circumstances	3:1-3 Circumstances	4:5 Circumstances
1:4 Crisis situation: The ship threatens to be wrecked	2:4 Crisis situation: Jonah threatens to drown	3:4 Crisis situation: Nineveh threatens to perish	4:1 Crisis situation: Nineveh threatens to continue to exist
1:14 The mariners' answer: The mariners pray	2:3, 8 Jonah's answer: Jonah prays	3:5-8 The Ninevites' answer: Penance and prayer	4:1-4 Jonah's answer: Rage and prayer
1:15b Adonai's answer: Ship is safe	2:7b, 10b Adonai's answer: Jonah is saved	3:10 Adonai's answer: Nineveh is saved	4:6-8 Adonai's answer: Kikayon, worm, east wind
1:16 The mariners sacrifice	2:10 Jonah sacrifices	3:10 God reconsiders his judgement	4:10-11 God asks Jonah to reconsider his judgement

with another goal. To understand the book correctly it is imperative to closely bear this in mind. Many people think that if one is convinced of the historicity of a bible story, one has already and somehow understood its message.[18] This is anything but right. A historicizing way of reading the bible stories leads to quite different questions than the ones which will be asked when the text is seen as a literary creation. Reading the text historically means that many elements of the story are entirely obvious. The principal character is called Jonah, for the simple reason that his name *is* Jonah. Nineveh, Jaffo and Tarsis are not under discussion, again for the simple reason that the events occur around those places. But the questions which *could* be asked are:

- How can Jonah sleep soundly when there is such a violent storm?
- How is it possible that Jonah was still alive after he had stayed in the fish's belly for three nights and three days?
- Are there any fish so big that this could be possible and if so, do these fish swim in the Mediterranean?
- Common historiography doesn't mention a mass conversion of Nineveh to the God of Israel? Why?
- How can a tree grow so big in one night only, that it gives enough shadow and shrivels up in one night next?

And so one can think of more, many more questions. However, when you take up the Book of Jonah as the product of the literary creativity of its author, it'll suddenly become obvious that the text can no longer be taken for granted. And quite different questions could be asked too:

- Why did the author call his principal character Jonah?
- Why did Jonah have to go to Nineveh and not to any other evil city?
- Why make him flee to Tarsis?
- Why does he tell a story about a storm at sea?
- Why must Jonah be thrown into the sea at all costs, when returning to the shore the ship will bring Jonah to dry land again?
- Why is the conversion of Nineveh's population not enough, but why is a command of the king and his ministers also needed?
- Why does the author make Jonah build a hut when just a bit later the Kikayon also gives the shadow wished for?
- Why is Jonah's anger not enough and why does he have to show, twice ànd dramatically, that he wants to die?

And yet a lot of questions could be asked which all amount to that one question: "Why did the author write the story in this and not in another way?

Whichever way one looks at it, the details of linguistic usage, style, narrative technique and composition do answer these questions hardly or not at all. Defining the character of the Book of Jonah as pure fiction,[19] legend,[20] novella,[21] a satiric-didactic short story[22] or something like that[23] doesn't solve this problem. Yet one should, on the basis of the accuracy of the composition of the text of the book, consider the possibility whether there is more behind the used images and themes, than one could suppose after a first, superficial reading. Does it say in fact what it says, when we read the Book of Jonah? This question can't be answered if we limit ourselves to simply reading the Book of Jonah only. We'll have to put the book in the context of the other literature known to us of the Israel of before, during, but also after the Book of Jonah was written. If we want to learn and understand the meaning of the images used, we'll have to turn to those books of Tanakh used by the author of the Book of Jonah. But also the way later generations of rabbis dealt with the book is important for the understanding of the book. They were the people who'd been closest to the author, albeit not in time, but certainly as far as the spiritual climate of Judaism was concerned. The Jewish-Hebrew world of thought of Tanakh, Talmud and Midrash makes up the most consistent frame we could interpret a book like Jonah in. That's why in the next chapters I'll turn to the Tanakh and the rabbinic tradition for the understanding of the Book of Jonah. Then it'll turn out that the Book of Jonah could best be described as a form of *midrash*.

3 Tell us

The Book of Jonah as Midrash

3.1 Jonah in canon and liturgy

Tanakh, the Hebrew Bible, traditionally consists of three parts, each with its own character:

Torah
The Hebrew word *Torah* is often poorly translated with 'Law'. A better word is 'Teaching'. Other designations are: *Chumash*,[a, 24] *Pentateuch* or simply 'Moses'.[b] The Torah consists of the five books of Moses: Genesis, Exodus, Leviticus, Numbers and Deuteronomy. Since the Babylonian exile the Torah is the literary and religious heart of Judaism. The service on sabbath has also been built up around the reading from the Torah. In the next section I'll pursue in greater depth the relation between the Book of Jonah and the Torah.

Nevi'im
The section of the *Nevi'im*, the Prophets, consists of two subsections:

- *The early prophets.* This subsection consists of the books Joshua, Judges, 1 and 2 Samuel, 1 and 2 Kings.
- *The later prophets.* The major prophets Isaiah, Jeremiah, Ezekiel, and the minor prophets Hosea, Joel, Amos, Obadiah, Jonah, Micah, Nahum, Habakkuk, Zephaniah, Haggai, Zechariah, and Malachi belong to this subsection.

The relation between the Book of Jonah and the other prophets will be further dealt with in the following as well.

---

[a] Chumash means 'a fifth part' and points in fact at the separate books of the Torah (see endnote).
[b] See e.g. Luke 16:30.

Ketuvim
This section is often called the section of the *Hagiographies* or The Writings. Here too we can distinguish three subsections:

- Psalms, Proverbs and Job;
- The so-called *Mêgilloth,* or the Feast Scrolls: The Song of Songs, Ruth, Lamentations, Ecclesiastes and Esther;
- Daniel, Ezra, Nehemiah, 1 and 2 Chronicles.

So the Book of Jonah has been included in the collection of the twelve minor prophets. And although it seems a matter of course, yet there is something peculiar about it. Because apart from one, single sentence (Jonah 3:4b) the book doesn't contain *any* prophecy. It's almost entirely a story about just one prophet, who hardly prophesies at all! It's true, more prophet stories happen in Tanakh, but these have all been included in a wider context. The best known examples are:

- Elijah   1 Kings 17:1 – 2 Kings 2:18;
- Elisha   1 Kings 19:19 – 2 Kings 13:19;
- Isaiah   Isaiah 36:1 – 39:8 en 2 Kings 18:1 – 20:21;
- Jeremiah   Jeremiah 36:1 – 43:7;
- Daniel   Daniel 1:1 – 6:29.

The story of Jonah is the only prophet story that has become a book in itself. And because it hardly contains any prophecy, it is in fact an alien element in the collection of the twelve minor prophets. Comparing Jonah with the other books of Tanakh, the similarity with 'novellas' like *Ruth* and *Esther,* which also belong to the collection of feast scrolls, is obvious indeed. In addition to this literary similarity there is a liturgical similarity as well. These feast scrolls are, as is in the name, books read on certain feasts in the synagogue. And although Jonah doesn't belong to the five feast scrolls, it is being read on a feast in the synagogue as well. These readings take place in the afternoon services on the corresponding feasts:

- Song of Songs   Pesach (Easter);
- Ruth   Shavu'ot (Whitsun);

- Lamentations 9th Ab (Day of Lament about the destruction of Jerusalem);
- Jonah Yom Kippur (Day of Atonement);
- Ecclesiastes Sukkoth (Feast of Tabernacles);
- Esther Purim.

The reading of Jonah during the afternoon prayer in the afternoon of the Day of Atonement is very old indeed. The Babylonian Talmud reads: "On the Day of Atonement one should read the section 'After the death' (Leviticus 16:1 ff.) and as a reading from the prophets the chapter 'For thus said the high and lofty One' (Isaiah 57:15 ff.). At the afternoon prayer one should read the section about incest (Leviticus 20) and as the final reading the Book of Jonah."[25]

The big difference between the Book of Jonah and the other prophetic books on the one hand and the remarkable similarities between Jonah and the feast scrolls on the other hand raises the question: Why does Jonah belong to the twelve minor prophets? Now there are clear indications that this has already been the case from very early times. In the book *Proverbs of Jesus Sirach*, from about 180 BCE, we read after Isaiah, Jeremiah and Ezekiel had been discussed: "May the bones of the twelve prophets flourish from their resting-place! Because they comforted Jacob and freed his children by inspiring them with confidence" (Jesus Sirach 49:10). It's obvious that these words point at the collection of the minor prophets and there is no reason, whatsoever, to presume that this collection differed then from the present one. This means that the Book of Jonah wasn't included with the feast scrolls, because it had already been part of the collection of the twelve minor prophets from time immemorial.[a] Therefore the editors of this collection must have had very good reasons indeed, contrary to the apparently non-prophetic character of the book, to attach it to the other minor prophets. As the Book of Jonah hardly expresses 'word of Adonai' and the bigger part of the text can't be attributed to Jonah's prophetic authority – the words 'prophet' and 'prophecy' don't even

---

[a] To include some of the feast scrolls into the canon, was still under discussion till the end of the 1st century CE. So the collection of the feast scrolls was compiled much later than the collection of the twelve minor prophets.

appear in the book – there must have been other weighty arguments to consider Jonah to be one of the minor prophets yet. These arguments can only be found in the text of Jonah to the extent it has a basis in the Torah and the other traditions. Therefore – in the next section – I'll examine how the author connected his book with them.

3.2 The Book of Jonah and the Torah (Genesis in particular)

Links between the Book of Jonah and the Torah are numerous. There is, for instance, this almost verbatim quotation of Exodus 34:6 in Jonah's description of God in Jonah 4:2. In this section, however, I'll restrict myself to the links existing between Jonah and the first chapters of the Book of Genesis, which are so remarkable that we're able to argue that the Book of Jonah is rooted in the Torah.

Many words, images and themes from Jonah 1 and 2, can be found again in the first creation story in Genesis 1. Jonah's confession in Jonah 1:9 – in the middle of the story of the storm at sea[26] – is a summary of Genesis 1, adapted to the situation. Moreover I'd like to point out the following similarities:

- The flood (Hebrew *têhom*), the point of assembly of the primeval waters (Genesis 1:2), Jonah had to go down in, to be able to appear again, converted (Jonah 2:6);
- The spirit/wind (Hebrew *ru'ach*) God uses to get the water going (Genesis 1:2; Jonah 1:4);
- The water(s) (Hebrew *mayim* plural) which God separate and which surround Jonah (Jonah 2:6);
- The seas or sea (Hebrew *jamim/hajam*) formed by God from the waters flowed together (Genesis 1:10), at which the drama of the storm takes place (Jonah 1:5 ff.);
- The heaven(s) (Hebrew *hashamayim* plural), the exclusive sphere of power of God (Genesis 1:1; Jonah 1:9);
- The dry land (Hebrew *hajabashah*) God makes appear from the water (Genesis 1:9; Jonah 1:9) and the mariners want to return to (Jonah 1:13);
- The fish (Hebrew *hadagah/hadag*), God appointed man to as ruler (Genesis 1:26) and Jonah was swallowed by (Jonah 2:1-2);

- This fish is described as 'big' (Hebrew *gadol*), just like the big marine animals (Hebrew *hataninim hagêdolim*) God created on the fifth day (Genesis 1:21).

Without any doubt the later rabbis noticed the similarities between Jonah and Genesis 1. A number of their midrashim on Jonah fit in closely with the first story of the Creation. In the text Pirke de-Rabbi Eliezer the discussion of the creation is interrupted between the fifth and sixth day by a chapter with stories about Jonah fitting in with the events from Jonah 1 and 2. In it Jonah's flight is seen as to belong to the events which took place on a fifth day of the week (Thursday). This link is based on the creation of the big marine animals on the fifth day.[27] The big fish that was to swallow Jonah later, belonged to these big marine animals. It is said that God destined this fish for its later task in the sixth day of the Creation.[28]

Now what meaning should we ascribe to the fact that Jonah 1 and 2 were written so obviously against the background of Genesis 1? Evidently, the author of the Book of Jonah wanted to indicate that the issues he brings up in his book, are about Gods original intentions with the world in every respect. And so he puts the relation between Jonah and Nineveh in the centre of the creation. After all it's about something that touches the centre of the existence of the world!

The parallels between Jonah and Genesis are not limited to Genesis 1. Also in the stories about the paradise, the first sin and the first murder of a human, we find a number of expressions and themes which evoke powerful associations with the story of Jonah, especially in Jonah 4:

- The deep sleep (Hebrew *tardeimah*) God caused to fall upon Adam (Genesis 2:21) and that Jonah had allowed himself to fall into (Jonah 1:5; Hebrew *jeiradam*);
- The question "What (is) this (now that) you have made?" (Hebrew *mah-zot asit(a)*) God asked Eve (Genesis 3:13), matches literally the question the mariners asked Jonah (Jonah 1:10);
- The expression 'away from before the face of Adonai' (Hebrew *milifnei Adonai*) is used both with Kain (Genesis 4:16) and Jonah (1:3) to indicate their estrangement from God;

- The indication 'east of' (Hebrew *mikèdem*) is used with the Garden of Eden (Genesis 3:24) and with Nineveh for the place where Jonah sits down (Jonah 4:5);
- Also the wind (Hebrew *ru'ach*) God approaches man with to call him to order, is found back in both stories: the cool of the day in Eden (Genesis 3:8; Hebrew *ru'ach hayom*), and the wind from the east in Jonah (Jonah 4:8; Hebrew *ru'ach kadim*);
- The words 'good' and 'evil' (Hebrew *tov* and *ra'ah*), that indicate a central theme in the paradise story (Genesis 2:9, 17; 3:5), play an important part in Jonah 4 in forms adapted to the situation (Jonah 4:1, 3, 8, 9);
- The motive of knowing (Hebrew *jada*) good and evil (Genesis 2:9, 17; 3:5, 22) we find in adapted wording in God's last word to Jonah which is about 'not know[ing] (what is) between their right hand and their left hand' (Jonah 4:11);
- The theme of life and death (Hebrew *chajah* and *meit*) is dealt with a number of times in different forms of the same verbs in both stories (Genesis 2:9, 17; 3:3, 4, 22; Jonah 4:3, 8).

In this respect two thematic similarities are conspicuous:

- The motive of the trees and the snake in Genesis 3 has its parallel in the motive of the Kikayon (gourd) and the worm in Jonah 4;
- In both stories the central figures try to protect themselves inadequately and then God offers them a more reliable protection; the girdles of fig-leaves, which are replaced by garments of skin (Genesis 3:7 and 21), find their parallel in the tabernacle replaced by the gourd (Jonah 4:5 and 6).

So it has everything to recommend that the Book of Jonah and especially the fourth chapter was written with the stories of the paradise and the original sin in the background. This can be explained in the continuation of the background of Genesis 1. If the relation between Jonah and Nineveh belongs to the centre of the creation, then his flight from Adonai and his unwillingness with regard to Nineveh is in line with the original sin. If Jonah doesn't fulfil his task with regard to Nineveh, the creation will deteriorate. This is the insight God wants Jonah to recognize. The task the Israelite Jonah has with regard to the world is a task that emerges directly from the first chapters of the Torah.

The description in the Book of Jonah of the city of Nineveh, of her evil and of God's reaction to this, reminds one very much of similar motives in the first Genesis stories. We come across Nineveh in the list of nations in Genesis 10. It's the first city built by Nimrod (Genesis 10:8-12). The expression 'the big city' (Jonah 1:2; 3:2; 4:11), in Hebrew *ha'ir hagêdolah*, is also found in Genesis 10:12, with identical words, the reason why the rabbis make them refer to Nineveh as well.[29] In Jonah 3:8 the evil of the inhabitants of Nineveh is described as violence (Hebrew *chamas*), an expression used twice for the generation from before the Flood (Genesis 6:11, 13). The forty days in Jonah's prophecy of doom (Jonah 3:4) evoke memories of the forty days and forty nights of downpour during the Flood as well (Genesis 7:12, 17). The expression "shall be overthrown" in Jonah's words to Nineveh are found, in other forms of the same verb, three times in the story of the destruction of Sodom and Gomorra (Genesis 19:21, 25, 29).

The intention of all these stories is not one of downfall. The essence of the Flood is not the destruction of the creation, but its renewal. Even the destruction of Sodom is not an end in itself, as Abraham's plea makes clear (Genesis 18). It's all about the extermination of evil and the restoration of the good in the creation. It's obvious that the author of the Book of Jonah wanted to associate himself with this typical Torah-issue.

Another, last comparison with Genesis may help us to get a better insight in his intentions. All names occurring in the Book of Jonah have an equivalent in the list of nations in Genesis 10. It's about the next five names:

- *Jaffo* (Jonah 1:3) has the same root as *Jafet*, Noah's third son (Genesis 10:1-2);
- The name of *Jonah* can be considered the female form of *Jawan*, the name of the fourth son of *Jafet* (Genesis 10:2,4);[30]
- *Tarsis* (Jonah 1:3) is the name of *Jawan*'s second son (Genesis 10:4);[31]
- We already saw that *Nineveh* was the first city built by Nimrod (Genesis 10:11-12);

- And finally the word *Hebrew* (Jonah 1:9) is derived from the name of *Eber* (Genesis 10:24) which – as is evident from Genesis 10:21 – takes up a central position in the list of Sem's descendants.

Of course, these similarities of names could be considered a chance coincidence. However, the accuracy the Book of Jonah was written with (see chapter 2) and the fact that the author linked his story closely up with the other stories from the beginning of Genesis, justify the supposition that there is a lot more going on than a story with only a number of 'catchy' names. In other words, it could have been the writer's conscious intention to link up the Book of Jonah with the list of nations. Anyway, he hasn't taken any pains to prevent any associations with Genesis 10. It's also remarkable that in this respect the later Midrash finds a connection between the Jonah story and the seventy nations of the world, the existence of which is derived from Genesis 10. With the verse of Jonah 1:5 "and they cry out, (every) man to his god" is told that there was a representative of all seventy nations on board.[32] So the ship became the world in a nutshell as it were. The conclusion we should draw from this is that it's about more than about only one prophet who does not or hardly performs his task. And that in the case of Nineveh it's about more than one, evil city. Are Jonah and Nineveh the representatives of Israel and the nations? If so, then the Book of Jonah is a call to Israel to save the world by teaching it its knowledge of Adonai. Then the creation can be restored by confronting the nations with the God of Israel. In chapter 5 I'll put this thought behind the Book of Jonah in the time the book was written in.

3.3 Jonah and the prophets (especially Elijah)

Relations between Jonah and a number of some other prophetic books can be pointed out clearly. In literature on Jonah one often points at the links with Jeremiah and Joel. However, I'll restrict myself to the books of 1 and 2 Kings only, especially to the Elijah stories.

The clearest link between Jonah and the books of Kings is the description of Jonah as 'son of Amitai' (Jonah 1:1). The figure of Jonah has been borrowed directly from 2 Kings 14:25, where Jonah is said to come from the village of Gathhepher, just north of Nazareth in the tribal territory of Zebulon (Joshua 19:13). This Jonah was a prophet in the days of Jeroboam II, king of the northern kingdom of Israel. Jeroboam II was the fourth and the last king but one from the dynasty of Jehu, who – by order of Elijah and Elisha – had been anointed king of Israel as the successor of the house of Ahab (1 Kings 19:16; 2 Kings 9:1-3). This dynasty ruled Israel for almost a century and produced the following kings:

- Jehu (845-818);
- Joachaz (818-802);
- Joas (802-787);
- Jeroboam II (787-747);
- Zechariah (747-746).

Jonah foretold the recapture by Jeroboam II of the lost territories (2 Kings 14:25). One time only Israel regained its old frontiers. Jeroboam's son Zechariah was the last king from the house of Jehu. He was murdered during an uprising (2 Kings15:8-12). Twenty-four years later the northern kingdom of Israel was over. It was destroyed by the Assyrian armies in 722 BCE.

The question that should be asked now is: Why did the author of the Book of Jonah with the expression 'son of Amitai' try to link up so clearly with this prophet in the latter years of the northern kingdom of Israel? Before being able to answer this question we should deal with other parallels first between the Book of Jonah and the books of the Kings. Some commentators point out, and with good reason, the great number of similarities between Jonah and the stories of the prophet Elijah (1 Kings 17:1 – 2 Kings 2:18). Especially the story of Elijah's journey to Horeb (1 Kings 19) is important in this respect.[33] And indeed, there are remarkable parallels:

- The calling of Jonah and Elijah by Adonai in Hebrew is worded in the same way: And (then) occurs a word of Adonai …. to say: "Rise up, go (Jonah 1:1; 3:1; 1 Kings 17:2, 8; 21:17).
- The words of Jonah's prayer to Adonai in Jonah 4:3 and 8 have been taken almost entirely from Elijah's prayer in 1 Kings 19:4, as shown clearly if we compare the Hebrew texts:

Jonah 4:3 and 8	1 Kings 19:4b
3 wê'<u>atah adonai kach</u>-na et-nafshi mimèni ki <u>tov</u> moti mechajai	<u>wajishal et-nafsho lamut wajomer</u>
8 <u>wajishal et-nafsho lamut wajomer</u> <u>tov</u> moti meechajai	rav <u>atah adonai kach</u> nafshi ki lo-<u>tov</u> anochi me'avotai

- Both Jonah and Elijah flee to a place where they lie down (Hebrew in both stories: *wajishkav*) and fall asleep (Jonah 1:5; 1 Kings 19:5).
- In both stories the relation between Israel and the nations play an important part: in Jonah Nineveh (Jonah 1:1; 3:1), in Elijah among other things Aram (1 Kings 19:15).
- In both stories the prophet had to set out on a mission to a foreign capital: Jonah to Nineveh, Elijah to Damascus (1 Kings 19:25).
- God manifests his authority in both series of narratives by means of natural phenomena: with Jonah the big wind, the big fish, the Kikayon (the gourd), the worm, the easterly wind, and with Elijah the draught (1 Kings 17:1 ff.), a big wind, an earthquake, a fire, a still small voice (1 Kings 19: 11-12).
- In both Jonah 4 and in 1 Kings 19 we come across a context of heath, sun, desert and scorching.
- Also the theme of a self-made, poor protection and the then sound protection from God's hand is found in both stories: with Jonah the tabernacle and the Kikayon (Jonah 4:5-6), with Elijah the broom-tree and the cave (1 Kings 19:4-9).
- In both stories the meeting between God and the prophet takes place at dawn (Jonah 4:7-9; 1 Kings 19:9).

It's quite possible to discover more parallels, however, on the basis of the above mentioned similarities the conclusion can be made that the author of the Book of Jonah has fitted in consciously with the stories about the prophet Elijah. Very probably the rabbis of old noticed that as well, for in the midrashim they tell about Jonah the prophet, they associate him very much with the prophets Elijah and Elisah.

The midrash informs us that Jonah was the son of the widow of Zarephath, who was revived by Elijah (1 Kings 17:9-24).[34] The young Jonah became Elijah's pupil and after Elijah's ascension, he joined Elisah's retinue.[35] He was the not named son of a prophet who lost the iron part of his axe when chopping wood (2 Kings 6:1-7).[36] Also the unnamed prophet appointed by Elisah to anoint Jehu king of Israel, is supposed to have been Jonah (2 Kings 9:1-13).[37] After Jehu had exterminated the house of Ahab, he was foretold that his sons would occupy the throne of Israel for four generations to come (2 Kings 10:30). Also Jonah told him this prophecy.[38] As Jonah lived in the days of Jeroboam II, the last king but one from the house of Jehu, almost a century after Jehu's anointment it's not amazing to hear that all prophecies to the house of Jehu were conveyed by Jonah.[39] Presumably Jonah died when Jeroboam's son Zechariah was king, at the age of a hundred and twenty years,[40] therefore as old as Moses.

The link between Jonah on the one hand and Elijah and Elisah on the other, so specifically stressed by the Midrash, does not only rest on the relation between the Book of Jonah and the Elijah stories. The books of 1 and 2 Kings themselves give very much rise to it. After the death of Elisah (2 Kings 13:14 ff.) just one prophet only appears in the northern kingdom of Israel and that is Jonah (2 Kings 14:25). So Jonah can be considered the successor of Elisah. After Jonah prophecy is silent in the realm of the ten tribes, which was left to its own devices, prophetically seen that is. The revolts followed each other rapidly and kings only ascended the throne by bloodshed (2 Kings 15:10-30). In the end the northern kingdom of Israel was destroyed by the Assyrian king Shalmaneser V (2 Kings 17:3 ff.). And it's exactly this country, Assyria, where Nineveh was, the city Jonah was sent to in the Book of Jonah. What could have moved the writer of this small prophet book to send Elijah's and Elisah's heir, to one of the most important cities in Assyria, the land that was to execute God's judgment on the kingdom of Israel, that had ignored its prophets? This question I'll try to answer in chapter 4. Here my conclusion is that the choice of Jonah, son of Amitai, as the main character of the Book of Jonah has everything to do with the fact that this Jonah in 2 Kings ended the period of the prophecy of Elijah and Elisah and the northern kingdom of Israel.

3.4 The Book of Jonah as midrash

After the previous sections it'll be obvious how much the Book of Jonah is rooted in the Tora and the Prophets. By linking up with certain stories the writer wanted to actualize a number of themes from Israel's tradition in his own situation by means of a new story. Therefore I'll describe the Book of Jona with the help of the term *midrash*. Elsewhere I have dealt with this notion of midrash elaborately.[41] Here I'll only give a concise description of this notion directed at the Book of Jonah.

A midrash story has an educational function first. It's meant to shed some light on contemporary problematical cases which happen in the community with the help of words and notions, themes and images from the tradition. First of all the midrash story will therefore fit in with existing, authoritative literature. Several literary means are employed to realize the connection with the background stories. In the Book of Jonah we'll find for instance:

- The use of the same or cognate words and expressions as those occurring in the background story, for instance the words for sleeping deeply in Jonah 1:5 and Genesis 2:21.
- Quoting literally or almost literally substantial pieces of text, as is the case with the prayer of Jonah and of Elijah (Jonah 4:3 and 8; 1Kings 19:4).
- The use of the same cognate images and themes as in the background story, like the image of the Kikayon and the worm in Jonah 4 and the tree and the serpent in Genesis 3.
- The identification of people, like Jonah and Elijah in Jonah 4 and 1 Kings 19.
- The choice of a central figure for one's own story from the background literature as happened here with Jonah, son of Amitai, from 2 Kings 14:25.

A midrash story doesn't describe historical events, fact by fact, event by event. History is transformed, so to speak, into "biblical history." It's not important whether the historical Jonah from 2 Kings 14:25 was ever in Nineveh or not, that is to say, was there once in a historical sense. However, it is important that he has been there in a theological sense, or rather: he *goes* there again and again when his book is being read in the synagogue on Yom Kippur. It's all about which message for the reader of the book lies in Jonah's assignment to go to Nineveh. What can be learned of Jonah's initial refusal and of his final recalcitrance towards God. That message is part of the didactical character of the book. A midrash story is not only written to teach a contemporary, but also a later listener, a certain outlook on the world he lives in. The aim is to move a reader or listener towards an attitude to life which could make the world a better place. The story is not only didactic but also polemic in character, insofar it adopts an attitude that confronts the opposite ideas among contemporaries. Besides one should consider that differences in notions on all sorts of essential matters were ànd are rather more usual than unusual in Judaism. In that context a midrash story like Jonah's will be a contribution to an ongoing discussion as well. In the chapters 4 and 5 I'll go into it more deeply.

An essential feature for the understanding of a midrash story is that abstract matters are worded with the help of concrete images. One of the biggest obstacles for us, modern Bible readers, is that we haven't been brought up on this Hebrew idiom. With regard to Jonah we'll have to try and recover the meaning of all sorts of words and names from other stories in Tanakh. The writer himself made so clear a connection with the Torah and the Prophets that this justifies the method of figuring out these images. But also later rabbinic literature can help us to retrieve the meaning of images and words from Tanakh, because this literature developed ànd emanated directly from the body of thought of Tanakh. In the next sections I'll try to explain the meaning of the city of Nineveh and the name of Jonah in this way.

3.5 Nineveh, that big city[a]

Before exploring the biblical meaning of Nineveh, passing a number of historical facts in review, will clarify the situation. In the biblical era Nineveh was one of the big cities of the world power Assyria. The Assyrians lived on the uppercourse of the Tigris River in the north of the present Iraq. People had already began to live in Nineveh in the 7th millennium BCE.[42] The Assyrian history started in the 2nd millen-

---

[a] A survey of the dates in this section can be found in table 3.1.

nium BCE and was characterized by varying periods of rise and fall.[43] Its last Golden Age began in the 9th century BCE under king Assurnasirpal II (883 – 859 BCE). Until its fall in 610 BCE Assyria developed into a powerful, belligerent nation, that was to scourge the entire region from Egypt to Persia with its ruthless armies. Ashurnasirpal II and his successor Shalmaneser III (859 – 824 BCE) went to war already against the small kingdoms along the Mediterranean. Their armies left a trail of death and destruction and many princes of the small nations made the best of a bad bargain by submitting themselves and paying a yearly tribute. As was done by the already mentioned king Jehu of Israel. In figures 3.1 and 3.2 we can still see today how he and his men paid their tribute to king Shalmaneser III of Assyria.

The threat of the Assyrian storm abated only temporarily from 782 to 746 BCE. Weak kings ruled the Assyrian nation and epidemics of plague caused the armies to return home without having achieved their aim. And exactly in this period the ten tribes kingdom of Israel was ruled by Jeroboam II. He used the Assyrian power vacuum to reestablish the old borders of Israel and during his reign the historical prophet Jonah made his appearance (2 Kings 14:25). This lee in the dwindling hostile power during which his action took place, could also be a reason why the author of the Book of Jonah made this Jonah, son of Amitai, the central figure of his small book. However, the question is whether that's all there is to it.[44]

Figure 3.1 *King Jehu of Israel hands over the tribute to king Shalmaneser III of Assyria.* [45]

Figure 3.2   *The bearers of the tribute of Jehu.* [46] *The accompanying text says: "The tribute of Jehu, of the house of Omri. I received from him silver, gold, a gold dish, a gold vessel, gold cups, gold buckets, tin, a royal staff and puruchtu-wood."*

After the actions of the historical Jonah Assyria's bloody history was to have another terrible sequel. The very height of the Assyrian power was reached with and from the reign of Tiglath-Pileser III (745 – 726 BCE). In figure 3.3 we see him in his ceremonial chariot. Now the question is: what is the meaning of the history of Assyria after 745 BCE for the interpretation of the Book of Jonah. In chapter 5 I'll deal with a large number of arguments for dating the Book of Jonah after the Babylonian exile (598 – 538 BCE). That means it was written when Assyria, fallen in 610 BCE, didn't exist any longer for almost a century or more. That doesn't alter the fact that its bloody history was still very much alive in the collective memory of all the nations in the Middle East. That's also very probably the reason why Nineveh and the Assyria of the 8th and 7th century must have evoked terrible memories in the minds of the author and the first readers of the Book of Jonah. So to understand the Book of Jonah, this history is highly important. The Assyrian kings were not only builders of cities and palaces, but also fearsome warlords. Assyria's foreign policy depended almost exclusively on military violence, wielded by the Assyrian warmachine (see e.g. figure 3.4), which distinguished itself by its effectiveness, and was checked continuously, renewed and strength-

Table 3.1

Chronological table of the most important periods of government in the kingdoms of Judah, Israel, Assyria and Babylon in the 9th – 7th century BCE.

BCE	JUDAH	ISRAEL	ASSYRIA	BABYLON	MEDIA/PERSIA	LYDIA	GREECE
880			883 Ashurnasirpal II				
870		878 Omri 871 Ahab					
860	868 Jehoshaphat	ELIJAH					
850		852 Ahaziah 851 Joram	859 Shalmaneser III |				
840	847 Joram 845 Ahaziah 844 Athaliah	845 Jehu	| | |				
830	839 Joash	ELISHA	| |				
820			824 †				
810		818 Jehoahaz	810 Adad-nirari III				
800	800 Amaziah	802 Joash	|				
790			|				
780	786 Azariah = Uzziah	787 Jeroboam II	| 782 †				
770		AMOS					
760		HOSEAH JONAH	Temporary decline of the Assyrian threat				
750	757 Jotham (regent)						From about 750 settling of colonies along the entire Mediterranean and the Black Sea.
740	742 Ahaz (regent)	747 Zechariah 746 Shallum 746 Menahem 737 Pekahiah	745 Tiglath Pileser III (Pul)	745 Revolt			
730	735 Ahaz (king)	736 Pekah 732 Hoshea					
720	726 Hezekiah	722 Fall	726 Shalmaneser V 721 Sargon II	729 Revolt 721 Revolt |			
710	ISAIAH MICAH			710			
700			704 Sanherib	703 Revolt			

Continuation of Table 3.1

BCE	JUDAH	ISRAEL	ASSYRIA	BABYLON	MEDIA/PERSIA	LYDIA	GREECE
690	697 Manasseh			694 Revolt |			
680			680 Esarhaddon	689			
670			668 Ashurbanipal				
660							
650				654 Revolt |			
640	641 Amon 640 Josiah			648			
630							
620	JEREMIAH ZEPHANJAH NAHUM		629 Ashur-etil-ilani	627 Nabopolassar	Cyaxares		
610			614 Fall 612 Nineveh destroyed				
600	609 Jehoiakim 598 Jehoiachin			604 Nebuchadnezzar			
590	598 Beginning of the Babylonian exile						

ened till the day of its fall.[47] Under king Ashurbanipal (668 – 629 BCE) the Assyrian army was not only equal to any task, but what's more, divided "scientifically" into specialized army groups. Tactically and strategically seen, the Assyrians believed strongly that the attack was the best form of strategy.[48] They pursued a foreign policy of relentless aggression to far beyond their borders. But the other side of this one-sidedly relying on military violence was that they could defeat everyone, but could not keep the defeated nations down for long.[49] For instance their conquest of Egypt had to be confirmed continuously by means of new campaigns: in 720, in 700, in 675, in 674, in 671, in 669, in 667 and in 663 the Assyrian armies marched against the Egyptians until they were driven out of Egypt between 658 and 651 without much further ado and left Egypt alone.[50] Even the Assyrian subjection of Babylon had to be fought again and again: in 745, in 729, from 721 to 710, in 703, from 694 to 689, from 654 to 648 and in 626.[51]

Figure 3.3 *King Tiglath-Pileser III of Assyria (745 – 726 BCE) in his ceremonial chariot.*[52]

The Assyrian way of warfare was characterized to a considerable extent by terrifying cruelty. When they besieged a town, it was surrounded by an impregnable ring. Who tried breaking out, was impaled on a pole before the city wall as a deterrent for the beleaguered[53] (see figure 3.5). After the conquest or surrender of the city, looting, arson, destruction and rape followed (see figure 3.6). The Assyrian soldiers caused a bloodbath, at which they piled up the heads of the defeated enemies at the feet of the king of Assyria. They spared the lives of young men and artisans to deport them to Assyria as convicts (see figure 3.7). The rest of the population was deported to another part of the Assyrian empire.[54]

One of the most important motives for campaigning against the neighbouring peoples was looting for state income. For the Assyrians warfare was a profitable affair for a long time.[55] King Sargon II (721 – 704 BCE) set out on his eighth campaign in 714. He'd been in power less than ten years. So it seems that such campaigns were organised on an almost yearly base.[56] Only those who surrendered to the Assyrian army, who bowed obediently to the Assyrian king and paid a big tribute, had a chance to survive.[57] If one didn't perform accordingly,

Figure 3.4   *Assyrian military equipment: a. Hoplite with a big shield and cuirass; b. lightly armed soldiers with round shields and cuirasses; c. Assault tower; d. Chariot for three soldiers.*

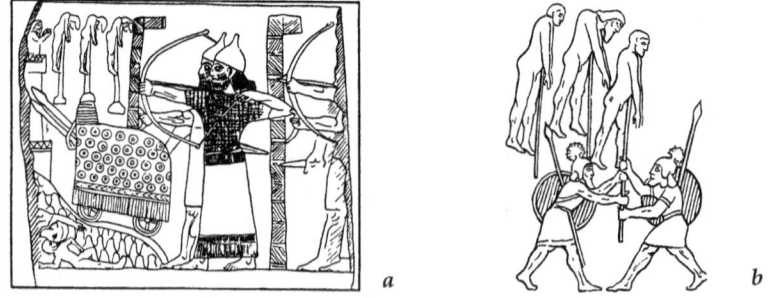

Figure 3.5   *a. King Tiglath-Pileser III sieges a town; b. Assyrian soldiers impale Judean captives from the town of Lachish.*

The Book of Jonah as Midrash

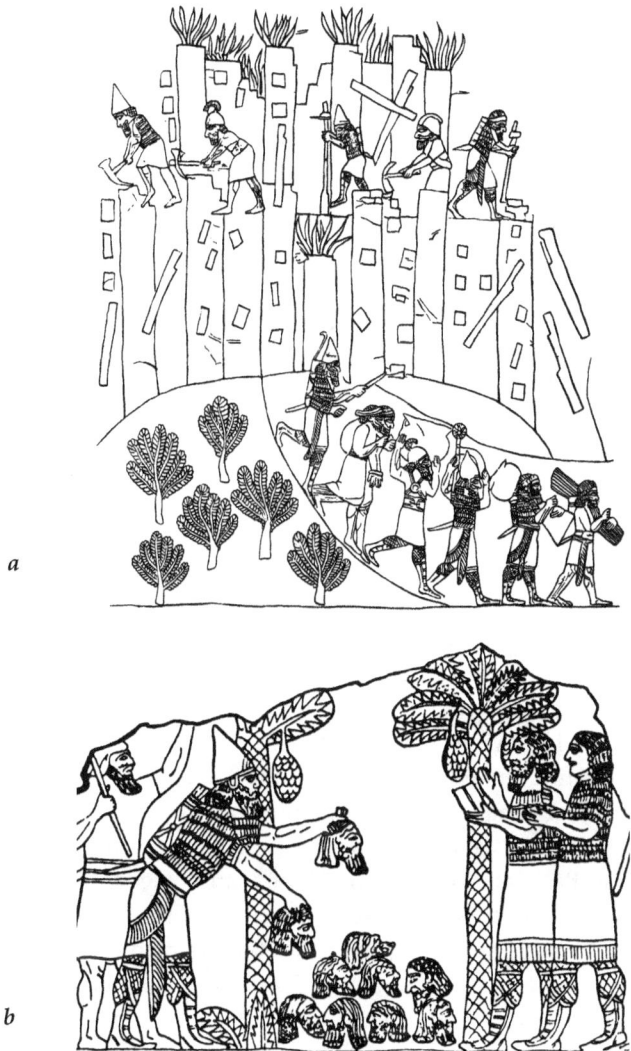

Figure 3.6 a. *The destruction of a conquered town; while soldiers laden with spoils lead the last inhabitants out of the gate, others break down the walls of the burning town.* [58] b. *Assyrian soldiers count the cut off heads.*

THE BOOK OF JONAH AS MIDRASH

Figure 3.7   *Deported captives setting out for their country of exile elsewhere in the Assyrian empire.*[59]

annihilation followed. This happened to Damascus in 732, Samaria in 722, Musair in 714, Babylon in 689, Sidon in 677, Memphis in 671, Thebes in 663, Susa in 639 in that order (see map 3.1). in 610 when finally Assyria's power had come to an end only two capitals of neighbouring nations were still intact: Jerusalem and Tyre.[60] Weakened by the continuous war effort, economic decline, depopulation, and the internal tensions of palace revolutions and peasants's revolts, the empire of Assyria went down in the war of 614-610. The united armies of the Babylonians, the Scythians and Medes took their revenge for almost two centuries of terror. The big Assyrian cities, among them Nineveh, met with the same fate as many a city of the neighbouring peoples had undergone and the Assyrian communities were swept from the earth's surface forever.

Against this background we should consider the biblical outlook on Nineveh and Assyria as Israel's biggest enemies. In the list of nations in Genesis 10 rather a lot of space is devoted to this Assyrian background. In Genesis 10:8-12 the enumeration of the generations is suddenly interrupted by an elaboration about Nimrod, who "began to be a mighty one in the earth" and he then appears to be the founder of four Assyrian cities of which Nineveh is the first. The Hebrew word *gibbor*, 'a mighty one', should better be translated with 'conqueror' or 'tyrant'. In this short story the tremendous threat of Assyria for the whole community of nations is personified by Nimrod. Tyranny and the building of enormous cities make of Nimrod a typically Assyrian ruler. So in the later Jewish tradition Nimrod is seen as the one who after the construction of the tower of Babel sets the entire world against the Holy One, blessed be He.[61] In the Midrash this Nimrod – placed in Abraham's days – plays the same oppressing part Pharao played in Mozes' days.[62]

From about 700 till its destruction in 612 BCE Nineveh was the capital of the Assyrian empire and therefore the residence of a notorious king like Sennacherib (704 – 680 BCE).[a] That's why Nineveh has become a byword for Assyria, just like Washington can be a synonym for the United States and Moscow for Russia. This Nineveh, this Assyria, was a threat to Israel and Judah for over a century. King Menachem of Israel (746 – 737 BCE) managed to escape the Assyrian

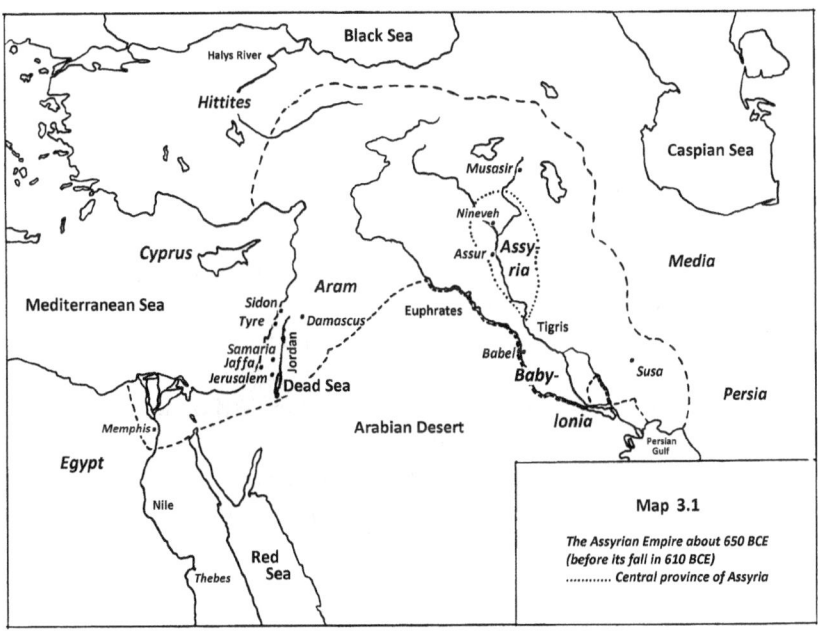

Map 3.1

The Assyrian Empire about 650 BCE (before its fall in 610 BCE)
.... Central province of Assyria

---

[a] See: 2 Kings 18:13; Isaiah 36:1; 2 Chronicles 32:1.

threat by submitting (himself) to Tiglath-Pileser III – in the Bible sometimes called 'Pul' – by paying an enormous tribute (2 Kings 15: 19-20). During the reign of king Pekach of Israel (736 – 732 BCE) Tiglath-Pileser III conquered the entire north of Israel yet, Galilee included, and deported the population to Assyria into exile (2 Kings 15:29). King Ahaz of Judah surrendered as a vassal to king Tiglath-Pileser in spite of Isaiah's warnings, to be able to hold out against the attacks of the kingdom of Israel and Aram (2 Kings 16:1-10). Then Tiglath-Pileser destroyed Damascus in 732, the capital of Aram. Not ten years later yet the remnants of the kingdom of Israel are overrun by Shalmaneser V, after king Hoshea of Israel (732-722 BCE) conspired against Assyria with Egypt. In 722 Samaria, the capital of Israel, is taken by the Assyrians and the population is exiled forever to the other end of the Assyrian empire (2 Kings 17:1-6).

But even after the fall of the northern kingdom of Israel the threat of Assyria for the southern kingdom of Judah is not over yet. Under king Hezekiah of Judah (726 – 697 BCE) the Assyrian king Sennacherib advances, occupies the entire kingdom of Judah and besieges Jerusalem (2 Kings 18:13 ff.). The second Book of Kings pays a lot of attention to this siege (2 Kings 18:17 – 19:36), which ends in a miraculous release, because "the angel of the LORD went forth, and smote in the camp of the Assyrians a hundred fourscore and five thousand." Sennacherib breaks off the siege, retreats into Nineveh and is murdered by his sons (2 Kings 19:35-37). Even though the Assyrian threat for Judah and Jerusalem continued for almost a century, the second Book of Kings was so composed that after this miraculous release the Assyrians played no longer a part in it.

In other prophetic books too, Assyria plays an important part. Isaiah, Jeremiah and Hosea regularly mention Assur/Assyria, being the force which was to execute the judgement of God on the unfaithful people, an interpretation of the events in 722 BCE, we also find in 2 Kings. [a] On the other hand, the fall of Nineveh and Assur is presented as a consolatory prospect and a just punishment of God.[b] Especially

---

[a] Isaiah 7:17-20; 8:4-8; 10:28-34; 20:1-6; 23:13; Jeremiah 50:17; Hosea 9:1-6; 11:1-5; 2 Kings 17:7-23.

[b] Isaiah 10:5-19; 11:11-16; 14:24-27; 27:13; 30:31-33; 31:6-9; Ezekiel 32:22-23; Hosea 11:7-11; Micah 5:4-5; 7:11-12; Zephaniah 2:13; Zechariah 10:10-11.

the little book of the prophet Nahum is devoted entirely to the fall of Nineveh. Moreover, in it we discover a vivid description of the image one had of Assyria and Nineveh: [63]

> "Woe to the city of blood, steeped in lies,
> full of prey, with no end to the plunder!
> The crack of the whip! The rattle of wheels!
> Galloping horses, jolting chariots,
> cavalry charging, swords flashing,
> spears glittering and hosts of slain,
> heaps of bodies; there is no end to the corpses;
> they stumble over their corpses" (Nahum 3:1-3).

Even after the fall of the Assyrian empire and after the destruction of Nineveh, the city and Assyria continue to live on as the incorporation of "the evil [which] comes up to God's face" (Jonah 1:2). Nineveh, "the city guilty of bloodshed" (Nahum 3:1), with "the violence that (is) in (the palm of) their hands"(Jonah 3:8), where a "bellicose king" lives (Hosea 5:13), still lingers on in the later Jewish literature as the designation for all the wrong and injustice, all violence and threat of Israel. In the apocryphal Book of Tobit we read that someone in Nineveh is found guilty of a capital crime by fulfilling his most elementary duty of mercy: burying the dead (Tobit 1:18-20). When after the Maccabean revolt halfway the 2nd century BCE the author of the Book of Judith looks back on the oppression by the Seleucids, he writes a story in which the enemy of Israel, king Nebuchadnezzar of Assyria lives in the big city of Nineveh (Judith 1:1), which is – historically seen – completely wrong after all. Nineveh, the historic city of Tiglath-Pileser and Sennacherib, has disappeared long since, simply and solely. The city became the incorporation of all evil, all violence and all injustice done to Israel in the course of the centuries. "All kingdoms indicated with the name of Nineveh, are thus mentioned because they enrich themselves at the cost of Israel," says the Midrash.[64] Small wonder Jonah takes to his heels, when he is ordered to go to Nineveh.

3.6   Jonah, the dove

Jonah means 'dove'. Only one other person in Tanakh bears the name of a dove: *Jemimah*, a daughter from Job's second family (Job 42:14). *Jemimah* means 'turtledove'. Furthermore, Jonah's name occurs in the Gospel of Matthew as well, as the name of Peter's father (Matthew 16:17)[a] and in the Talmud for two rabbis and the father of a rabbi. One should think that it wasn't a very common or popular name in early Judaism. But a too distinct conclusion shouldn't be drawn from such a fact. Animal names happen more often in Tanakh – like *Rachel* which means 'ewe lamb' or 'sheep' – but they are a minority among the proper names.

The dove is the bird that of all birds adapted its life most to humans. Sparrows like living in villages and cities in the midst of people as well but they always keep some distance. Doves on the other hand are easier to feed, to catch and to keep as a pet. That was already the case in the old days as doves are mentioned very often in Bible and Talmud.[65]

This familiarity with the life of doves[66] resulted in the fact that the dove, and the white dove especially was to play an important part in the entire eastern culture.[67] And in the culture of Israel as well. In the world of those days various observations and ideas concerning the dove existed everywhere. For instance doves, being peaceful birds, were assumed to have no gall. Love and loyalty to the partner and their young were also ascribed to the dove.[68] In the love poems of the Song of Songs the dove is mentioned various times as an indication of the loved one (Song of Songs 2:14; 5:2, 12; 6:9). However, in Israel the dove has never become the attribute of some goddess of love, as in so many pagan cults.

The fact that the dove is mentioned in the Song of Songs is particularly important for our view on the Book of Jonah. After much rabbinic deliberation the Song of Songs finally found its way into the canon of Tanakh, because the exegesis that the Song of Songs was an ode to the love between God and Israel already existed for a long time and

---

[a]   It is possible that this name as a midrash-motive has been derived from the prophet Jonah to characterize Peter as someone who is inclined to escape from a difficult assignment.

prevailed in the end. In the Song of Songs the beloved is compared with a dove and so it's not surprising that in the rabbinic exegesis the dove became – apparently – a symbol of Israel. Various rabbinic sayings could be quoted here:

- "Abisai, son of Zeruja, said: the congregation of Israel is compared with a dove." [69]
- In the Midrash quite a list of characteristics is to be found which Israel is supposed to have in common with doves.[70]
- A commentary on the Song of Songs reads: "The Holy One, blessed be He, says: 'I call Israel a dove, as is written: And Ephraim is become like a silly dove, without understanding (Hosea 7:11). For Me they are like a dove, but for the nations they are like various kinds of wild animals.'" [71]
- Rabbi Eliezer explains one of the prescribed offerings in Genesis 15:9 by means of two texts in the Song of Songs: "And a young dove (Genesis 15:9): This refers to Israel, which is like a young dove, as is said: 'O my dove, in the clefts of the rock' (Song of Songs 2:14). For your voice is sweet in prayer[a] and your face is lovely with good deeds.[b] And [once more] a young dove (Genesis 15:9): This refers to Israel which is like a young dove (as is said): 'But she is unique, my dove' (Song of Songs 6:9)."[72]

Now the problem is that the above-mentioned phrases were put in writing after the canonisation of Song of Songs and much later than the Book of Jonah. May we not use then the identification of Israel with the dove (= Jonah) for the exegesis of the Book of Jonah? This is the question indeed.

The fact that a certain idea was put down in writing in later times, doesn't necessarily mean that this idea had not existed in the preceding centuries. Therefore we should consider that in antiquity ideas and notions were not written down because they were new and original, but because one wanted to make old proven traditions subservient to the contemporary generation. This is especially the case for the imagery of the Midrash that was older and more widespread than

---

[a] Allusion to the cooing of doves.
[b] Allusion to the cock-pigeon's display.

the time and place in which the traditions in their present form came into being. If that had not been the case they wouldn't have had any power of expression for the greater part of Judaism.[73] So a specific imagery which used the dove as designation for Israel could have existed already long before the sayings of Abisai, son of Zeruja, and of Rabbi Eliezer were put down in writing. Already in the oldest writings of Tanakh clues for it can be found. For in the earlier quoted verse of Hosea 7:11 we read: "And Ephraim is become like a silly dove, without understanding." And in Hosea 11:11 we read about Israel: "They will return in fear and trembling like birds from Egypt, like doves from Assyria, and I will settle them in their homes, declares the LORD." Could one think of a bigger contrast than between Assur and the dove?

> "Remember how the enemy hurls insults, O LORD,
> and how a foolish nation blasphemes your name!
> Do not hand the life of your dove over to a wild animal!
> Do not continue to disregard the lives of your oppressed people!"

These words from Psalm 74:18-19 may indeed have been the basis for a kind of imaginary that already existed in the days the Book of Jonah was written and in which the dove was synonymous with Israel. In the same psalm we read (verse 21):

> "Do not let the afflicted be turned back in shame!
> Let the oppressed and poor praise your name."

This psalm is a lament on the destroyed temple. The image of the dove here is put in the context of suppression and misery, a same kind of context in the above quoted verse of Hosea 11:11. A saying from the Talmud fits in with this theme: "One should always belong to the persecuted and not to the persecutor," because no birds are more persecuted than turtledoves and young doves and yet the Tanakh considers them worthy enough to be sacrificed on the altar.[74]

It's this complex of meanings of "Jonah – the dove – Israel" which becomes especially important against the background of Nineveh which I discussed in the last section. Here the more than violent

Nineveh opposes the dove Jonah as the representative of the oppressed Israel. Which attitude should be adopted by the persecuted and oppressed people of Israel in respect of the world and especially in respect of its persecutors? And don't think that the answer to this question will be a simple one!

3.7 Summary and preview

Before I'm going to look for the meaning of the Book of Jonah in the next chapters, I'd like to conclude what went before about the literary character of Jonah with a short review and preview.

In chapter 2 we discovered that the Book of Jonah, including the Psalm of Jonah, is a very well thought-out literary composition. In chapter 3 we saw how closely the Book of Jonah fitted in with some writings in Tanakh and in which way the imagery of the book can be "decoded" with the help of other books of the Bible and the Jewish-rabbinic tradition. And at the same time I described the literary genre as "midrash." There are at least two strong links between the Book of Jonah and Tanakh, namely the one with the first chapters of Genesis and the one with the Elijah stories. I'll try to further explain the meaning of these links in chapter 4. The meanings of Nineveh and of the name of *Jonah*, as discussed in the preceding sections, should be interpreted more accurately as well against the background of the time when the Book of Jonah was written. An important part of chapter 5 is devoted to this.

4 And call against her

The ethics of the Book of Jonah

4.1 Jonah, Tanakh and the nations of the world

In the previous chapter we saw that the author of the Book of Jonah in his choice of themes, fitted in very closely with Genesis, the first book of the Torah and especially with its first chapters. What else could have been the reason for this than the universal vision the author had about Israel's place among the nations? Via Jonah – Israel's representative – God maintains his relation with the nations of the world, with the entire creation even. The author of the Book of Jonah shows clearly that this universal vision was derived from the Torah itself. The entirety of the creation in Genesis is not only the stage on which the history of Israel will be enacted, but it's also and ultimately

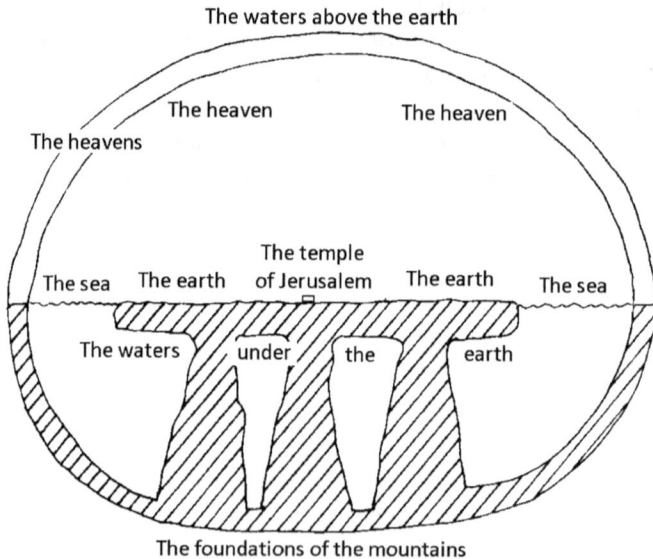

Figure 4.1   *The biblical image of the world as supposed in Jonah 2 with the Temple of Jerusalem in the centre.*

the manifestation of God's majesty. The whole creation will recognize his kingship. By fitting in the Jonah story so closely with Genesis the author undoubtedly wanted to point at the fact that Jonah (Israel) – nolens volens – must play a part in the improvement and completion of the creation, and the conversion of the nations of the world should be an integral part of it.

Therefore it's no surprise that the Book of Jonah is one of those parts of Tanakh in which the biblical image of the world comes up very clearly (see figure 4.1). We come across the basic lay-out of the creation: the heaven, the sea and the dry land (Jonah 1:9). The waters below the earth, being the Sheol, surround Jonah (Jonah 2:3). He descends to the foundations of the mountains on which the earth rests (Jonah 2:7a). Also the Temple in Jerusalem, that was the centre of the earth, is mentioned (Jonah 2:5, 7). And there is Tarsis, situated on the Atlantic coast of Spain near the Guadalquivir estuary, then a place, one thought, at the end of the world (Jonah 1:3). By now it should be clear that the Book of Jonah is a lot more than a story about *one* prophet sent to *one* evil city. In the end, it's about the entire creation. Apparently the city of Nineveh plays a part of great significance. And it is apparent as well that there, in the city of Nineveh, a lot of work should be done on the recovery of the creation! But it won't be easy to accept and undertake this task.

Jonah is ordered to go to Nineveh, an assignment which is not exactly welcome, and so Jonah runs away. But even when he's running away he fulfils, unwillingly, his prophetic assignment. The testimony forced out of him aboard the ship (Jonah 1:9) and the fate of the 'suffering servant'[75] he's also forced to accept (Jonah 1:11-15), cause the mariners' conversion (Jonah 1:16). And then Jonah receives, as if nothing has happened, again the assignment to proclaim God's message in Nineveh. This time Jonah goes to Nineveh indeed, but the way in which he carries out his assignment, doesn't give the impression that he falls to his task enthusiastically: "And (then) begins Jonah to go into the city by going a day, (only) *one*," although the city is "(very) big before God with a going of *three* days" (Jonah 3:4a and 3b). The unconditional cry: "Yet forty (times) a day and Nineveh shall be overthrown" (Jonah 3:4b) is rather a cry of triumph than a call to conversion. He doesn't speak about the God who passed judgement on Nineveh, he doesn't convey any arguments about the why of this judgement. And yet Jonah causes the conversion of Nineveh (Jonah 3:5-9) by this reluctant "prophecy", so that God regrets his intention to destroy Nineveh. "And not (at all) He does (it)" (Jonah 3:10), to Jonah's great dissatisfaction (Jonah 4:1).

It's clear that the author of the Book of Jonah evokes a sharp contrast between Jonah's intentions and actions on the one hand and God's intentions and the effects of Jonah's actions on the other. Whatever Jonah does, the result is that the pagans convert to Jonah's God. So, the improvement and the perfection of the creation only comes closer, if and when Jonah makes the nations of the world share the reverence for Adonai, the God of heaven and earth. Whether he wants it or not, Jonah must fulfil his assignment. So the author of the Book of Jonah seems to show a concerned and forgiving attitude towards the pagans: Israel will have to benefit the nations of the world by its actions. Who now thinks that therefore Jonah is a unique and exceptional book in Tanakh, errs. I'll explain this in short by means of some parts from the Torah and the Prophets.[76]

This attitude, directed at the nations of the world, can already be observed "in the beginning" of the Bible. The Torah even needs the whole Book of Genesis before Israel as a nation begins to participate in the already long existent, surrounding world. And even though in this world a history developed of the patriarchs – Abraham, Isaac and Jacob – this history is preceded by a primal history which results in a big enumeration of all seventy nations of the world (Genesis 1-10). That all people descend from one man, Adam and later again from Noah, fundamentally unites the fate of all people, the fate of Israel and of all the other nations. When God makes his pact with Noah, it is as much a pact with all living beings (Genesis 9:9-11). And when Abraham's story begins to to emerge from the community of nations, it is expressly in the sign of the common good for the nations, because " all peoples on earth will be blessed through you" (Genesis 12:3). Also the change of his original name *Abram* into *Abraham* is a sign of this. The new name is explained as 'father of many nations' (Genesis 17:5). A clear example of the way in which Abraham could be a blessing for the nations is found in the story of the destruction of the amoral cities of Sodom and Gomorra. Before God sends his messengers down to Sodom, He allows Abraham to plead in defence of the world (Genesis 18:17 ff.). Again we read in God's motivation that with

Abraham all nations of the earth will be blessed (v. 18). And again this motive returns after the binding of Isaac. And then the content of this "blessing for the nations" is further specified with the words: "because you have listened to my voice" (Genesis 22:18). Apparently one can only then be a blessing for the nations, if one's willing to stake everything, even the most precious thing one possesses.

Keeping on reading we notice that Abraham's assignment with regards to the community of the nations is not something limited specifically to him, but passes to his posterity as well. Isaac is the first (Genesis 26:4b). The motivation is accentuated, as it were: Because Abraham "listened to my voice and kept my watch, my commandments, my laws, and my instructions." That's why Isaac inherits this, his father's assignment (Genesis 26:5). So we can see here that being orientated on the world of the nations can indeed go hand in hand, at least should do so, with the laws and instructions "from above", that is the Torah. The last word of Genesis 26:5, 'instructions' is in Hebrew put in the plural of *Torah: Toroth*. But this orientation on the world of the nations can result in assimilation, adaptation to the non-Jewish surroundings and way of life. Hereafter we'll see that this area of tension keeps the Tanakh and Judaism occupied permanently.

Jacob, Isaac's son, also gets the assignment to be a blessing for humankind (Genesis 28:14). Moreover Genesis pays a lot of attention to Joseph's stay in Egypt. If anywhere it's in these stories that it's shown clearly what it means to be a blessing for the nations (Genesis 39 – 41). Joseph is in all sorts of respects a man of the exile. At the cost of persecution and imprisonment he keeps up his God-inspired style of life (Genesis 39:9). But he doesn't hesitate to make his contribution to the welfare of Egypt if he gets the chance to do so (Genesis 41). It's as if the Torah wants to say that it's exactly because of this attitude in life that Israel as a nation will stay alive (Genesis 42:1 ff.). Also in the Book of Daniel, written much later, the same theme comes up once again, albeit in different circumstances. The area of tension between on the one hand living according to God's assignments and on the other participating in a non-Jewish society in order to be a blessing, comprises the effort of these stories of Joseph and Daniel.

The undercurrent of Tanakh, aimed at the nations, only sounds very loud and well-articulated in the performance of Deutero-Isaiah during the Babylonian exile (586 -538 BC). Fitting in with a tendency which can already be discerned in the first Isaiah (e.g. Isaiah 19:23-25), the prophecy of Deutero-Isaiah grows into a worldwide perspective (e.g. Isaiah 42:1-7; 45:22-25; 49:1-7; 56:1-8). We also come across this attitude with the prophet Zechariah, who made his appearance after the exile (Zechariah 8:20-23). One gets the impression that it was exactly the Babylonian exile, which gained many Israelites the insight into the potential meaning of Israel for the nations. Jonah is one of the fruits of this insight, an insight that has kept strong support also among the Jews in post-biblical times.

4.2   Jonah, Ezra-Nehemiah and the Persian Empire[a]

Many Christian commentators take the view that the Book of Jonah was written in or after the days of Ezra and Nehemiah. According to them the Book of Jonah was aimed especially against the so-called narrow-minded, religious nationalism of these Jewish leaders after the Babylonian exile. You see, in the books of Ezra and Nehemiah we read about measures against marriages of Jews with non-Jewish women (Ezra 9:1 ff.; Nehemiah 13:23-27). Also some non-Jews are denied their rights in Jerusalem (Nehemiah 2:20). In that case these measures are interpreted as a form of "narrow-minded, religious nationalism" against which the Book of Jonah was supposed to preach a "humane universalism." [77] However, there is not a single substantive relation between the problem of mixed marriages in Ezra and Nehemiah and the message of doom of Jonah to Nineveh. If only because of this, that outlook on the message of the Book of Jonah should be distrusted. But there is more.

The designation "narrow-minded, religious nationalism" for the actions of Ezra and Nehemiah is based on a faulty reading of the books of Ezra and Nehemiah. Indeed for a correct interpretation of the measures of both Jewish leaders against some non-Jews and against the marriages of Jews with non-Jewish women we should consider its context. The three non-Jews Sanballat, Tobia and Gesem are deprived of their rights in Jerusalem as a reaction on the ridicule, contempt and

---

[a]   A survey of the most important events from this period can be found in table 4.1.

Table 4.1
Timetable of the most important periods of government and events in Judah, Samariah (formerly Israel), Babylon and Persia in the 6th and 5th century BCE.

vCJ	JUDAH	ISRAEL/SAMARIAH	ASSYRIA	BABYLON	MEDIA/PERSIA	LYDIA	GREECE
610		614-610 Fall of Assyria					
600	609 Jehoiakim			604 Nebuchadnezzar			
590	598 Jehojachin / Fall Jerusalem Beginning of the Babylonian exile						
580							
570							
560						Croesus	
550				555 Nabonidus	559 Cyrus II the Great		
540				DEUTERO-ISAIAH 539 Belshazzar	547 Cyrus conquers Lydia		
530	537 Return led by Zerubbabel			538 Cyrus conquers Babylon			
520	520 Reconstruction of the Temple Jeshua High priest				529 Cambyses 522 Darius I		
510							
500							
490							
480					486 Xerxes I		
470							
460					465 Artaxerxes I		
450	458 Ezra goes to Jerusalem						
440	445 Nehemiah Viceroy	Sanballat Viceroy					
430	433 Nehemiah returns to Persia						
420					424 Xerxes II 423 Darius II		

insinuations they voiced with regards to the Jews who repaired the walls of Jerusalem (Nehemiah 2:19-20). Also the measures of Ezra and Nehemiah against the marriages with non-Jewish women should be seen in the light of the behaviour of the non-Jewish inhabitants of Judea and the ensuing influence on the Jews. Ezra's main task was to put the Torah again in the centre of the Jewish community after the exile (Ezra 7:10). In this society the Jewish element was threatened constantly by assimilation, adaptation of the Jews to their non-Jewish surroundings. Before these steps were taken, the why of them was mentioned three times: the intermarriage of Jews with non-Jews, which caused the Jews to begin to adopt the "horrors", i.e. the idolatrous and immoral practices of the non-Jews (Ezra 9:1, 11,14). Especially because of the central part the women play in Jewish education, there was a danger that very little or nothing would come of a Torah true Judaism. So Ezra's measures were not taken and enforced rashly and without reflection. Lawcourts were set up to reach a correct settlement of the divorces (Ezra 10:13-17). Though not mentioned it would have been very well possible that divorce could be prevented by conversion to Judaism after the example of Ruth, the Moabite. The danger of assimilation is underscored once more in Nehemiah 13:23-27, which says that marriages with women of Ashdod, Ammon, and of Moab would lead to their children's estrangement of Israel. Anyway this shows that Ezra's measures had hardly any effects a decade and a half later.[a]

So in this context it's important to make a clear distinction between "narrow-minded, religious nationalism" on the one hand and measures against assimilation on the other. This last mentioned needn't be at a variance with a positive attitude directed at the community of nations, but it could be the other, unavoidable side of it. A universalism that leaves the assimilation unimpeded, isn't a universalism in biblical sense. The tension of sticking to a life on the basis of the Torah on the one hand and being a blessing to the nations on the other, especially because one lives on the basis of the Torah, that tension is also the commitment of the books of Ezra and Nehemiah. The fact is that one cannot deny these books a positive setting directed at the community of nations as well.

---

[a] Ezra appeared in the seventh year of king Artaxerxes (Ezra 7:8), while Nehemiah took these measures in or after the twenty-third year of king Artaxerxes (Nehemiah 13:6).

For example it's remarkable that a Persian king takes a decision four times in favour of the Jews. King Cyrus II acts as the "servant of Adonai" and orders the exiles to go to Jerusalem and to rebuild there the temple of Adonai on his behalf (Ezra 1:1-4). When the reconstruction has ceased after the opposition of the non-Jewish population of Judea and is resumed again at the urging of the prophets Haggai and Zechariah (Ezra 5:1), King Darius gave his explicit consent (Ezra 6:6 ff.). Later Ezra returns from Babel to Jerusalem with King Arthahsasta's consent (Ezra 7:11 ff.) and later still the same applies to Nehemiah (Nehemiah 2:1 ff.). The reconstruction of the temple before the arrival of Ezra, the embellishment of the temple by Ezra (Ezra 7: 12 ff.) and the reconstruction of the walls and gates of Jerusalem by Nehemiah, this all happened always with the consent of the Persian kings. King Darius even orders to continue the sacrificial service, so that "they can pray for the king and his sons" (Ezra 6:10). There is nothing in both books that points at the fact that the Jewish leaders would free themselves of the Persian authority. On the contrary, their attitude with regard to the Persian empire is one of complete loyalty in every respect.

That loyalty appears for instance from the fact that the reconstruction of the temple stops when the Persian king on the basis of false information orders this (Ezra 4:24). Again and again the builders have to defend themselves against the non-Jewish inhabitants who accuse them of the intention to rise in rebellion against Persia (Ezra 4:12-16; Nehemiah 2:19b). Nehemiah who was the cupbearer at the Persian court initially (Nehemiah 1:11) and acted as a governor of Judea later on (Nehemiah 8:9; 10:1; 12:26), returns dutifully to the Persian court when his term of office has expired (compare Nehemiah 2:6 with 13:6). Influence of the Persian court on the course of events in the temple is also mentioned (Nehemiah 11:23). When Nehemiah reads a lesson, he ends with mentioning that the Persian dominance has been imposed on Israel by God Himself, and he leaves out every prayer of deliverance (Nehemiah 9:37). So the anti-pagan measures of Ezra and Nehemiah should be seen especially as a fight against assimilation and not as a manifestation of nationalism. Yet even with them remained room for non-Jews who sincerely wanted to join the Jewish people, as is proved by Nehemiah's remark: "Moreover there were at my table of the Jews and the rulers a hundred and fifty men, beside those that came unto us from among the nations that were round about us". (Nehemiah 5:17).

At the end of this section I'd like to add that the above observations in the books of Ezra and Nehemiah have consequences for the understanding of the messages of the Book of Jonah. If indeed the Book of Jonah was written during or directly after the days of Ezra and Nehemiah, how should Jonah be read against the background of the then political relations in the world. In other words, shouldn't it be possible that 'Nineveh' not only refers to an already vanished Assyria, but also to the Persian empire which had subjected Israel after the Exile? And if so, won't the Book of Jonah be a direct continuation of the books of Ezra and Nehemiah? In chapter 5 I'll pursue these questions in greater depth.

4.3 Jonah, the rabbis and proselytism

It can be clarifying for the understanding of the message of the Book of Jonah to consider Jonah as part of an age-long development which continued among the rabbis during the post-biblical period. It is remarkable indeed that the on the nations oriented attitude we see in many places in the Torah and with the prophets, is expressed regularly in the later rabbinical tradition as well. The following quotation is an example of this phenomenon:[78]

> "The Torah was given publicly [in the Sinai wilderness], visible for all, in public. Had the Torah been given in the land of Israel, this nation could have said to the nations of the world: 'You are extraneous to it.' That's why the Torah was given in the wilderness, in no-man's-land, in public, visible for all. And everyone who wants to receive the Torah, can come and receive it."

In the rabbinic tradition there are many statements in the same tenor: Anyone from the nations who comes to Israel to obtain the knowledge of Adonai, should be received with open arms. And even though Judaism didn't and doesn't implement the idea of "mission among the nations",[79] generally speaking that is, it will be clear that this open attitude made it possible that many non-Jews linked up with Judaism or even converted to it. This conversion from paganism to Judaism, called 'proselytism', was a frequent phenomenon in antiquity. The enormous size of the Judaism in the days of the Roman Empire can be explained from this.[80] Therefore I'll concentrate my discussion of the above mentioned attitude of the rabbis', on their attitude towards the proselytes.[81]

In the rabbinic literature of the first centuries CE the generally accepted attitude towards proselytes is usually positive. From the end of the first century those, who joined Judaism from conviction, were mentioned in the Eighteen Benedictions prayer before the just and the pious. Famous rabbis like Shemaiah and Avtalion, Rabbi Akiva and Rabbi Me'ir descended from proselytes. They were even supposed to be the offspring of evil people like Sisera, Sanherib, Haman and Nero. Most rabbis from the first centuries followed the tradition: "When a proselyte comes to be converted, you should receive him with an open hand to bring him under the wings of the divine presence."

However, there have been some exceptions to this general rule. Character and temperament, but also the circumstances one lived under or the experiences with proselytes one had acquired, caused some rabbis to judge negatively about proselytism. One comes across some characteristic discussions. For instance, once Rabbi Eliezer ben Hyrcanus objected to the acceptance of proselytes. Aquila the Proselyte was amazed and asked him: "Is this all the love Adonai has given the proselyte, as is written: 'And He loves the stranger to give him bread and clothes?'" This answer made Rabbi Eliezer angry with him, but Rabbi Joshua agreed with him and said: 'Bread means Torah […], clothes means the prayer shawl: the man who's worthy to possess the Torah, will also receive its commandments. His daughters are allowed to marry priests and their grandchildren will sacrifice on the altar. One sees that in such a discussion the positive point of view has, so to speak, the last word. Elsewhere the following statement by Rabbi Eliezer about proselytes can be read: "They return to their evil ways." Obviously his experiences with proselytes were not very agreeable. But even a positive statement of him has been preserved: "If someone comes to you in sincerity to be converted (to become a Jew), don't reject him but encourage him on the contrary.

Under certain circumstances especially, an anti-proselytes attitude could develop on the basis of bad experiences. In times of prosecution and forced by circumstances proselytes often went over to the enemy and betrayed their former co-religionists and indicted them. A similar context explains the extremely fierce statement of Rabbi Simeon: "Those (among the pagans) who were God-fearing were an obstacle for Israel [...], the best of the pagans: one should put them to death." All the same he's also of the opinion that proselytes who are loved by God can be compared with the sun when it rises in its power. The statements by Rabbi Chiyya and Rabbi Chelbo fit in too with this context of unfaithfulness and treason. The first said: "Do not trust a proselyte at all, until twenty-four generations have passed, because so long evil will remain in him." The last said: "Proselytes are like a rash for Israel."

However, in spite of these negative eruptions the main theme remains also in later centuries: "Proselytes are loved. He [God] looks upon them as parts of Israel." In the 3rd century two rabbis, Rabbi Jonathan and Rabbi Eleazar, derived independently and from different verses in Tanakh that "the Holy One, blessed be He, caused Israel to go into exile among the nations only to make their numbers grow through adding proselytes." Rabbi Eleazar said: "Who takes a proselyte under one's protection, is considered as if he created him." There is a continuous line of this on the nations of the world directed attitude of the Torah and the Prophets to the acceptance of proselytes by the rabbis. The Book of Jonah is an early exponent of that attitude.

Finally, if we compare the Book of Jonah with Tanakh and rabbis on the point of openness towards the nations, the following attracts the attention. Jonah 1 and 2, with the exception of the assignment to go to Nineveh, don't differ essentially with the positive attitude we so often come across in Tanakh and with most of the rabbis. The main features of that attitude are: maintain a way of life on the basis of the Torah and be open to your pagan surroundings, so that you may be a blessing to them and receive the interested pagans with an open mind. It's this attitude we also see reflected in Jonah 1. When asked, Jonah tells the mariners about his God (Jonah 1:9). And then he shows them how to find a way out of the storm (Jonah 1:12). Though Jonah certainly doesn't want to convert them and wasn't asked to do so, the effect of his presence and his behaviour aboard the ship is that the men do convert to Adonai and even offer Him sacrifices (Jonah 1:16). If one should think of proselytism in this case couldn't be said with certainty,[a] but yet it looks very much like it. The words "and (then) the men feared a fear (very) big [for Adonai]" may indicate indeed that they became God-fearing men, a preliminary stage of proselytism.

The chapters 3 and 4 of Jonah go further in one respect than any other story in the Tanakh: Jonah is charged with the task to prophecy among the pagans in order to save them from their fall.[b] This story goes far, and we could wonder why? Missionary activities don't come up anywhere in Tanakh or in the rabbinic tradition. Nowhere the Israelite or Jew is purposefully called up to approach the pagans in order to convert them to the God of Israel. Why then does this seem to be the case in the Book of Jonah?

In this respect we should pay attention to a subtle feature in the Jonah story, which is of importance for answering the above question. Jonah's message in Nineveh doesn't imply at all proclaiming the God of Israel. Jonah even doesn't speak about Him (Jonah 3:4 in contrast to Jonah 1:9). Presumably it's not the purpose of this message to get the Ninevites to know the God of Israel. And so the name of God doesn't occur at all in the story of Nineveh's conversion (Jonah 3:5-10). The central point in Jonah's words to Nineveh is the fate of this city: for Jonah its destruction, for God its salvation (Jonah 3:4). Jonah's assignment with respect to Nineveh is not an assignment of mission in the later, Christian sense of the word. The purpose is not to convert Nineveh to Judaism, but to save the city from its fall. Even a non-Jewish city can find favour in the eyes of Adonai, provided it turns away from the evil that is in it. In this respect the Book of Jonah is in line with Abraham's plea for Sodom and Gomorrah (Genesis 18:16-33).

4.4   From seer to prophet

When we are looking for the message in the Book of Jonah, we can't ignore the strange argument between God and Jonah as it reaches its climax in Jonah 4. What's the background of this difference of opinion

---

[a]   For sacrifices could also be made by or on behalf of non-Jews in the Temple of Jerusalem.
[b]   Comparable is only, in a way, Elijah's mission to Damascus (1 Kings 19:15), but this was directed at one person only.

between God and his prophet? Jonah's unconditional prophecy of doom has not been fulfilled. On the contrary, Nineveh is not overturned like Sodom and Gomorrah, but remains – converted as a remorseful city – straight up.[a] And this to the annoyance of Jonah, because this degrades him, in his own eyes at least, to a false prophet according to the criterion of Deuteronomy 18:21-22. Since it says in Deuteronomy that a prophet whose prophecy is not fulfilled is a false prophet who has not spoken on behalf of Adonai. Whereas Jonah has experienced personally that Adonai has done everything to force him to fulfill his task. He called out half the cosmos, a storm, the sea and a big fish. No prophet can be more profound convinced to have spoken on behalf of Adonai than in fact Jonah. Not surprisingly Jonah would very much prefer to die than to live. He isn't a false prophet, God made him a false prophet after the event.[82] And this quarrel becomes more remarkable when we read that Jonah himself says having foreseen this outcome. He didn't flee to escape from his assignment, but to prevent this outcome – the deliverance of Nineveh (Jonah 4:2-3). He could have foretold it, so to speak, but in his unconditional message to Nineveh he didn't. Is this not the friction in Jonah's way of acting? On the one hand he knows of God's mercy and on the other hand he doesn't mention a single word of it in his message to Nineveh. Is here perhaps the key of the problem to be found why Jonah belongs to the Minor Prophets and not to the feast scrolls?[83] Isn't this about the nature of prophecy itself?

In section 3.3 I showed that the author of the Book of Jonah linked up closely the story in Jonah 4 with the stories about the prophet Elijah. In the midrashim of the rabbis this link between Elijah and Jonah is further developed. There Jonah is introduced as one of the most important pupils of Elijah. In that case we should realise that Elijah belongs to the so-called Former Prophets. These Former Prophets – among them Samuel – distinguish themselves from the Latter Prophets – among them Isaiah and Jeremiah – because their prophecies are unconditional. Tanakh itself shows this difference in places with

---

[a] See for both these meanings of the word "overthrown" the commentary on Jonah 3:4 in chapter 8.

the help of the word 'seer'.[a] In 1 Samuel 9:9 we read the remarkable statement: "Before time in Israel when a man went to inquire of God, thus he said: 'Come and let us go to the seer.' For he that is now called a prophet was before time called a seer." And as for these seers: what is spoken, is spoken. A sentence is unconditional and irrevocable. At best the sentence is commuted, but it will be executed. We'll show four examples of this phenomenon.

Samuel
In 1 Samuel 15 we read how Saul is ordered to eradicate Amalek, Israel's primal enemy, root and branch. Amalek's action against Israel in the wilderness is explicitly referred to, as described in Exodus 17:8-16. If the story is read carefully, it's clear that Amalek already attacks Israel (Exodus 17:8), when Israel's army must still be put together (Exodus 17:9). Amalek represents in Tanakh the cowardly mentality which attacks innocent, defenceless fellow men and women to destroy them. It's hardly surprising that the memory of this Amalek mentality should be "utterly blotted out from under heaven" (Exodus 17:14). Saul gets this assignment and indeed he defeats Amalek, but instead of destroying it utterly he gathers a rich booty. In the way he gathers this booty one recognizes Amalek's mentality: the best of the small stock, the cattle and the lambs is spared, worthless and inferior matters are destroyed (1 Samuel 15:9). The mentality Saul was supposed to destroy, he appears to possess himself. What's more, he takes king Agag home as a prisoner of war. The princes of those days were in the habit, if they were successful in waging wars, of keeping a household of captured kings and princes. And evidently Saul planned to be a king like the kings of all other nations in this respect (compare 1 Samuel 8:5, 19-20). After this Samuel's reaction is unrelenting. He informs Saul that his kingship won't persist. And all remorse shown by Saul (1 Samuel 15:20-21, 24-25, 30) can't change anything of it at all (1 Samuel 15:23, 26, 28-29). The only thing Saul achieves is that Samuel commutes the punishment slightly by not letting him down in the face of the nation (1 Samuel 15:30-31). After all these events Samuel returns

---

[a] Hebrew: *ro'eh* instead of *navi*, 'prophet', the last word meaning literally 'announcer'.

home to Rama. Till his death he didn't see Saul again, but he did mourn Saul (1 Samuel 15:34-35).

Nathan

David's punishment by the prophet Nathan is a similar case. After David's adultery with Bathsheba, the wife of his officer Uriah the Hittite, and after he had caused this Uriah to be killed in the war (2 Samuel 11), the prophet Nathan appears before David and announces his judgement (2 Samuel 12:1-12). When David immediately shows remorse the punishment is commuted in the sense that David won't die but the son born from this adultery (2 Samuel 12:13-14). Whatever David tries to do to save the boy's life: it's to no avail (2 Samuel 12:15-18). The verdict is not set aside (2 Samuel 12:22-23).

Gad

In 2 Samuel 24 we read how David orders Joab and his officers to count the people of Israel. They give up their initial resistance when the king's command appears to be stronger than their objections. A census like that had no other than a military purpose as appears from its result: Israel had 800,000 warriors who could wield their swords (2 Samuel 24:9). Now it is precisely the military side of kingship which at the time filled Samuel with the greatest possible objections against kingship (1 Samuel 8:11-12). It's typical of David that he already began to feel remorse for his action yet before a prophet turned up at his palace. However, the next morning the prophet Gad appears. He's explicitly announced as the "seer of David" (2 Samuel 24:11). The punishment is inevitable. The only moderation is that David is left the choice, so that he can choose the slightest severe punishment: a seven year's famine, three months of civil war or a plague of three days. Here too we see the unconditional message of the seer.

Elijah

King Ahab of Samaria obtained, via the machinations of his Phoenician wife Queen Jezebel, Naboth's vineyard illegally (1 Kings 21). On his first tour of inspection across the newly obtained property he meets Elijah the Tishbite, who foretells him that this injustice will not only be the end of his kingship, but also of his dynasty and his entire family (1 Kings 21:20-24). All will be eaten by the dogs. The effect of that message is that Ahab "rent his clothes, and put sackcloth upon his flesh, and fasted, and lay in sackcloth, and went softy" (1 Kings 21:27). But this can't nullify the sentence, at the most it can be commuted. Only a stay of execution is granted: not during Ahab's life, but only after his death the sentence will be executed on his family and dynasty (1 Kings 21:28-29). But it's also executed on himself. After being killed in action near Ramoth in Gilead, the dogs lap up his blood from his chariot at the pool where the harlots wash themselves (1 King 22:34-38). By order of Jehu – who according to the midrash was anointed king by Jonah – Jezebel was thrown down from a window and eaten by the dogs (2 Kings 9:30-37). Then Jehu exterminated Ahab's entire family: "So Jehu smote all that remained of the house of Ahab in Jezreel, and all his great men, and his familiar friends, and his priests, until there was left him none remaining" (2 Kings 10:1-7).

Now there can be sensed a large similarity between:

- Samuel's message to Saul;
- Nathan's message to David;
- Gad's message to David;
- Elijah's message to Ahab;
- Jonah's message to Nineveh.

All five of them are unconditional. The first four, those of the seers Samuel, Nathan, Gad and Elijah were fulfilled literally. Jonah too speaks as a seer: unconditionally. But – and that is the big difference – his prophecy is *not* fulfilled literally. Nineveh's penance prevents the execution. Nineveh fulfils the condition Jonah didn't state. And that is something Jonah doesn't understand. The Talmud says: "Jonah didn't understand the message he had to deliver on behalf of Adonai very well." He understood a destruction like that of Sodom and Gomorra. But Adonai meant: a reversal of conviction."[84] Atonement as on Yom Kippur, the Day of Atonement, the day one reads aloud the Book of Jonah in the synagogue.

With it Jonah does not only stand chronologically (the time of Jeroboam II), but also "theologically" on the borderline of seers and prophets. A seer's characteristic is his unconditional message. The prophets' characteristic is the conditionality of their message: "If you don't repent, a disaster will follow, but if you repent, welfare will follow." And so Jonah is a false prophet, not because his message remained unfulfilled – so the Talmud says – but because he kept back his true message. And this does not only refer to his flight "away from the face of Adonai"! Jonah also kept back his message by withholding Adonai's name from Nineveh and not mentioning His mercy and grace although he knew very well of this.[85]

In the afternoon service of Yom Kippur the story of Jonah is read, the story of the man who must be converted by Adonai Himself from seer to prophet. The story of the man who must be converted from a visionary judgement to prophetic empathy. Small wonder that this story had not been set aside in a separate collection of feast scrolls, but is put among the other prophets. The story of Jonah is a key story to the understanding of prophecy.[86]

4.5 Jonah and the Jewish-biblical feasts

At first sight the relation between the Book of Jonah and the Jewish-biblical feasts seemed limited to Yom Kippur, the Day of Atonement. Already long, long ago the Book of Jonah was read in its entirety in the synagogue in the afternoon service on the Day of Atonement. The Talmud states the following about that: [87]

> "On Yom Kippur one reads (the part) *After the death* (Leviticus 16:1 ff.) and as a reading from the prophets (the chapter) *For thus saith the High and Lofty One* (Isaiah 57:15 ff.). During the afternoon prayer one reads the part on incest (Leviticus 20) and as a final part (the Book of) Jonah."

As regards content there is, as we'll see later in this section, a big thematic similarity to discern between this prophetic book and this Jewish-biblical feast. However, the relation between the Book of Jonah and the Jewish-biblical feasts doesn't turn out to be limited to the Day of Atonement. Further research will reveal that the Book of Jonah shows a thematic structure that runs parallel with the annual cycle of the Jewish-biblical feasts. As the story of Jonah evokes the entire worldview of his days,[88] it also calls up for us the entire liturgical year. Not from the Day of Atonement to the Day of Atonement however, but from the Feast of Tabernacles to the Feast of Tabernacles. There are indications from which it can be gathered that one was still aware of this phenomenon in the Judaism of the beginning of the Common Era.

Table 4.2 contains a survey of the most important Jewish feasts. Some of them had only come into being in an era when the Book of Jonah already existed. So traces of these feasts can't be expected to be found in the Book of Jonah. This is certainly the case with Chanukah, the feast of the Rededication or Renewal of the Temple that was instituted in the days of the Maccabees (2nd century CE). It is also believed with regard to the feast of Purim that it is later than the Book of Jonah,

Table 4.2
Survey of the Jewish-biblical months and the most important biblical and post-biblical Jewish holidays.

Number of the month	Name of the month	Date	Holiday	Period
7	Tishri	1	Rosh Hashanah/New Year's Day	Yamim Noraim/ 10 Conversion days
		10	Yom Kippur/Day of Atonement	
		15 t/m 22	Sukkot/Feast of Tabernacles	
		23	Simchat Torah/Rejoicing of the Law	
8	Cheshvan			
9	Kislev	25 t/m	Chanukah/Feast of Dedication	Rainy season
10	Tevet	2		
11	Shevat			
12	Adar	14	Purim	
1	Nissan	15 t/m 21	Pesach/Easter	
2	Iyar			
3	Sivan	26	Shavuot/Pentecost	
4	Tammuz			
5	Av	9	9th Av/Destruction of the Temple	
6	Ellul			Month of shofar blowing

although this is more difficult to determine. In 2 Maccabees 15:36 this festival is already called "the day of Mordechai".[a] Of the other festivals, like Rosh Hashanah (the Jewish New Year) and Simchat Torah (the Day of Celebrating the Torah), it is not certain when they came into being and when they got the character they still have in Judaism. By and large one could say that the festivals are of a considerable earlier date than the time they are mentioned in writing for the first time. After all, such references are based on the fact that those festivals were already known generally. My investigation into the liturgical background of the Book of Jonah will even yield some arguments with regard to some feasts for an earlier date of origin than is rather widely assumed. I'll discuss the liturgical background in the relevant chapter.

a. The liturgical background of Jonah 1
There is an old rabbinic tradition which says that the word of Adonai came to Jonah (Jonah 1:1) during his stay in Jerusalem. He'd gone there as a pilgrim on the occasion of Sukkot (the Feast of Tabernacles). This feast is celebrated from 15 to 22 Tishri (Numbers 29:12-38). It begins five days after the Day of Atonement. Sukkot is pre-eminently a feast of joy. It is among other things a harvest-festival that ends the summer and that heralds the winter, the rainy season. On the last day of this festival a water ceremony was performed in the temple in Jerusalem, celebrating the beginning of the rainy season. Now this old rabbinic tradition says that the word of Adonai came to Jonah (1:1), when he was watching the performance of this water ceremony.[89]

This "dating" of the beginning of the Book of Jonah on the last day of the Festival of Tabernacles links up remarkably well with the further course of the story and that because of two reasons. In the first place it is probable that in early times already in many synagogues the last two chapters of Deuteronomy were read on the day after the Festival of Tabernacles.[90] This means that on this day – which became later known as Simchat Torah (Rejoicing of the Law) – the order of the readings of the Torah was closed. But in the days afterwards – or perhaps on the same day as is the case today – the new cycle of Torah readings was begun with the Book of Genesis.[91] Now it is remarkable

---

[a] Hereafter in this section (under a.) we'll find an indication that perhaps Purim already existed in the time the Book of Jonah was being written.

that the story in Jonah 1, as we already saw,[92] with regard to theme and choice of words fits in closely with the Creation story in Genesis 1.

In the second place I'd like to mention the fact that from the last day of Sukkot the rainy season has begun, which included the autumn and winter and lasted till Pesach the next spring. And it was precisely the winter season when in antiquity one sailed the Mediterranean as little as possible because of the dangers of bad weather and storm.[93] The story about the storm at sea in Jonah 1 fits in thematically and entirely with the time that follows Sukkot. Jonah's wish to escape must have been very big and his action is characterized in this way as highly irresponsible.

Leaving aside Chanukah as a festival of later date, the next feast that occurs on the Jewish calendar is Purim, that is celebrated on the 14th of the month Adar. This month comes at the end of the rainy season. Purim owes its name, according to Esther 9:26, to throwing the *pur*. 'Pur' is an Assyrian-Babylonian word that means 'dice of fate'. It's also translated as such in the Book of Esther (Esther 3:7; 9:24). This theme of throwing the dice of fate occurs also in Jonah 1:7 remarkably enough. Both in Jonah and in Esther the same verb (*napal* = throw, cast) and the same noun (*goral* = "dice of fate") are used.

Esther	Jona
3:7 hipil pur hu hagoral	1:7 w'napilah goraloth
9:24 w'hipil pur hu hagoral	1:7 wajjapilu goraloth
	1:7 wajjipol hagoral

There are also more thematic similarities and contrasts between Jonah 1 and the Esther stories. The dice of fate are cast in both cases by pagans: in Jonah by the mariners, in Esther by Haman and his cronies. In both cases the "fate" of the Israelite is decided by it: in the Book of Jonah the fate of Jonah, in the Book of Esther the fate of Mordechai and all other Jews. Besides these similarities there are two remarkable thematic differences between both stories. In Jonah the pagans certainly don't want to kill the Israelite. After having determined Jonah's involvement, the mariners are doing their utmost to put him ashore unharmed (Jonah 1:13). Only after a prayer to Adonai and at their wits' end they throw him overboard (Jonah 1:14-15). In the Book of Esther it is the explicit intention of the pagan Haman and his accomplices to exterminate Mordechai and the Jewish people. The following difference is closely connected with it: Jonah does indeed suffer the fate of the Sheol, but Mordechai and his people are saved from the death by the courage of one woman (Esther 8 and 9).

It would be getting too far here to fully examine the connection between Jonah 1 and Purim from a religious perspective.[94] It's enough to observe that the author of the Book of Jonah obviously lived in a time when something like a form of Purim already existed. In section 5.1 I'll put forward yet other arguments for this presupposition. So it is quite possible that the scene of the casting of the dice was added in the story of the storm at sea with an eye to "something like a Purim feast".[95]

b. The liturgical background of Jonah 2

The rainy season, the winter season, ended with Pesach (Easter) halfway the month of Nissan in spring.[96] There are now a lot of clues that Jonah 2 should be read as a Pesach story. In the first place there is of course the theme of the passage through the water of the sea, which also occurs in Exodus 14 and 15. In the second place about three expressions occur in the Psalm of Jonah which show a strong relationship with similar expressions in the Song of Moses sung after the passage through the Red Sea (Exodus 15:1-18):

- The words "in the heart of the seas" (Jonah 2:4) strongly resemble the words "in the heart of the sea" (Exodus 15:8);
- The words "to the temple of your holiness" (Jonah 2:5) correspond to the words "unto your holy habitation" (Exodus 15:13);
- The word "weeds" in Jonah 2:6 (Hebrew: *suf*) occurs also in the Hebrew words for the Red Sea in Exodus 15:4 (Hebrew: *jam suf*).

In the third place, when we compare the Psalm of Jonah with the song of Moses, it's obvious that they've almost the same structure:

Themes	Exodus 15	Jona 2
Opening words in the first person	1-3	3
Description of the deep	4-12	4-7a
God saves	13a	7b
Mentioning the temple	13b	8
Mentioning the pagans/idolaters	14-16	9
God's dwelling, resp. to sacrifice	17	10a-b
Final observation about Adonai	18	10c
[Mentioning the saving action of God]	[19]	[11]

So it's obvious that we have to take the story of Jonah's stay in the fish's belly and the Psalm of Jonah liturgically as a Pesach story. In later Judaism we also find clues that this is and was seen in this way.

In one of the rabbis' midrashim the men of the ship say in the storm to Jonah: "Call out to your God, perhaps He will perform for us such wonders as He did for the Jews at de Red Sea in the olden times."[97] Here then a clear connection is made between the rescue from the storm and the story of Pesach. Also is next to the word "weeds" in Jonah 2:6 (Hebrew: *suf*) told that the big fish in whose belly Jonah stayed, showed Jonah the place where the Israelites went through the Red Sea (Hebrew: *jam suf*).[98] A clear example that Jonah 2 was seen in later times as a Pesach story we also find in the Gospel of Matthew. In Matthew 12:40 Jonah's stay of three days and three nights in the fish is linked up with Jesus' death and resurrection which according to Matthew happened around Pesach (Matthew 26:17 ff.).

From the above can be concluded that Jonah 2 has the Pesach feast as a liturgical background.

c. The liturgical background of Jonah 3
Without any doubt the liturgical background of Jonah 3 should be looked for in the time and theme of the present New Year's feast, Rosh Hashanah. *Rosh Hashanah* means literally "Head of the year". Yet it's not the first day of the first, but of the seventh month, the month of Tishri which falls in the autumn. In the Torah the name *Rosh Hashanah* is not used. However, the first day of the seventh month comes up as a special day: a day of rest when special sacrifices were made and the shofar (the ram's horn) was blown (Leviticus 23:23-25; Numbers 29:1-

6). This New Year's Day happens ten days before the Day of Atonement and has undoubtedly from olden times a preparatory function for Yom Kippur, the king among the Jewish-biblical feasts. And that preparatory function has never been anything else than what Rosh Hashanah still is today, namely that of *Jom Hadin*, "Day of the Court of Justice" or "Judgement Day". It is the day on which God according to the Jewish idea passes judgement on the actions the people have done during the past year. Blowing the shofar can in this context be understood as a signal of the approaching judgement.[a] On this day God decides by reason of their actions what the fate of the people will be in the coming year: whether they will be happy, rich or poor, sick or healthy, whether there will be war or peace, abundance or famine and so on. However, after Rosh Hashanah nine days follow to Yom Kippur. Together they are called the ten *Yamim Noraim*, the "Days of Awe".

During these ten days people have the opportunity to convert, distance themselves from their evil actions, repair the disturbed relations with their fellow men and to resolve to live better in the coming year. When God passes an evil judgement on a man on Rosh Hashanah, this judgement is suspended to Yom Kippur. Everyone has ten days left to better his life. Who converts sincerely during the ten days of conversion can count on God forgiving him his sins on the Day of Atonement, the day of forgiveness, and giving him a new chance to be a better man.

These themes occur in Jonah 3 in a similar way. Nineveh is notified of the fact that on the basis of its action it will be sentenced. She will have however forty days of grace, a period which according to Jonah 4:2 God indeed meant to give Nineveh the opportunity to turn away from her evil, so that the verdict can be changed. It is plausible that the function of Rosh Hashanah as preparation for Yom Kippur (Day of Atonement) in the time the Book of Jonah was written, wasn't limited to the first day of the seventh month, but that there was a longer period preceding Yom Kippur with this function. This can be gathered from the period of forty days the inhabitants of Nineveh are granted, and which in the liturgy of the synagogue agrees remarkably well with a "second" period of preparation for Yom Kippur not last-

---

[a]   See e.g.: Amos 3:6; Zephaniah 1:16.

ing ten but forty days. During the entire month of Ellul preceding Rosh Hashanah, the shofar is blown in the synagogue daily – except on the sabbath – to herald Rosh Hashanah and Yom Kippur. So penance and conversion are also the themes of this month of Ellul. In the Midrash the period of 1 Ellul to 10 Tishri is regarded as a period of forty days.[99]

It can be concluded from these data that the time around Rosh Hashanah and Yom Kippur is the liturgical background of Jonah 3.

d. The liturgical background of Jonah 4

The transition of the themes of Rosh Hashanah and the conversion days to Yom Kippur (Day of Atonement) already takes place in Jonah 3:10 when God watches the doings of the people of Nineveh, so that He regrets the evil He'd threatened them with. The climax of these Yom Kippur themes we then find in Jonah 4:2b which describes God as a God who is "gracious and compassionate, slowly (becoming) angry and abundant in kindness, repenting of evil." Next we find in Jonah 4 a reference to Sukkot (Feast of Tabernacles). In Jonah 4:5 Jonah has built a tabernacle east of the city. In Hebrew the word used for 'tabernacle' is indeed *sukkah* (the singular of Sukkot). This link with the Feast of Tabernacles now also declares why this verse (Jonah 4:5) must be in this place in the story and not, according to some commentators, between Jonah 3:4 and 3:5.[100] This verse was not put in a different place when it was copied out later, so they think, but the author of the Book of Jonah put it here definitely on liturgical grounds.

From Jonah 4:5 the story shows a lot of similarities with the story of the Fall in Genesis 2 and 3.[101] From a liturgical point of view we are in the time after the Feast of Tabernacles, a period that begins with Simchat Torah (Rejoicing of the Law). During this period the Torah reading starts again with among other things Genesis 2 and 3 on the next sabbath. And then it attracts the attention that in Jonah 4:6 the verb stem of *simchat* occurs twice: "And (he) rejoices, Jonah, ... (with) a joy, (very) big" (Hebrew: *wajjismach jonah ... simchah gêdolah*). And so we are back again in the liturgical period we began with in Jonah 1:1.

In table 4.3 is a survey of the parallels between the Book of Jonah and the Jewish-biblical feasts discussed in this section. In the table we

Table 4.3
Survey of the parallels between the Book of Jonah and the Jewish-biblical liturgical year.

Jonah 1 and 2	Festival of the period
1:1 The calling of Jonah during Sukkot (jT Sukkah 5:1)	Sukkot/Feast of Tabernacles (15-22 Tishri) – Water ceremony in the temple
1:4 ff. Many parallels with Genesis 1	Simchat Torah/Rejoicing of the Law (23 Tishri) – Torah reading from Genesis 1
1:4-15 Storm at sea (happened especially in the winter season)	Rainy season from the last day of Sukkot to the first day Pesach
1:7 Throwing the dice	Purim/Feast of the Dice (14 Adar)
2:1-11 Big similarity with the Song of Moses (Exodus 15)	Pesach/Easter (15-22 Nissan) – Passage through the Red Sea

Jonah 3 and 4	Feast or period
3:4 Forty days to convert for Nineveh	1 Ellul to 10 Tishri – a period of 40 days of penance and conversion
3:4 Judgement on Nineveh	Rosh Hashanah/New Year's Day (1 Tishri) – Day of Judgement
3:5-9 Conversion of Nineveh	Yamim Noraim/ Days of Awe (1-10 Tishri) – Conversion days
3:10 God reconsiders the judgement on Nineveh 4:2 God is gracious and compassionate	Yom Kippur (10 Tishri) – Day of penance and forgiveness
4:5 Jonah builds a tabernacle (sukkah)	Sukkot/Feast of Tabernacles (15-22 Tishri)
4:6 Jonah rejoices (simchah)	Simchat Torah/Rejoicing of the Law (23 Tishri)
4:6 ff. Many parallels with Genesis 2 and 3	Reading Genesis 2 and 3 on the sabbath after Simchat Torah

see that Jonah runs parallel with the liturgical cycle of a year. This is of great importance for the message of the Book of Jonah. It appears from it that the author saw the beneficial orientation of Israel on the nations of the world[102] and the liturgical service to God in the temple as inextricably bound up with each other. What should be celebrated in the liturgy, should be realized in the world. And that which is brought about in the world should be based on the liturgy. The service to the world and the service of sacrifices, prayers and the study of the Torah need one another. Jonah celebrates the Feast of Tabernacles, but does he allow Nineveh to celebrate Yom Kippur?

5 By the decree of the king and his big ones
The Book of Jonah in its time

5.1 The time of the origin of the Book of Jonah

There are different opinions about when the Book of Jonah was created varying from the 8th to the 3rd century BCE. However, most scholars take the view that the book was written in the time of the Persian rule of the land of Israel. This Persian period (538-332 BCE) followed the Babylonian exile (598-538 BCE) and ended with the conquest of the Greeks and Macedonians commanded by Alexander the Great (332 BCE). In this section I'll discuss briefly the most important arguments which play a part in this dating discussion and join those who place the origin of the Book of Jonah in the Persian time. Starting from that historical background I'll try to understand in the following sections Jonah as an actual midrash.

The earliest possible dating of the Book of Jonah falls halfway the 8th century BCE in or directly after the time in which the historical Jonah from 2 Kings 14:25 lived. That was during the reign of Jeroboam II of Israel (787-747 BCE). The Book of Jonah should – supposedly – have been written by one of Jonah's contemporaries with the intention of bringing up Jonah's performance for discussion. However, there are a number of facts which don't agree with such an early, historizing dating.

In the first place Nineveh wasn't the residence of the kings of Assyria in the time of Jeroboam II as told in Jonah 3:6. Assur was the city. Only half a century later, during the rule of king Sennacherib (705-681 BCE), the residence was moved from Assur to Nineveh[103] (2 Kings 19:36 still refers to it). In this respect it's remarkable that the title "king of Nineveh" (Jonah 3:6) is not historical.[104] Even in the time when Nineveh was the capital the kings of Assyria were called "king of Assur" (see for instance 2 Kings 20:6; 23:29). This could indicate that the author of the Book of Jonah did no longer have a clear image of the actual situation in the time of Jeroboam II, or that he wasn't really interested in a historical and qua facts correct story. What's more, the size of the city of Nineveh as described in Jonah 3:3 is legendary.[105] The historical Nineveh was at the time of her destruction in

THE BOOK OF JONAH IN ITS TIME

612 BCE nowhere bigger than 2.5 km wide and 5 km long. The circumference of the city was about 13 km, a distance that can be walked in almost 4 hours (see map 5.1).[106] This also makes it clear that the author of Jonah didn't intend to write an exact historical description of the events which would have taken place in or before his own days. All this gives sooner the impression that he lived later, in a time when Nineveh and the size of Nineveh could fulfil a specific part in the

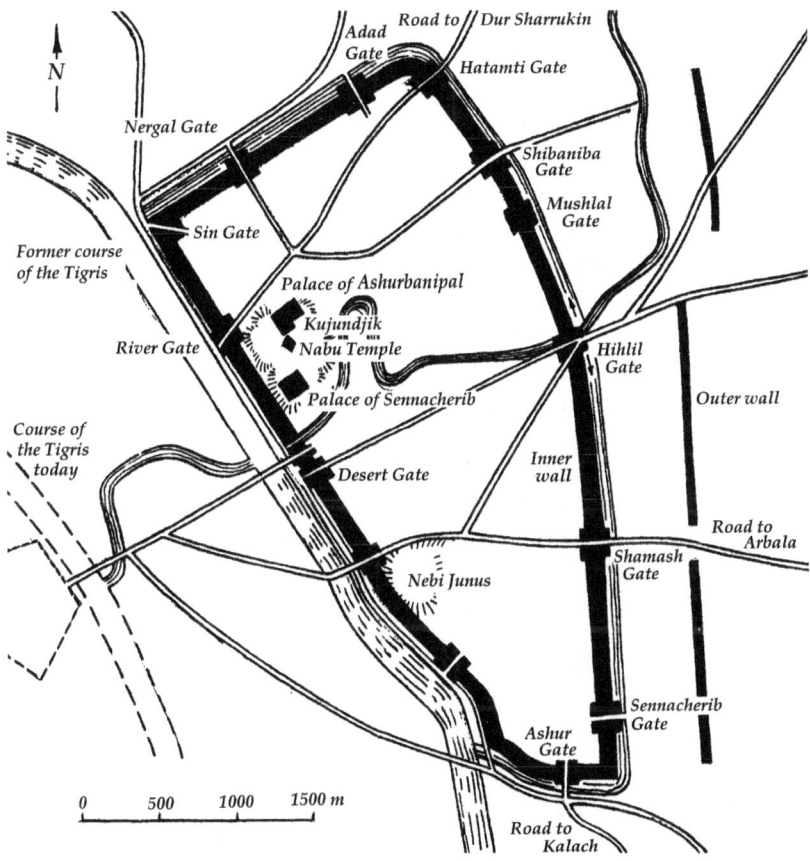

Map 5.1   *Map of Nineveh: The Northwesterly wall is only 2 km long, the easterly one hardly 5 km.*

argument of his story and so a part which surpassed the part of the historical Nineveh by far.

Besides the 8th century BCE as the earliest dating of the Book of Jonah there is also a last dating possibility. From a number of Apocrypha written in the 2nd century BCE, it's obvious that the Book of Jonah already existed. In Tobit 14:4 and 8 the fall of Nineveh in 612 is seen as a late fulfilment of Jonah's doom prophecy concerning the city. Also in the book the Wisdom of Sirach, of about 180 BCE, we find an indication that the Book of Jonah was known at that time. In it, Sirach 49:10, is spoken of the twelve prophets. Obviously the twelve lesser prophets, because there is no reason whatsoever to take it for granted that the group of twelve lesser prophets Jesus Sirach had had in mind was composed differently than the present collection in Tanakh. That implies that at that time already the Book of Jonah must have been authoritative. And since some time passes by before a text becomes authoritative, we can simply assume that the Book of Jonah had already existed for a longer period at the beginning of the 2nd century BCE. This means that in all probability the book had already come into being before the year 300 BCE. And that's in line with the most important arguments in the dating discussion, which all point into the direction of the 5th or the 4th century, the time of the Persian occupation of the land of Israel.

There is a great number of philological facts in the Book of Jonah which point in the direction of the time after the Babylonian exile as the time when the book had come into being. That time the Hebrew language became very much influenced by the Aramaic language and the Book of Jonah shows many features of it.[107] So in the text occur many expressions which are not of Hebrew but of Aramaic origin:

- The word *malach* ('mariner, sailor') in Jonah is Aramaic originally.[108]
- The word *jitasheit* ('changes his mind') in Jonah 1:6.[109] This word, as well as its stem of which it was derived, doesn't happen in the Hebrew parts of Tanakh. The Hebrew verb that could have been used here is *zachar*.[110] The stem *jitasheit* only occurs in the Aramaic part of the Book of Daniel (Daniel 6:4), which indicates that this too is a word of Aramaic origin.

- The word *bêshèlêmi* ('for whose cause') in Jonah 1:7.[111] This word has been made up of four parts: *bê* (= 'for' or 'by'), *shè* (from *asher* = 'the one'), *lê* (= 'to') and *mi* (= 'who'). Compound words like that don't occur in the pre-Babylonian exile Hebrew.
- Even the words *vêshèli* ('for my sake') in Jonah 1:12 and *shèbinlailah* ('a son of the night') in Jonah 4:10 are examples of Aramaisms. As in *bêshèlêmi* these words are made up with the help of the relative pronoun *shè*, a construction which only began to occur in Hebrew after the exile.[112]
- The word *wêjishtoch* ('so that it may be calm') in Jonah 1:11 and 12. The stem *shatach* of which it was derived, is used in Tanakh only here and in Psalm 107:30 and Ecclesiastes 26:20, and is probably an Aramaism.[113]
- The word *ta'am* ('command') in Jonah 3:7.[114] This is a corruption of the Assyrian-Babylonian word *temu*, a technical term for a royal command. This word only occurs in Tanakh in its Aramaic form in Ezra 6:13 ff. and in Daniel 3:10 and 29.
- Also the expression *lêhatsil lo mera'ato* ('to draw him away from his anger') in Jonah 4:6 can be seen as an Aramaism.[115]
- And finally the word *ribo* ('ten thousand') in Jonah 4:11 is a word that in the later texts of Tanakh replaces the older Hebrew word *rêvavah*.[116]

The expression 'the God of the heavens' in Jonah 1:9 follows naturally the foregoing and is an expression characteristic for the Persian official language and which occurs only in the texts of after the Babylonian exile with the exception of Genesis 24:7.[117] Especially in the 5th century BCE this was a popular expression.[118] In Tanakh we find this indication for God when Persian kings or,[a] just like the Jews who addressed Persian civil servants or other strangers.[b]

In this respect Jonah 3 contains also a number of important facts. I already pointed at the Assyrian-Babylonian origin of the word *ta'am* ('command') in Jonah 3:7. However, the whole description of the royal performance in Jonah 3 shows strong Persian features. With the 'big ones' in Jonah 3:7 princes, high civil servants and advisers are meant.

---

[a] Nehemiah 1:4, 5; 2:4, 20; compare also with Daniel 2:18, 19.
[b] Ezra 5:11, 12; Jonah 1:9; compare also with Daniel 2:37, 44.

Such individuals existed also at the Assyrian court. The procedure of the king and his high advisors making laws and commands *together* is unknown with Jews as well with Assyrians, but it does occur at the Persian court (Ezra 7:14; Daniel 6:18; Esther 1:13).[119] Also the nature of the decision that is sent out by the king and his big ones (Jonah 3:7-9), is neither Israelitic nor Assyrian but looks clearly like the nature of the decisions of the Persian kings (Ezra 7:12 ff.; Daniel 6:7-10; Esther 1:13-22).[120] Also the literary reproduction of such decisions has only become a custom after the Babylonian exile in Jewish texts.[a] In older books there are initiatives of this kind to be found, but they sooner give the impression to be excerpts of the relevant documents than a complete reproduction.[b] Anyway, we have to bear in mind that here we're dealing with a figure of speech and not with copies of real historical records.

According to me no other conclusion from all these facts is possible than that the Book of Jonah is a text which was written after the Babylonian exile and so in the Persian period. It's also remarkable that the later Jewish tradition considers this time to be the time in which the Book of Jonah was supposedly written. The author should have been a member of the so-called Great Assembly, a governing body which after the Babylonian exile governed the Jews who had gone back to the land of Israel.[121] This further agrees with what we saw in the chapters 3 and 4 with regards to the similarities between the Book of Jonah on the one hand and some other books of the Tanakh and the Jewish calendar of festivals on the other hand. Furthermore, the connections between Jonah 1 and Genesis 1 I discussed in section 3.1, point at the origin of the Book of Jonah in a period when the Torah already existed in its present form. If the Torah really underwent its final editing – as is stated by many scholars – in or directly after the Babylonian exile, it means that the Book of Jonah must have been written in the Persian period. This also applies to the thematic link between Jonah 1 and – possibly – an already existing Purim feast as discussed in section 4.5.a. In the following sections I'll further explain

---

[a] Ezra 5:6-17; 6:2-12; 7:11-26; 1 Maccabees 8:23-28; 10:18-20, 25-45; 11:30-37; 12:6-18; 13:36-40; 14:20-23, 27-34; 15:2-9, 16-21; 2 Maccabees 1:1-9; 1:10-2:8; 9:19-27; 10:16-21, 22-26, 27-33; 11:34-38.

[b] E.g. 2 Kings 19:10-12; compare also with 2 Chronicles 32:9-19.

what kind of time the Persian period was, seen historically and politically, and what kind of traces of it could be recovered in the Book of Jonah.

5.2 From Assyria to Persia: the Babylonian Exile

In section 3.5 we saw how the Assyrian empire terrorized the entire Middle East for two centuries till its fall in 610 BCE. However, all military efforts of the Assyrians could not prevent the Medes from building up a powerful empire in today's Iran. They were to pose a considerable threat to Assyria in the 7th century BCE. When in 627 BCE Nabopolasser of Babylon arose against the Assyrian authority, it wouldn't take long before a strong alliance was established between the Medes and the Babylonians, an alliance which would result in the fall of the Assyrians in the war of 614-610 BCE. The old Assyrian empire was divided by both superpowers. Babylon got the territory of the Euphrates and the Tigris and would soon extend its influence to Egypt. The Medes conquered the highlands north of former Assyria and advanced to Asia Minor. There they came into conflict with the Lydian empire. Only in 585 BCE they concluded the peace with the Lydians and the river Halys becomes the frontier between both powers (see map 5.2).[122]

During all these historical events before and around the fall of Assyria, the kingdom of Judah had managed to maintain its independence. To be sure, it was a vassal state of the great Assyrian empire, but as long as it didn't provoke the Assyrians, it needn't fear a fall. However, with the arrival of the Babylonians the political situation became more insecure, an insecurity which eventually would end in the fall of Judah and Jerusalem.

Because of the power vacuum which arose during the breakdown of the Assyrian empire, Egypt managed to expand its influence in the entire land of Israel as far as Syria. In 609 BCE pharao Neklo replaced king Jehoahaz of Judah with his brother Eliakim, who then changed his name into Jehoiakim (2 Kings 23:31-34; 2 Chronicles 36:1-4). This Jehoiakim would remain loyal to his Egyptian master as long as pos-

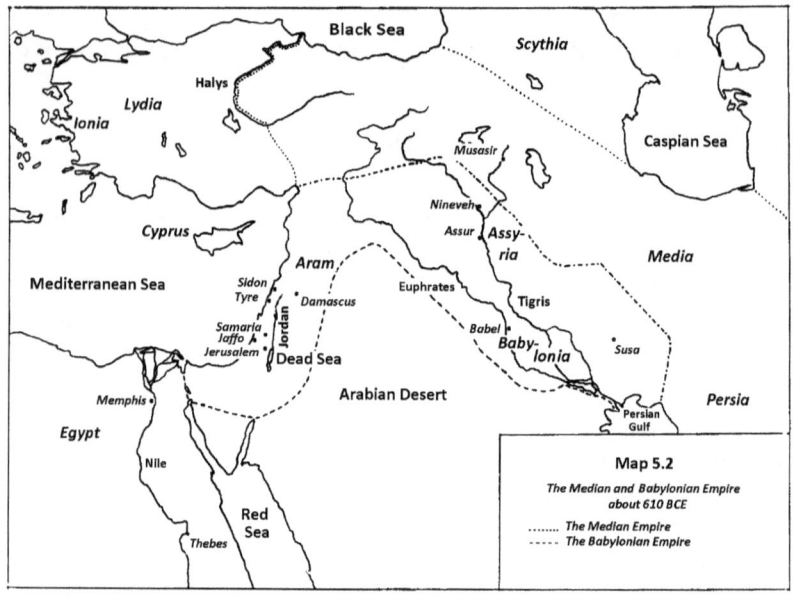

Map 5.2
The Median and Babylonian Empire
about 610 BCE
.... The Median Empire
- - - - - The Babylonian Empire

sible. However, in 605 BCE the Babylonian crown prince Nebuchadnezzar inflicted a crushing defeat on the Egyptians at Karkemis. When, a year later, he also conquered Ashkelon, Jehoiakim submitted to the Babylonians. Yet, three years later, in 601 BCE Nebuchadnezzar was defeated by the Egyptians and Jehoiakim joins again his old ally Egypt. Before Nebuchadnezzar could subject him, Jehoiakim died in 598 BCE and was followed by his son Jehoiachin, whose government would only last three months and ten days (2 Chronicles 36:9). After a short siege Nebuchadnezzar captured Jerusalem in the spring of 597 BCE. King Jehoiachin, his mother Nechusta, his court and many inhabitants of Jerusalem are deported to Babylon: the beginning of the Babylonian exile. Nebuchadnezzar appointed Jehoiachin's uncle Mattanja in Jerusalem as his successor who then adopted the name Zedekiah. Although the prophet Jeremiah warns him not to rise against Babylon (2 Chronicles 36:12), Zedekiah didn't manage to withdraw from the influence of those who wanted to release Jerusalem from Nebuchadnezzar's clutch. And he dumps Babylon. However, the Babylonian army immediately advanced to lay siege to Jerusalem. Although Jeremiah called on to surrender the city to the besiegers

(Jeremiah 38:17-18), Zedekiah lacked the courage to do so. In the summer of 587 BCE Jerusalem was captured by the Babylonians and destroyed thoroughly. The population was deported for a greater part to Babylon and Judah became a Babylonian province. The exile has finally got its definitive character.[123]

But in the course of the Babylonian exile a development occurred east of Babylon which will turn the history of Israel in quite a different direction again. The Median empire which together with Babylon had overthrown the old arch-enemy Assyria, experienced an important change from within. The form of government of this Median empire has not been the form of the usual unitary state. It was probably a federation of rather autonomous principalities ruled by vassals of the Median sovereign. In the middle of the 6th century BCE Cyrus II, vassal of the territory of the Persians, managed to bring and unite a number of his fellow-vassals under his authority. After that he established politic relations with the Babylonian king Nabonidus (556-539 BCE). In 550 BCE he conquered the Median empire, which from then on for more than two centuries would play the leading part in the Middle East as the Persian empire.

Initially Cyrus, who later was to be called 'the Great', left Babylon alone. First he turned to the Lydians in Asia Minor. In 547 he crossed the river Halys and conquered the Lydian empire. Immediately afterwards the first confrontation between Persians and Greeks occurred, a confrontation that would last the entire existence of the Persian empire and was to lead to its fall in the end. From 546 BCE the Ionic-Greek cities on the coast of Asia Minor were conquered systematically by the Persian armies (see map 5.3).

In 540 BCE Cyrus started a campaign against Babylon. In the mean time king Nabonidus had alienated himself thoroughly from his subjects. The Deutero-Isaiah[1] wasn't probably the only one in Babylon who watched out for Cyrus as a possible liberator. The theme of the whole of Isaiah 40-44 is the approaching liberation by the Persians. In Isaiah 45:1 Cyrus (Kores) is even called *messiah*, 'the anointed one of Adonai.' And so it happened in 539 BCE, that Babylon fell into the hands of Cyrus the Great as an easy prey, who turned out to be a tolerant ruler. He took the hand of the statue of the Babylonian supreme deity Marduk as a sign that he didn't want to rule Babylon as a for

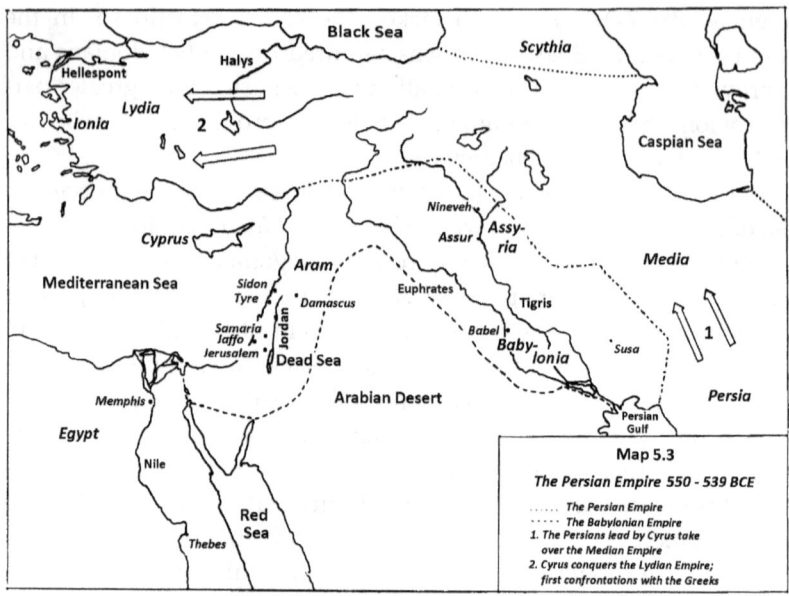

Map 5.3 - The Persian Empire 550 - 539 BCE
...... The Persian Empire
- - - - The Babylonian Empire
1. The Persians lead by Cyrus take over the Median Empire
2. Cyrus conquers the Lydian Empire; first confrontations with the Greeks

eigner. He then conquered the Babylonian empire at high speed to the border of Egypt (see map 5.4).[124] From that time the Jews would be subjects of the Persian empire for well over two centuries. Also with regards to them Cyrus showed himself to be a tolerant prince. According to 2 Chronicles 36:22-23 and Ezra 1:1 he commanded the Jews in

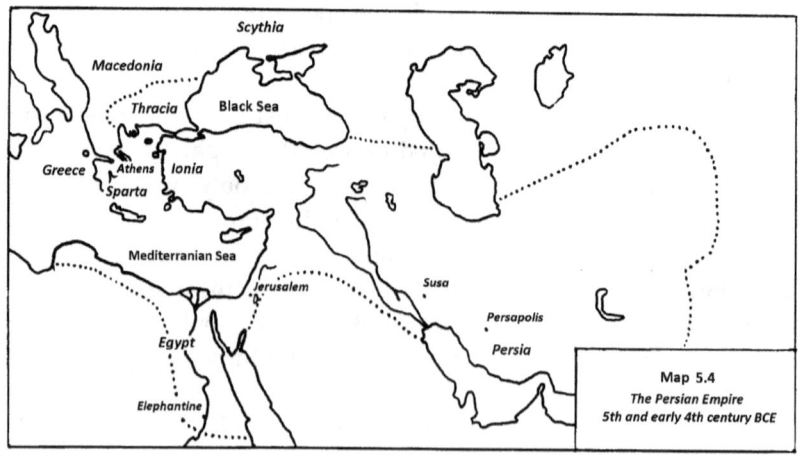

Map 5.4
The Persian Empire
5th and early 4th century BCE

the first year of his rule already to return to Jerusalem, to go and work on the restoration of the temple. This tolerant attitude was continued – as we saw in section 4.2 – by most of his successors. In the land of Israel the Jews received, certainly in the domain of religion, a certain measure of autonomy supervised by the Persian authority.

Now we should ask the question after the meaning of this historical context for the understanding of the Book of Jonah. In sections 4.1 and 4.5 we saw that the Book of Jonah not only evokes the entire image of the world of that time, but also the course of the Jewish-biblical liturgical year. So the question is also whether the course of Israel's history to the Persian time finds its repercussions in the structure of the book or not. And indeed there are a number of facts which point into this direction. The structure of the history of Israel of those days shows a division in three parts we find back in the Book of Jonah in similar form and provided with cognate themes:

- In the Assyrian era the kingdom of Judah remained independent amidst a tempestuous, historical situation.
- In the Babylonian era Judah lost its independence, Jerusalem and the temple was destroyed and a large part of the Jewish people was deported (swallowed up) to (by) Babylon.
- In the Persian era the Jewish exiles received permission to return to the land of Israel and was, in the sphere of religion, allowed a limited measure of self-rule supervised by the Persian authority.

- In Jonah 1 Jonah is an independent man who goes his own way amidst the representatives of the nations of the world.
- In Jonah 2 Jonah looses his independence and is swallowed by the big fish and in its inside he looks out for the temple and his liberation.
- In Jonah 3 and 4 Jonah appears, once liberated from the fish, with limited independence in a Nineveh described after a Persian model.[125]

The parallelism between both divisions in three parts can also be supported by a great number of facts derived from Tanakh. Without aspiring to completeness I'd like to point out the following similarities.

From the Jonah story it's obvious that Jonah's stay in the belly of the Sheol (Jonah 2:3) is the consequence of his refusal to carry out God's order. Whatever the men of the ship try (Jonah 1:13), the storm goes on till they've thrown Jonah overboard. That's God's judgement on Jonah's refusal and Jonah himself – he is after all the only one on board who knows this God – puts this into words and can't do anything else than accept (Jonah 1:12). Entirely similar is the situation with regard to the exile. The prophets make it clear – in many places in Tanakh – that the exile is the result of Israel's refusal to obey God's orders. That's already the case with the Assyrian exile that hit the inhabitants of the kingdom of Israel. In 2 Kings 17:7-23 we find an extensive discourse in which the deportation to Assyria is considered a consequence of the unfaithfulness to Adonai. Remarkable is the text in 2 Kings 17:19-20a which also puts the later exile in the same light here. Oftener even we come across the theme of the exile as a result of being unfaithful to Adonai with the prophets Isaiah, Jeremiah and Ezekiel.[a] In the Book of Ezekiel we read e.g.:

> "The word of the LORD came to me:[17] 'Son of man, when the house of Israel lived in their own land, they defiled it by their ways and their deeds. Their ways before me were like the uncleanness of a woman in her menstrual impurity.[b] So I poured out my wrath upon them for the blood that they had shed in the land, for the idols with which they had defiled it. [19] I scattered them among the nations, and they were dispersed through the countries. In accordance with their ways and their deeds I judged them" (Ezekiel 36:16-19 NKJV).

---

[a] See e.g. Isaiah 5:25-30; 47:6; 8:5-8; Jeremiah 25:1, 5-11, 15-18; Ecclesiastes 1:12, 15, 17-18; Ezekiel 36:16-19.

[b] Here the monthly menstruation is meant which played an important part in the fertility rites of the surrounding Semitic peoples in the idolatry of the gods and goddesses and which because of that were avoided in the Jewish worship. Ezekiel's reproach is that the Jews took part in the idolatry of the surrounding peoples which were dominated largely by the idea of fertility.

Besides, it will be clear now that the prophets accepted this judgement of God on Israel. And in this also Jonah shows himself to be a representative of his people: He accepts God's judgement as the consequence of his own unfaithfulness (Jonah 1:12).

Next to it there are even clearer clues that Jonah 2 should be read against the background of the Babylonian exile. In section 4.5.b I showed the parallelism between the Psalm of Jonah and the Song of Moses at the Red Sea. So this prayer of Jonah is a typical song of an exodus from hostile captivity. The exodus from Egypt in the Book of Exodus is the prototype of the exodus from every hostile oppression. Like the Song of Moses, the Psalm of Jonah is not a call for rescue but a song of thanksgiving for the salvation received. This song of Jonah is as such a representation of the certainty prophets like the Deutero-Isaiah (Isaiah 40-55) and Ezekiel in Babylon had, that God would deliver Israel from the exile. Besides, the language of images used in Jonah 2, evokes strong associations with the images in other writings of the Tanakh used to describe the hostility of the nations, the oppression and the exile.[126]

In the language of the Tanakh there is a complex of images which uses words like: 'sea', 'waters', 'deep', 'waves', 'Sheol', 'seeth', 'stream' etc. Generally this complex of images refers to hostility and oppression, especially towards Israel. The sea is in this particular language of images 'the face of the underworld' (literal translation of Genesis 1:2). The sea, or the ocean as such, are the remnants of the primal flood from which God called forth the dry land on the third day of the Creation. He put a check on the sea (Genesis 9:14-15; Jeremiah 5:22; Psalm 104:9; Job 38:8-11). However, by doing so the sea, the Sheol, has not yet been overcome. The victory over the primal flood waits till the end of time when the sea will be no more (compare Revelations 21:1). Until then, beyond the bounds made by God, death, destruction and fall will rule. In this context the sea, the deep and the Sheol mean all those places and situations where God isn't praised and where knowledge of the Bible and wisdom are not found (Psalm 6:6; Job 28:14; Ecclesiastes 9:10). God will cast the sins of Israel in the deep of the sea when He will have mercy on them (Micah 7:19). It's the same primal flood that swallowed up the pharao and his army (Exodus 15:4-5). A fate that also hits Tyre when it exulted at the fall of

Jerusalem, just like Babylon that deported Judah into exile (Ezekiel 26:2-3, 19; 27:34; Jeremiah 51:42).

However, the sea and the deep of the waters are not only an abode of evil, safely stored behind frontiers made by God. They rather pose a threat, because they are inclined to exceed these God-made frontiers again and again. God has to maintain his rule continuously against "the raging of the sea, when its waves rise…" (Psalm 89:9 NKJV). As such the sea, the waters, the deep and the Sheol are firmly connected to the threat that emanates from God's enemies towards Israel.[a] When God gives David the power over his enemies, one of the images expressing this is: "Also I will set his (David's) hand over the sea, and his right hand over the rivers" (Psalm 89: 25 NKJV).

It fits within this framework that the liberation from the power of the enemies is visualized as a way through the sea, a path through the waters.[b] These images are used especially for the prototype of the liberation from the exile: the liberation from Egypt.[c] But not only Israel's stay in Egypt is in the language of images of Tanakh connected closely with the depth of the sea. The sea, the waters and the Sheol often and also form an image of the nations which threaten Israel and especially the superpowers Egypt, Assyria and Babylon.[d] The 'nation from afar' (i.e Assyria) will roar against Israel like the roaring of the sea (Isaiah 5:30). The roaring of the seas and the roaring of their waves represent the uproar of the nations (Isaiah 17:12-13; Psalm 65:8). More specifically this is an image of the advance of hostile armies:

> "Thus says the LORD, Behold, a people comes from the north country, and a great nation shall be raised from the sides of the earth. They shall lay hold on bow and spear; they are cruel, and have no mercy; their voice *roars like the sea*; and they ride upon

---

[a] 2 Samuel 22:4-6; Psalm 42:8, 10-11; 69:2-5, 15-16; 89:10-11; 124:4-5; Ecclesiastes 3:52-54.

[b] 2 Samuel 22:17-18; Isaiah 8:23; 43:1-3, 16; 51:10; Zechariah 10:11; Psalm 18:17-18; 68:23-24; 144:7.

[c] Exodus 15:1-21; Isaiah 63:11-13; Psalm 77:15-21; 78:13; 106:9-10; 114:3; Psalm 136.

[d] Isaiah 5:13-14; 10:26; 11:15; 19:5; 21:1; 28:2; 57:20; Psalm 46:3-4, 7, 10; 74:13.

horses, set in array as men for war against thee, O daughter of Zion" (Jeremiah 6: 22-23).[a]

One can easily imagine such an advancing army: undulating through the rolling landscape, from afar the stamping on the earth could be heard as the roar of enormous, not to be stemmed waters. The Sheol itself approaches!

This complex of images now is extremely important for the exegesis of the Book of Jonah. In the Psalm of Jonah we come across a large concentration of words and images belonging to this complex of images:

- the Sheol (Jonah 2:3);
- the deep (Jonah 2:4);
- the heart of the seas (Jonah 2:4);
- the floods (Jonah 2:4);
- wrecking billows (Jonah 2:4);
- waves (Jonah 2:4);
- the waters (Jonah 2:6);
- the deep (Jonah 2:6);
- the corruption (Jonah 2:7).

The parallel between Jonah 2 and the Babylonian exile I sketched above, is supported strongly in the Psalm of Jonah by the use of this complex of images. Within that framework the following observation is of importance. Jonah says his psalm in the belly of the big fish, although there is no connection whatsoever between the contents of this psalm and the stay of three days. Big sea animals only occur a number of times in Tanakh and are then images of the superpowers which threaten Israel.[b] So we read in Isaiah 27:1 about the "Leviathan, the fleeing serpent" (Assyria), the "Leviathan, the twisted serpent" (Babylon), and the "reptile that is in the sea" (Egypt).[c] In Ezekiel 29:3 the pharao of Egypt is called "a great monsters, who lies in the midst

---

[a] See also Jeremiah 46:7-9; 47:2-3; 51:55-56; Ezekiel 1:24.
[b] Isaiah 51:9; Psalm 74:13; 89:11; Job 9:13; 26:12.
[c] The fast reptile is the fast-moving river Tigris along which Assyria laid. The twisting serpent is the slow-moving and winding Eufrat of Babylon. The monster of the sea is Egypt.

of his rivers" (i.e. the arms of the Nile). Also the primal monster Rahab-Hem-Shebeth ("Turbulence" or "Ebullient") is a sea monster that is an image of Egypt (Isaiah 30:7; Psalm 87:4). Moreover the statement in Jeremiah 51:34 is important for the Book of Jonah:

> "Nebuchadrezzar the king of Babylon has devoured me, he has crushed me, he has made me an empty vessel, he has swallowed me up like a dragon, he has filled his belly with my delicates, he has cast me out."

In this context Jonah's stay in the big fish can only be explained as an image of exile in general and as a reminder of the Babylonian exile in particular.

5.3   The political situation in the Persian age[a]

As we have seen in the previous sections, we should take it for granted that the Book of Jonah was written in the period of the Persian occupation of the land of Israel (538-332 BCE). We've also seen that the Book of Jonah not only reflects the world view of that time and the order of the Jewish-biblical, liturgical year, but also the actual history of Israel of that time.[127] Therefore we could further ask ourselves whether the then political and religious situation left its stamp on the Book of Jonah. And indeed, many indications can be found for this phenomenon. In this section I'll paint a picture of the political situation in the Persian time and of the foreign political relations of the Persian empire in particular.[128]

The political situation in the 5th and 4th century BCE was characterized especially by the discord between the free Greek world in the west and the Persian empire in the east. Long before one could speak of a Persian empire, Greece was already a powerful and influential nation in the entire Mediterranean. In the period of 750-550 BCE the Greeks settled with a series of well-considered undertakings across the entire length and width of the Mediterranean and the Black Sea, as "frogs around a pond", according to the words of Plato. Almost 250 colonies were founded in this whole area.[129] But Greece itself wasn't a

---

[a]   A survey of the years in this section is found in Table 5.1.

unitary state. It consisted of a great number of independent city-states spread out across the entire Greek peninsula, Crete, Cyprus, the islands in the Aegean Sea and the western coast of Asia Minor. All these city-states founded their own colonies as hometowns. The Ionic Greeks especially – they were the Greeks settled along the west coast of Asia Minor (Turkey today) – were very active and enterprising in the colonisation of the area.

Not surprisingly the Persian empire had already been confronted with the Greeks, even before it had reached its full size. When the Jews still groaned under the yoke of the Babylonian exile, the first combats between the Persians and the Greeks were already taking place. When Cyrus II the Great had conquered the Lydian empire in Asia Minor in 547-546 BCE, his generals seized the Ionic-Greek cities along the west coast of Asia Minor one by one. This was the beginning of largely two centuries of war and skirmishes between both nations. The next events illustrate these strained relations between Persians and Greeks.

When in 525 the Persians under Cambyses II (529-522 BCE) attacked Egypt, the Egyptian pharaoh Ahmose II was defended by Greek mercenaries. These however betrayed the Egyptians and Egypt became a Persian province with among other things a garrison of Jewish mercenaries on the isle of Elephantine in the river Nile. Under the Persian king Darius I (522-486 BCE) the fighting between the Persians and the Greeks really began. In about 515 Darius crossed the Hellespont and set out on a campaign to Scythia, the territory north of the Black Sea, with the intention to deprive the Greeks of their "granary." This campaign however came to a dead end and Darius was forced to retreat. But it left the Persians with a bridgehead at the Hellespont. In the next years the Persians reclaimed a number of strategic islands in the Aegean Sea from the Greeks. When in this campaign they suffered a defeat at the isle of Naxos, the Greeks in the Ionic cities at the western coast of Asia Minor rose against the Persian authority. It'd last till 493 until the Persians had suppressed this rebellion. In 490 Darius undertook a large invasion into Greece. He crossed the Aegean Sea with about 25.000 soldiers. At Marathon however, the Persian army was beaten surprisingly by the Athenians. The Persians began to realise that the "Greek problem" was bigger than at first they'd thought.

Table 5.1
Chronological table of the most important confrontations between Persians and Greek from 647-323 BCE.

	JUDAH	ISRAEL/ SAMARIA	ASSYRIA	BABYLON	MEDIA/ PERSIA	LYDIA	GREECE
560						Croesus	From about 750 founding of colonies along the whole Mediterranean and Black Sea
550	Babylonian exile			555 Nabonidus	559 Cyrus II the Great		
540				DEUTERO-ISAIAH	547 Cyrus conquers Lydia and the Ionian cities		
				539 Belshazzar			
530	537 return led by Zerubbabel				538 Cyrus conquers Babylon		
520	520 Reconstruction of the Temple Jeshua High priest				529 Cambyses
522 Darius I		
510					515 Campaign to Scythia		
500							
490					499 Uprising of the Ionian cities
490 Darius's invasion into Greece		
480					486 Xerxes I
480 Xerxes's invasion into Greece		
470							
460					465 Artaxerxes I		
450	458 Ezra goes to Jerusalem				459 Athens supports the Egyptian uprising against the Persians		
440	445 Nehemiah Viceroy	Sanballat Viceroy			448 Peace between Persia and Athens		
430	433					439 Athens attacks the Persians
431 Peloponnesian war		
420		TIME OF COMPOSITION			424 Xerxes II
423 Darius II		
410		OF THE BOOK OF JONAH				412 Recapture Ionian cities
404 Artaxerxes II   404 Fall of
401 Rebellion of Cyrus   Athens
400 War with Sparta; support of Athens		
400							
390							
380						387 Persian peace in Greece	
370							

	JUDAH	ISRAEL/ SAMARIA	ASSY-RIA	BABYLON	MEDIA/ PERSIA	LYDIA	GREECE
360							
350					358 Artaxerxes III		
340							
							339 Persians expelled from Europe
					338 Arses		338 Philippus of Macedonia
					336 Darius III		336 Alexander the Great
330							
320			BEGINNING OF HELLENISM				323

Preparations were made for a large, coordinated invasion. But then Darius died in 486.

This large Persian invasion into Greece was only executed by Xerxes I (486-465 BCE) on land and at sea as well in 480. Athens was conquered and burned down. However, in September of that year the Persian fleet was destroyed devastatingly at Salamis under the eyes of Xerxes. This would turn out to be the turning point in the Greek-Persian relations. In the following months the Persians were pushed back step by step. And in the following years the Greeks also managed to push further back the influence of the Persians in the Aegean Sea and along the Ionic coast of Asia Minor. Especially at sea the Greeks established their power definitively and the Persians were no longer interested in conquering Greece. From 459-454 BCE the Athenians and their allies were able once more to support a revolt in Egypt against the Persian authority.[130] Nevertheless in 448 BCE a peace treaty was agreed between the Athenians and their allies on the one hand and the Persians under Artaxerxes I (464-425 BCE) on the other. Yet this peace won't last long. In 439 the Athenians violated the peace by attacking the isle of Samos.

The now following period was a period of great tensions between the Greeks among themselves. On the Greek peninsula the Peloponnesian War was raging now and again from 431-404 BCE between the Greek city states and Sparta. First the Persians committed themselves to one party and then to another. Initially the Persians supported Athens against Sparta, but from 413 under Darius II (423-404 BCE) they supported the Spartans. In 412 they restored their authority of the Ionic cities of the western coast of Asia Minor. In 404 Persian gold and Spartan soldiers brought Athens down.

However, the confrontation between the Persians and the Greeks did not only occur in the Greek area. In 401 the Persian prince Cyrus the Younger revolted for the second time against the authority of his brother Artaxerxes II. From Asia Minor he marched eastwards to conquer the throne at the head of 10.000 Greek mercenaries. In Mesopotamia he was beaten by Artaxerxes. However the unit of Greek mercenaries remained, although battered, intact and managed via a long march and in good order under the inspiring leadership of among others Xenophon to escape to the north to the Black Sea and from there homewards. Probably no other event has showed the Greeks clearer how intrinsically weakened the Persian empire already was in this period.

During the rule of the Persian king Artaxerxes II (404-359 BCE) Sparta, as the leading Greek nation, again waged war against the Persians. The conflict which lasted from 400 to 387, passed off at the disadvantage of Sparta and again the Persians supported Athens which was recovering from its defeat in the Peloponnesian War. In 387 Artaxerxes II imposed peace on the Greeks, but wasn't able to subject one of both Greek parties or to bind them permanently.

In the following decades Greek mercenaries kept playing a part in the theatre of war of the Persian empire. One time they fought on the side of the Persians and another time on the side of their adversaries. In this period however, Greece was no real threat for Persia. Because the Greek political organisation in numerous independent city states was too broken up. But in the course of the forties of the 4th century this changed a lot. Then the kingdom of Macedonia came forward as the realm that was to combine the Greek power. In 339 the Persians were driven away from the Continent, and in 338 Philip of Macedonia dominated Greece entirely. After that the fate of the Persian empire was soon sealed as well. In the period of 334 to 330 Philip's son Alexander would conquer the Persian empire and the entire territory from Greece to India and he'd try to change it into a Hellenistic empire.

As far as the history of Israel is concerned it's obvious that the days of Ezra and Nehemiah fell in the midst of this Persian period.

They appeared between circa 460 and 430 BCE. It's the time of Artaxerxes I. Then Judea had already been under Persian rule for almost a century. In the field of foreign policy the Persian attempts to submit the Greeks had already failed for some decades at that moment. Even during the Peloponnesian War between Athens and Sparta, that was about to begin at that moment, the Persians wouldn't be able to subject the Greeks. The Persians had to learn to live with the "Greek problem" at their northwesterly borders. However, not only there.

The confrontation between the Persians and Greeks was not only an armed confrontation in the borderland of each other's territories. The activities of the Greeks extended out far into the Persian empire and at all sorts of fields of life. It would even be possible to say that in spite of the continuous tensions between the Persians and the Greeks the Persian empire depended to a large extent on the restless activities of the Greeks. Greek mercenaries made out an essential part of the Persian army.[131] The Persian foreign trade was dominated by Greek merchandise.[132] Greek silver and also its imitations in the 4th century was the currency in the Persian empire.[133] A lot of relics of the Greek influence of those days are also found in the land of Israel.

Though there are few historical and archaeological facts of the history of the Jews in this period, there are clear signs that in the Persian time the influence of the Greek culture on the entire land of Israel had been extensive, an influence that already went back to the 7th century BCE, that is to say from before the Babylonian exile.[134] Especially the Phoenicians played as a trading nation a mediating part initially.[135] But later the Greeks also manifested themselves everywhere in the Middle East. The Greek trading route to Arabia went through the south of the land of Israel and in Greek literature a Greek trading centre is mentioned in Acco in the middle of the 4th century BCE.[136] Remnants of Greek earthenware are found in many excavations in the land of Israel even in the area around Jerusalem.[137] Also in Israel, as elsewhere, a lot of Greek coins have been found in excavations, the oldest ones from the second half of the 6th century, directly after the Babylonian exile. In the period of 450 to 350 BCE even an abundance of small Greek coins was in circulation. Originally these coins came from Athens and other Greek cities. The Athenian coins which showed the head of Pallas Athens and the owl – her holy bird – set the price of the money in the entire eastern basin of the Mediterranean. This coin, the

111

owl type, was accepted to such an extent that it was imitated frequently by the local governments. In Judea coins were also struck after the Athenian type in that period (see picture 5.1). At least six kinds have been found with the inscription *Jehud*, Aramaic for 'Judea", in old-Hebrew script. On one of the coins the name *Hezekiah* can be read too, which could be the name of the high priest Hezekiah.[138] Under Greek influence the Persian 'Darics' were often called by their Greek name *drachmen* in the land of Israel as well.[139] Several Greek myths were known also in the land of Israel, and already in the middle of the 4th century the seaport Jaffo was mentioned in Greek literature in connection with the legend of Perseus and Andromeda.[140] To this fact in particular we'll return later in connection with the Book of Jonah.

All this means that the Jews in the land of Israel in the Persian time were acquainted with the Greek culture and that meetings of Jews and Greeks must have taken place regularly in whatever circumstances. Besides it's probable as well that the contact of Jews with the Greek culture not only occurred in the land of Israel itself. In this period a lot of Jews must have settled in the Greek world, either forced as slaves, or voluntary as merchants or as farmers. In this respect the prophet Joel was clear when he reproduced God's words to Sidon, Tyre and Philistea: "You sold the children of Judah and Jerusalem to the Greeks that you might send them far from their homeland" (Joel 3:5, NKJV). The Ionians were the Greeks who populated the western coast of Asia Minor. In addition to this the final chapter of Isaiah mentions among other things Jawan (i.e. Greece) and the faraway coastal cities from which the dispersed Jews would return to Zion (Isaiah 66:19; see

Picture 5.1   *Coins from the Persian time. a. Double Daric (gold), Persian coin with the image of Darius I (522-486 BCE); b. and c. Judean coins (silver) from the 4th century BCE with the Athenian owl and the Hebrew legend 'Judah'.*

also Zachariah 9:13). Being slaves initially, many of them would have tried to buy their freedom. Some would have used their freedom to return to Judah and Jerusalem. Others settled in Greece or in the Greek colonies as merchants or farmers.[141]

Given the great influence of the Greeks in the Persian empire and their great mobility throughout the entire area of the Near East, the Jews settled in Greece would have kept in touch regularly with their fellow Jews in the land of Israel. Besides it's quite conceivable that many Jews in and around Jerusalem felt attracted to the economic and social atmosphere of the free, Greek, western world which could be characterised as being republican, more or less egalitarian and secular. Which of course was very much contrary to the world of the Persian empire with its monarchist, hierarchic and priestly character.[142] And even though the Persian occupation of the land of Israel was tolerant generally, especially from a religious viewpoint, in times of poverty and heavy taxation, the resistance against the Persian authority would have struck root among the Jews (see e.g. Nehemiah 5:4; comp. also Ezra 4:13 and 7:24). What is more, there were great tensions continuously anywhere in the Persian empire. Rebellions occurred in all parts of the empire with clock-like regularity. In this situation it should have been a source of inspiration for the subject peoples, that the Greeks with their vital culture managed to outdo the Persians in a number of fields, even in the greater parts of the Persian empire. The persistent military resistance the Greeks, in spite of their own internal discord, managed to offer to the Persians, must have been greeted with assent by many of the subject nations in the Persian empire. Although the attitude of the Jewish leaders Ezra and Nehemiah towards Persian authority had always been a loyal one (see section 4.2), there is no reason at all to assume that feelings and actions of resistance and rebellion towards the Persian occupation did not occur among the Jews, as they did among the other nations.

Also among the Jews there should have been many who had looked out for the opportunity to throw off the Persian yoke and the restoration of national independence. That, in this case, the Greek were seen as obvious allies is sooner self-evident than uncertain. It's possible that others, forced by circumstances, had left the land of Israel in order to build a better life in the free Greek world instead of working together in the restoration of a Jewish society around Jerusalem under Persian rule. In such a situation there had been cause enough in the circles of the Jewish leaders around Ezra and Nehemiah to write a story with a conclusive argument in the fields of international politics. In that story the orientation of Jews on the free, Greek world could best be worded in images pointing directly to that free Greek world. That perhaps the Book of Jonah could be meant as such an argument, can be demonstrated by means of the following facts.

It's exactly the situation of a world divided into two we come across in the Book of Jonah: in the west the free world of the Mediterranean dominated by Greece (Jonah 1 and 2) and in the east the occupied world of the Persian empire, hidden here behind the name of the evil city of Nineveh (Jonah 3 and 4). I'll specify the associations between Jonah 3 and 4 and the Persian empire in the next section.[143] I'll finish this section with the strong associations between Jonah 1 and 2 an the world of the Greeks.

In the first place there is this remarkable mention of three names related to names in the list of nations of Genesis 10, all pointing in the direction of Greece:[144]

- The name of *Jaffo* (Jonah 1:3) is cognate to the name of *Japheth* (Genesis 10:1-2). In the list of nations of Genesis 10 Japheth is the ancestor of the peoples from the north, to which the Greeks belonged as well. And the name of *Japheth* is also cognate to the name of Lapetus in the Greek mythology, the father of Atlas and Prometheus.[145]
- The name of *Jonah* is the female form of the name of *Javan*. Javan is the fourth son of Japheth (Genesis 10:2). The name of *Javan* is in the list of nations the designation for the Greeks![146] The word is cognate to the words 'Ionia' and 'Ionians', the name of the Greek tribe inhabiting the western coast of Asia Minor. The name of this border tribe was transferred to all Greeks in Hebrew.[147] On the basis of this affinity between Jonah and Javan (Greece) it's obvious that the author of the Book of Jonah has taken his principal character as a Jew oriented on the free, Greek world against whose attitude he makes a stand.
- The name of *Tarsis* (Jonah 1:3) is the name of the second son of Javan (Genesis 10:4). The source of this name and its meaning in the frame of the list of nations is not clear. Two places could be

thought of. The first place to be considered is the town of Tarsis in Cilicia at the southern coast of Asia Minor. It was a Phoenician trading colony. In the Persian time periods of Persian authority followed periods of own autonomy in this Tarsis, as was exactly the case with the Ionian-Greek cities at the western coast of Asia Minor.[148] Maybe the author of the Book of Jonah had this situation in mind, the more so because Tarsis was considered to belong to the sphere of influence of Javan/Greece in Genesis 10. However, a second possibility is that Tarsis also reminds one of Tartessos, a Phoenician trading colony at the southwestern coast of Spain beyond the Strait of Gibraltar. This place was solidly in the hands of the Carthaginians, who guarded the sea route to it jealously. The only mariners who had managed to reach Tartessos in antiquity, were the mariners from the Ionian city of Phokaia.[149] The author of the Book of Jonah could also have thought of this place. Tartessos was the remotest place in the west known in those days. As such this place fits into the story of Jonah's flight to the western part of the continent. Besides there is also a chance that both meanings of *Tarsis* had been in the author's mind. Anyway, Tarsis had been for him a place in the western part of his world, which in his time was strongly under the influence of the Greeks.

There is another indication yet that the author of the Book of Jonah in the first two chapters had wanted to associate with the Greek world. The themes of the flight across the sea, the journey through the depth of the waters, of being swallowed by a sea monster, of staying in the bowels of it and reaching land uninjured, all this together are themes which don't occur anywhere in Tanakh in similar forms. However, we do find a great concentration of images belonging to this theme in Psalm 107 and Ezekiel 27, but there is no motive at all of a stay in the belly of a sea monster in these texts. What is more, Israel has never been a seafaring nation and therefore stories of shipping are rare in Tanakh. In this respect there is a remarkable story of the only fleet ever built by the southern kingdom of Judah. It was wrecked so that it couldn't sail to Tarsis (!) (2 Chronicles 20:37). This story has both the motive of the shipwreck and the goal of the voyage in common with the Jonah story and may have played a part at the background of the

Book of Jonah. The image of the big fish seemed to be borrowed from texts like Jeremiah 51:34 as well, as we saw in the previous section, but the image of a man going down into the depth of the sea who survives the confrontation with a big sea animal, can't be found anywhere in Tanakh.

This theme of Jonah's stay in and return from the Sheol demonstrates a strong affinity with the mythology of the neighbouring peoples. Such stories of heroes who land in the depth of the sea because of all sorts of reasons and are confronted there with a sea monster or a big fish and end up on dry land again, occurred in all coastal areas from the Indian Ocean to the Aegean Sea.[150] But for the Book of Jonah one of these stories is very important and that is the Greek myth of Perseus and Andromeda. Andromeda is being sacrificed by her father, king Cepheus of Ethiopia, when a sea monster threatened his land. At that moment the Greek demi-god Perseus passes by and falls in love with Andromeda. He saves her by throwing himself into the sea and by killing the monster.[151] That story has of course quite another course than the Jonah story, but – as I already indicated above – it is important that this myth very probably already before or early in the Persian time was associated with port Jaffo, the same town where Jonah went aboard![152] One used to show somewhere around the city of Jaffo (Greek: Joppe) the remains of the chain which would have nailed Andromeda to the rocks to sacrifice her to the sea monster.[153] It's unimaginable that the author of the Book of Jonah, who appeared to have a sound grasp of the shipping of his days, hadn't known such myths and especially this combination of Perseus with Jaffo.

However, there is no sense in asking the question whether the Jonah story developed from the myths of the peoples.[154] Discussions of the phrasing of such a question ignore the nature of a Jewish-biblical story like Jonah's. The author of the Book of Jonah hadn't been a narrator who had seen in the Greek myth a suitable theme for an exciting story. And yet it would have been perfectly possible that he'd derived the theme of Jonah's stay in the Sheol from pagan mythology. But then we have to ask ourselves why he'd done so.

In the first place he could have copied these images from the myths of the peoples and especially from the myths of the Greeks because he wanted to argue that his story had everything to do with the world of the Greeks. In the second place he uses these specific images especially because they fit in the structure of his argument precisely. Besides we don't have to think that his 'argument in the form of a story' was directed towards the Greeks themselves. We should rather see it as follows: Many Jews in the land of Israel, who'd had enough of the Persian empire, probably had looked longingly to the free Greek world in the west. Perhaps they even expected to be supported there in any attempts to rid themselves of the Persian authority. Or they recognized in the Greek world a mental climate of political, social, economic and religious freedom, in which they could thrive better. It's this hostility towards the Persian empire and towards the orientation to the free Greek world involved, that the writer of the Book of Jonah makes a stand against. In the following sections I'll work out how the writer of the Book of Jonah has set up his argument.

5.4 The Book of Jonah and the Persian empire

Now that we've come to the conclusion that the foreign political situation of the Persian empire is reflected in the Book of Jonah, we should bear in mind that certain domestic political or religious aspects of the Persian empire could be recognized in his book. In section 5.1 I already showed an example of it: The way in which in Jonah 3 the court of Nineveh reacted to Jonah's prophecy of doom, shows strong Persian features. The promulgation of a decree to the population by the king together with the great ones of his empire is a procedure known only of the Persian court. There are however in Jonah 3 and 4 still other elements which call forth strong associations with the Persian empire. I'll devote a short discussion to some four of them.

In the first place there is the aspect of the language. The Persian empire consisted of many different peoples which spoke almost as many different languages. The Persians themselves spoke Old-Persian, a southwestern Iranian dialect, which was only put in writing for the first time under Darius I. In addition to Old-Persian the Persians also used the languages of the Babylonians and the Elamites. The language most commonly used in the government of the empire however, was Aramaic.[155] According to the Book of Ezra the correspondence between the land of Israel and the Persian court was conducted in this language (Ezra 4:7-7:26). It's also this language, as we saw in section 5.1, that strongly influenced the linguistic usage of the writer of the Book of Jonah.

In the second place there is the aspect of the social organisation of the Persian society. The traditional Iranian societies were feudal of character. There were three classes. An aristocratic class of rulers and military, which can be compared with the European nobility in the Middle Ages. Then came a religious class of priests and finally a class of farmers and cattlemen.[156] Traces of all three can be found back in the Book of Jonah:

- The first reaction caused by Jonah's prophecy of doom in Nineveh (Persia), is of a religious nature: The men of Nineveh believed in God, and "they called a fast and put on sackcloth from their biggest (ones) and to their smallest (ones)" (Jonah 3:5). Although they aren't called 'priests' but 'men', we can assume that here members of the Persian class of priests are meant. After all, such a religious reaction without the instigation of the class of priests is less probable in a feudal society. That in the story these men aren't called 'priests' is hardly surprising: The writer of the Book of Jonah has only acknowledged the Levitical priests of Israel as priests of the one God. A pagan priest who turns to the God of Jonah, is – from Israel's point of view – still 'a common man'.
- In Jonah 3:6-7 we next meet the king and his big ones, the representatives of the classes of the nobility and the military.
- In the decree of the king and his big ones we finally find the third class of the farmers and cattlemen, to whom this order is directed: "The humans and the beasts, the cattle and the sheep, not (at all) they taste anything, not (at all) they feed, and the waters they shall not drink. And they cover themselves (with) sackcloth, the humans and the beasts …" (Jonah 3:7-8).

This class background does not only explain the disproportionate attention given in the order to the cattle, but also to the remarkable course of the story. First the reaction of the class of priests is a religious one. The class of the nobility takes this reaction up and renders it into an instruction for the class of the farmers and the cattlemen. So there is no reason at all to consider the decree of the king and his big ones as a *nachholende Erzählung*, that is *mentioning information afterwards*[157], in which one comes back to something that, presumably, had taken place before, that is before Jonah 3:5. The social structure of the Persian society is the background which makes the story in Jonah 3 transparent.

The third point is the word 'big' or 'great' (Hebrew: *gadol*) which occurs remarkably often in the Book of Jonah. This word played an important part in the terminology of all big empires of that time (see for instance 2 Kings 18:19, 28). The word 'big' was frequently used in the official language of the Persian empire as well. Not surprising because the Persian empire was the biggest known empire in the Near East then. In the historic literature on the Persian empire one frequently comes across expressions like 'the great king', 'the great empire', 'the great army', and so on. The Persian kings were called 'great king' and two of them – Cyrus II and Darius I – have entered history with the title 'the Great'. For instance Cyrus was described as: "Son of Cambyses, the great king, king of Anshan, grandson of Cyrus, the great king, king of Anshan, descendant of Teispes, the great king, king of Anshan, from stock which has always held kingship."[158] About Darius I was said: "The great king, king of kings, king of the lands with all kinds of peoples, king of this great, far and wide earth."[159] Also all later Persian kings, like Artaxerxes III, had titles as "the great king, the king of all lands of the earth".[160] In this respect it's remarkable that Alexander of Macedonia was only called "the Great" when he was in the heart of the former Persian empire. Only in Ecbatana, one of the former Persian capitals, he allowed the Orientals to address him as "great king, only king among many, king of the lands of the earth". And this even contrary to the wish of his fellow companions.[161]

It's against this background that the use of the word 'big' or 'great' can be explained best. Six times it's used for Nineveh or its inhabitants, the Ninevites (Jonah 1:2; 3:2, 3, 5, 7; 4:11), which undoubtedly refers to the greatness of the Persian empire. Eight times it's used for the means God uses and for the reactions His actions bring about: a big wind (Jonah 1:4), a big storm (Jonah 1:4, 12), a big fish (Jonah 1:17), a big fear (Jonah 1:10, 16), a big evil and a big joy (Jonah 4:1, 6). It looks as if the writer of the Book of Jonah had wanted to put the greatness of Nineveh (Persia) into the shadow of the greatness of the God of Israel. A case in point is the one time that a verb form of the verb 'become big/be big' is used. In Jonah 4:10 it's said of the Kikayon (the miracle tree) that Jonah "not at all [has] caused [it] to become big." Then, in Jonah 4:11 this Kikayon is compared with Nineveh. Here the greatness of God's contact with the people and the greatness of the Kikayon-Nineveh-Persia come together: It's God who gives the Kikayon-Nineveh-Persia its greatness and who also determines what should come of this greatness in the end. With all these big images of wind, storm, fish, fear, fury, joy and Kikayon the writer has placed Jonah in the area of tension of Nineveh-Persia on the one hand and the greatness of God's actions on the other. And together with Jonah his audience, which daily experienced and knew the Persian rule.

As fourth and last point we'll have to deal with the religious situation in the Persian empire and especially so with the religion of the Persians themselves. The religions of the peoples in the big Persian empire were – every one of them – polytheistic. One experienced reality as the field of activity of many different gods, who all should be served in their time and place. The religion of the Persians however, was an exception to this rule. It was for the greater part monotheistic just like Israel's religion. Probably about 600 BCE the great religious prophet and teacher Zoroaster (often called *Zarathustra* as well) appeared in the northeast of Iran. His teachings were of a highly ethical quality and stressed continuously that man should act righteously, speak the truth and detest the lie. He degraded the old Iranian gods to demons which belonged to the realm of the lie. The only god Zoroaster acknowledged, was Ahura Mazda, the "Wise Lord".[162]

This monotheism was connected with an moral dualism. Ahura Mazda was involved in an ongoing battle with his opponent Ahriman, the "Lie", with the life of man at stake. This Ahriman embodied the evil principle as did his followers, who'd chosen him of their own volition. This contrast between the principle of good and that of evil consists already from the beginning of the world. But Ahura Mazda is Lord over both principles and will overcome the spirit of evil in the end.[163] Animal sacrifices were probaply renounced by Zoroaster and in the Zoroastrian cult fire became the central symbol of the truth.[164]

It's not clear in all respects to what extent the Persian kings were adherents of the Zoroastrianism. Possibly Cyrus II the Great was already one, probably Darius I the Great and almost certainly Xerxes I

Picture 5.2   *Monument of Darius I in Behistun: The beaten rebels brought before the king; over them the god Ahura Mazda.*

and his successors. For example Darius I only mentions Ahura Mazda in his inscriptions (see picture 5.2). As the substitute of Ahura Mazda he laid claim to rule the entire world.[165] Xerxes and his successors also called other gods by their names, but Ahura Mazda always remains elevated far above them. The tone of Darius' words is the tone of Zoroastrianism and archaeological excavations show that in Persepolis, one of the residencies of the Persian kings, animals were not sacrificed. Fire on the other hand played an important part in the religion of the Persian kings. Under Artaxerxes I the Zoroastrian calender was accepted as the official calender of the Persian empire. However, in the days of Artaxerxes II the old Iranian god Mithra and the goddess Anahita return again in the royal religion and are placed next to Ahura Mazda.[166]

Although the Persian court has not always fully adhered to a pure monotheism, nevertheless the monotheistic Zoroastrianism has greatly influenced Persian rule. Undoubtedly the moral quality of this monotheism has been the cause that the Persian kings ruled from quite another spirit than the Assyrian and Babylonian kings before them. The tolerance they managed to show for the many different popular cultures united by their empire, must have been a relief for many in those days (compare for instance picture 5.2 with picture 3.6b). Within the big empire – concerning communication – the Per-

121

sians showed concern with their subject nations. In big parts of the empire they didn't use their own language, Old-Persian, but Aramaic as official language. Contrary to the kings of the former superpowers, which wrote their inscriptions in their own language only, the Persian kings also used the language of their subject nations when drafting their monumental inscriptions.[167] But more important even is the following.

The Assyrians and Babylonians used to uproot the defeated peoples by deporting the upper class of the population, thus creating a uniform mass of subjects about which they organised the government. The Persians by contrast have given the peoples deported by their predecessors permission to return to their original home-grounds (Ezra 1:1 ff.). They respected the traditions and institutions of the subject peoples and took care that the services for the local gods should be performed according to the traditional rules.[168] Within the scope of this policy the Jews under Cyrus the Great received permission to rebuild their temple. In general it could be said that the Persians ruled their empire with great tolerance. In many cases rebellious peoples, governments or rulers were granted forgiveness. Bloody suppression and acts of revenge happened rarely.[169]

The monotheistic influence of the Zoroastrianism on Persian rule with its supporting ethical tendencies and tolerance with respect to other traditions, could perhaps have been the reason, why in books like Ezra, Nehemiah and Esther the relation between the Persian kings and the Jews is almost always presented positively. Monotheistic pronouncements about the God of heavens, in which no distinction is noticeable between the God of the Persian kings (Ahura Mazda) and Adonai, the God of Israel, were made on behalf of Cyrus (Kores), Darius and Artaxerxes (Arthahsasta) (Ezra 1:2; 6: 9-10; 7:12). This monotheistic tendency of the Persians is also of the utmost importance for the understanding of the Book of Jonah. We come across at least three cases of this phenomenon in Jonah 3:

- Contrary to Jonah 1 (Jonah 1:5) there is no trace of polytheism in Jonah 3. Although Jonah doesn't proclaim his prophecy of doom on behalf of a god (Jonah 3:4), the inhabitants of Nineveh immediately understand that the message comes from God. They react as if they are already acquainted with the service to one

single God. This must have been unthinkable in the Assyrian Nineveh of centuries before, but in Nineveh alias Persia this completely connects to the monotheism of Zoroastrianism.
- Also the problematic nature of good and evil, borrowed from Genesis 3 and 4, that only comes forward expressively in Jonah 3 and 4, fits in entirely with the background of Zoroastrianism with its dualistic ideas in the field of ethics. Words derived from the verb stem "to be evil" occur seven times in Jonah 3 and 4 (Jonah 3:8, 10a, 10b; 4:1a, 1b, 2, 6). Words derived from two cognate verb stems occur five times in Jonah 4 (Jonah 4:3, 4, 8, 9a and 9b).
- In line with this is the reaction of the Ninevites which is especially ethical-religious of nature. This is contrary to the reaction of the sailors in Jonah 1, which is cultic of nature (Jonah 1:5, 16). The theme of making a sacrifice we do see in Jonah 1 (Jonah 1:16), is lacking entirely in Jonah 3, which is in accordance with the absence of bloody sacrifices in Zoroastrism.

All this evokes the question which argument the writer of the Book of Jonah has wanted to put into words for the Jews in the Persian time.

5.5 Summary and conclusions

If we put together all data and facts discussed in the preceding chapters and sections, a clear and consistent image arises about the 'message' of the Book of Jonah. Fitting in with the intention of the Torah, directed at mankind as a whole, and of some of the prophets (section 4.1) the Book of Jonah puts into words the same attitude of loyalty towards the Persian empire, we come across in the books of Ezra and Nehemiah (section 4.2), as part however of another discussion. In this story Jonah is the Israelite, who sees himself as the representative of the old Israel from before the Babylonian exile (section 5.2), and who concentrates on the restoration of national independence. Therefore he focussed his attention on the free Greek world in the west, his natural ally as it were, in resisting the authority of the Persian empire (section 5.3). In doing so he places himself with regards to this empire in the tradition of the old, unconditional seers for whom a judgement was a judgement (section 4.4). The evil which in his eyes the Persian empire has also brought to Israel and which can be compared with the evil of Assyria, should be blotted out. The newer tendencies in Israel's prophecy which he knows indeed (Jonah 4:2), he certainly doesn't consider applicable to other peoples than Israel itself. On the other hand the author of the Book of Jonah states that the Persian empire isn't so invariably evil as Jonah with his memory of Assyria thinks it is, and that the conditional nature of the prophecy of doom is indeed applicable to the Persian people as well. In addition to the monotheistic tendency in the Persian empire, which is strongly ethical by nature (section 5.4), he sees the possibility and necessity that the Jews should contribute to the ethical edification of this empire and in doing so of mankind in its entirety. This assignment is closely connected with the liturgies of temple and synagogue (section 4.6). They not only borrow its inspiration from these liturgies, but even makes them only really possible and justified (compare for instance texts like Hosea 6:6). And so the message of the Book of Jonah is not only of importance for a specific group of Jews in the Persian era, but also for all Jews and all humans of all times.

6   And he goes down
Annotations to Jonah 1:1-16

Jonah 1:1

> And (then) occurs a word of Adonai to Jonah, son of Amitai, to say:

And (then) occurs. Hebrew: *wajêhi*. This word is often translated with 'and it happened'. It's about the Hebrew verb which means 'to become', 'to be', 'to appear' and 'to happen/to occur'. This verb has a dynamic character. We have translated it with 'occur' as much as possible to express the dynamic character of the event either.[a] In Hebrew it's quite usual to begin a story with the word *wajêhi*. The books of Joshua, Judges, 1 and 2 Samuel, Ezekiel, Ruth and Esther, all begin with this word. All these books have not been written to record history, but to teach Israel something about its history for the future with the help of stories. In that sense the word *wajêhi* connects the past with today and the future.

A word. Usually the Hebrew word *davar* is translated with 'word', but in fact it's an untranslatable word. It does not only mean 'word', but also 'thing', 'matter', or 'act(ion)'. We could just as well translate here: "an action of Adonai occurs to Jonah." The elementary connection of name and thing, word and action, language and behaviour, cannot be reproduced in our language in that way. One of the chief features of Hebrew thought is that speaking is a form of acting and acting is a form of speaking, that actually words and actions should support one another and have no meaning when used separately.[170] For the exegesis of the Book of Jonah, this means among other things, that the actions of God and Jonah in the story form a language, making known their ideas. So we'll have to look upon their actions as expressions of their ideas and points of view.

Adonai. The Hebrew text gives here the Name of God, consisting of four letters, which isn't pronounced. Instead one does read *Adonai* (= LORD) or *Ha-Shem* (= the Name). So the word *Adonai* replaces the

---

[a]   Occasionally we have translated this word with (a form of) 'to be' (e.g. in Jonah 3:4).

Annotations to Jonah 1

Name. I think it's not correct to render the Name literally in translations. This isn't done anywhere in the RKJV, the Septuagint and in the New Testament as well.[a] The use of these replacement-words like 'LORD', 'Adonai' or 'Ha-Shem' does more justice to the Bible as a Jewish book and could be a sign today that Christians take the dialogue with Judaism seriously.[b] Instead of 'Adonai' I will also use 'LORD' now and then in the future.

In the Book of Jonah two different indications for God are used. In addition to the Name we also come across the word 'God' (Hebrew: *eilohim*) e.g. in Jonah 1:9). The word 'God' is not God's Name, as many assume erroneously. 'God' is nothing else than a common noun, comparable to words like 'man', 'animal', 'planet', and so on. In the world of Tanakh there are many gods (see Jonah 1:5), whose existence isn't denied because everything can be a god for humans.

We do not only come across the words *eilohim* and *adonai* separately but also combined together as *adonai eilohim*, translated by me with 'Adonai God' (Jonah 4:6). However, different meanings should be ascribed to both words. The basis for the difference between *eilohim* and *adonai* could already be found in the first chapters of the Torah. In the first story of the Creation (Genesis 1:1-2:3), in which the creation of the heavens and the earth is described, God is referred to solely with the word *eilohim*. That's the reason why this word especially represents God as the creator and judge of humankind. In the second story of the Creation and the companion story of the Paradise (Genesis 2:4-3:24) the word *eilohim* is almost always preceded by the Name, by me represented with 'Adonai' or 'LORD'. Why this double name of God?

The name itself is derived from the same verb stem as the word *wajêhi*, that is to say H-J-H with the meaning 'to become', 'to be', 'to occur'. For the meaning that could be given to the Name, especially the text in Exodus 3:13-14 is very important. When Moses asks God what Name he shall mention when the Israelites ask him for it, the answer is: *èhjèh ashèr èhjèh*. These words are often translated with: "I am who I am." However, this translation is too static and doesn't

---

[a] Greek uses *Kurios* (= Lord) as the translation of Adonai. The RKJV uses 'Lord'. English speaking Jews usually translate it with 'Lord' also.
[b] I propose a *halachah* (a rule of life) for Christians: The Name shouldn't be pronounced and shouldn't be reproduced literally in translations.

express time nor place. And that is quite inconsistence with the dynamic verb H-J-H which denotes an occurrence taking place in space and time. Therefore one could better translate this *èhjèh ashèr èhjèh* with "I am the One who will be there." So the Name of God is especially a description of God's association with people and especially with the people of Israel. Therefore it's rather significant that in the Torah the meaning of the Name is only revealed at the moment that God through the person of Moses singles out for Himself the people of Israel from the community of nations and makes a special pact with them. The second story of the Creation and the story of Paradise (Genesis 2 and 3) has been built up entirely around God's association with people as well. This God turns out to be – and this contrary to the gods of the nations – a God who always associates with people, who teaches them, who has compassion with them, but who also calls them to account, and all this from His partnership with them.

In the Book of Jonah He is not indifferent as well to what happens with Nineveh and what idea Jonah has about Nineveh. So God is not only *eilohim*, that is to say: the creator and judge of the world, He's also Adonai, the LORD, that is to say: the guide and discussion partner of man. It is this ambiguity that is professed in Deuteronomy 6:4 as a fundamental unity: "Hear, O Israel, *Adonai, Eiloheinu* (the LORD, our God), *Adonai* is one!" So with what image could the God of Israel better be compared than with the image of a father or mother in association with their children? Like parents bringing their children in the world, who decide about them, educate them, punish them if necessary, teach them, accompany them to adulthood, impart own responsibility to them and who call them to book, that's the way the LORD God associates with his people.

Jonah, son of Amittai. In the previous chapters we've seen which associations the name of the principle person calls forth. By adding the words 'son of Amittai' a clear relation is established between this Jonah and the prophet Jonah who appeared in the time of king Jeroboam II of Israel (2 Kings 14:25). We also saw in section 3.6 that the name *Jonah* (with the meaning 'dove') may already have been a designation of the oppressed and persecuted Israel in old times. And next there is the fact that the word *Jonah* is the female form of the Hebrew word *Jawan*, a designation for the Greeks and especially of the Ionians among them. It is probable that the author of the Book of Jonah who –

as we saw in chapter 5 – lived in the Persian time, had been thinking of all these three meanings. There must have been many Jews in the land of Israel ruled over by the Persians, who longed fervently for the restoration of Israel/Judah as an independent nation. They experienced the Israel of their days as a nation suppressed and pursued. The resistance offered by the Greeks to the Persians, could have inspired them in their anti-Persian attitude. Especially the ongoing struggle of the Ionian-Greek cities on the coast of Asia Minor trying to get out of the Persian authority, was their example. Historically seen the prophet Jonah in 2 Kings 14:25 must have been an important source of inspiration for them. After all it was this historical prophet Jonah who prophesied the restoration of Israel's borders as they'd been in king Solomon's time. The choice for Jonah, son of Amittai, as the central figure of this small book of the prophet Jonah could have had a polemic background indeed. What is the writer going to tell us about this fellow-Jew who's yearning for the freedom and the restoration of Israel's independence?

Amittai. This name is derived from the expression *èmet adonai*, meaning 'Adonai is true' or 'Adonai is faithful'.[171] We should pay attention to the link between Jonah and God's truth. However, it's too easy to draw the conclusion that Jonah doesn't show himself to be in the least a representative of God's faithfulness[172]. The fact that the writer mentions the name of Jonah's father could not be explained as a reference to the historical Jonah only. In that case he could have named him 'Jonah of Gath Hepher' as well (2 Kings 14:25). Some meaning should sooner be ascribed to the mention of 'son of Amittai' as well as part of the argument of the Book of Jonah. For instance Jonah himself couldn't certainly be charged with disingenuous conduct: After all, he attempts everything to back out of his assignment and finally performs very poorly, only because it couldn't be done otherwise. Why is it then that this Jonah is called 'son of *Adonai-is-true*'? Could it be because he dare raise the question after the truth of Adonai so clearly (Jonah 4:2)? Doesn't this Jonah compete with God in truth? And shouldn't we take therefore Jonah's behaviour and ideas most serious indeed?

To say. (Hebrew: *leimor*.) This expression means that Jonah is obliged to pass this message of God on to others. It is remarkable that this element of obligation is not entirely clear from the words which follow: Jonah must go to Nineveh because of its evil, but what he should foretell the inhabitants of this city, can't be gathered from God's words. However, the word *leimor* does seem to imply this message indeed.[173]

Jonah 1:2

> "Rise up, go to Nineveh, that city, the big one, and call against her, for up comes their evil to my face."

Rise up. This is a usual introduction to a divine command to go somewhere with a special assignment.[a] It's a call to come into action.

Nineveh. In section 3.5 we saw that Nineveh is the representative of the Assyrian empire. The image of Nineveh the Tanakh hands down, is one of the bloodtown where King Pugnacity resides. A remarkable command then, which Jonah gets here. He must brave the lion in his den, the place which emanates the greatest threat for Israel. Here a couple of questions emerge. Why should Jonah go to Nineveh and not to the Assyrian town of Assur, which was Assyria's capital in the days of the historical prophet Jonah? The answer to that question is obvious when we take the story of Jonah as a midrash. In the Tanakh the memory of Assyria is more connected with Nineveh than to Assur or any other Assyrian town. Moreover we'll understand from later tradition that Nineveh pre-eminently becomes the symbol of being the capital of Israel's enemies (for instance in Judith 1:1 and Tobit 1:3 ff.). All kingdoms which are indicated with the name Nineveh are called thus, because they enrich themselves at the expense of Israel, according to the later rabbinic Midrash.[174]

A second question is why the town Jonah is sent to doesn't evoke a more direct association with the Persian empire. As we have seen in section 5.4, it was indeed the Persian empire the author of Jonah had in mind. The answer to this question is twofold. First of all we could argue that if the author of a midrash story uses the historical figure of Jonah to attach his argument to him, he will also make use of other

---

[a] See e.g. Jeremiah 1:17; 13:4, 6; 18:2; Ezekiel 3:22; Micah 2:10.

Annotations to Jonah 1

Table 6.1
The stratification in the use of images and the argument of the Book of Jonah.

Period	Historical situation	Bible story
Halfway the 8th century BC	Assyria was weakened in those days, but would later return strongly and threaten Israel. Nineveh was an Assyrian city but not yet its capital.	The historical Jonah from 2 Kings 14:25 foretells the recapture of the territories lost by Israel, using if possible the weakness of Assyria at that moment.
5de en 4de eeuw vCJ	The Persian empire dominates the entire Middle East and has occupied the land of Israel. The Jews were allowed to return from Babylon.	Jonah, the central figure of the book of the same name, has to preach in Nineveh in order to prevent her fall (Jonah 3 and 4). Now Nineveh is the model of the Persian empire.
	Especially the Greeks of the West offered resistance against the Persians. Among the readers of the Book of Jonah were Jews who wanted to free themselves from the Persian authority.	Jonah takes refuge to the west, the Greek world, to escape his assignment (Jonah 1 and 2).

historical data from the days of Jonah, that is, if these date come in handy in his story. If Jonah, son of Amittai, serves as a model for certain groups of fellow Jews in the time of the Persian empire, groups which long for freedom and independence, then Nineveh can serve as a model for the Persian empire itself, or for the image these fellow Jews had of this empire. Next it won't be necessary to have Jonah go to a city that calls up more direct associations with the Persian empire. In the first place the Persian empire didn't exist yet in the days of the historical Jonah. In the second place the Persian empire never had one distinct capital. In the third place the author probably does not call up his own image of the Persian empire, but the rather one-sided image of those against whom he makes a stand. There is also a chance that he wants to say the following: Suppose the Persian empire is so evil as was Nineveh, even then it's Jonah's (Israel's) mission to take its fate to heart! In table 6.1 I have tried to clarify the stratification in the argument of the Book of Jonah schematically.

That city, the big one. I'll return to this expression in the commentary on Jonah 3:3.

And call against her. The Hebrew verb *qara* knows – depending on the context it's used in – various differentiations. But almost always it means 'calling out loudly', 'proclaiming publicly'. Prophets don't speak or preach, they call or shout. This is lost in many translations. Is calling or shouting thought too noisy? Compare this for example with Jeremiah 20:7-9. A prophet performs in full sight of the the people and in doing so he calls out loudly because he wants to be heard by as many people as possible.

For. In Hebrew: *ki*. This word can mean both 'for' and 'that'. That's why this sentence has in fact a double meaning, which can't be rendered into English. 'And call against her, *for* …' gives the reason why Jonah should call something against Nineveh. 'And call against her, *that* …' gives the content of what should be called against Nineveh. It appears from the words Jonah calls against Nineveh in Jonah 3, that Jonah hasn't taken the words following *ki* for the content of the message he had to deliver to Nineveh. From this can be concluded that Jonah has understood the word *ki* as causal, while perhaps God has only meant to confront Nineveh with the fact that her evil came up to his face without immediately considering the destruction of the city.[175] We'll come across such double bottoms in the story more often. Then it'll appear also that the one meaning is the meaning Jonah evidently attaches to the words, while the other meaning is the meaning God could possibly have meant with the words.

Their evil. The word 'evil' (Hebrew: *ra'ah*) appears ten times in the story of Jonah (Jonah 1:3, 7, 8; 3:8, 10; 4:1a, 1b, 2, 6). It can denote all kinds of crimes, iniquity and injustice, but not idolatry. The concept of *ra'ah* includes especially moral evil, moral depravation, cruelty against one's fellow man, social injustice etc. (cf. Jonah 3:8). As the reason for the flood we twice come across a word for 'evil' with the same stem in Genesis 6:5. Here it's about evil actions towards the fellow man, with which the generation of Noah forfeited its right to live in God's creation. Serving idols doesn't play a part in any of these stories and the Ninevites aren't charged with this in the book as well.

To my face. The Hebrew word *panim* ('face' or 'countenance)' is recognized in the Yiddisch word *poneim*. The word is derived from the verb *panah*, which means 'to turn to'. If you turn to your fellow man you show him or her your face. The expression 'before my face' alludes to commitment and interaction. God doesn't look away from the evil of Nineveh but turns to it instead. He is not an indifferent God, but he watches the evil (cf. Genesis 6:11-12) and acts to make it disappear from the earth. This teaches us that man, created in Gods image, should recognize the evil in the world and fight it as well.

Jonah 1:3

> And up rises Jonah to flee towards Tarsis away from before the face of Adonai. And down he goes to Jaffo and he happens upon a ship (there), going to Tarsis. And he gives the fare thereof and down he goes into it, to go with them towards Tarsis away from before the face of Adonai.

To flee. There are more stories in the Tanakh of someone who flees. Jacob flees from Esau (Genesis 27:4-28:9). Moses flees from Pharao (Exodus 2:13-15), David flees from Saul (1 Samuel 19:1-24) and later from Absalom (2 Samuel 15:13-37). Elijah flees from Jezebel (1 Kings 19:1-8). However, Jonah's flight differs from all these other flights in three respects. First Jonah doesn't flee because he is in danger of losing his life. In the second place he flees from God and not from his enemies. And thirdly, this is the only story in which a flight across the sea is described, while the sea has never been a favourite element for the Israelites to embark upon.[176]

If we compare Jonah's reaction to his calling with the reactions of some other prophets, we'll see that he isn't the only unwilling prophet. Moses too demurred to his assignment and put forward his speech impediment as an excuse (Exodus 10:17). Very piously Isaiah confesses his unclean lips and had to burn himself on the fire of the altar first, before he's willing to set off (Isaiah 6:5-8). Jeremiah declares himself – very modestly – much too young (Jeremiah 1:6). And later God too has always to exert himself a lot to get Jeremiah to work (Jeremiah 20:7-9). But none of these unwilling prophets goes so far as to flee from God immediately after his calling and to ignore his assignment completely. But Jonah does so and moreover, he doesn't give a single motive for his extraordinary action as well. No wonder that the commentators have come up with a great deal of motives for his conduct.

In the first place we could assume that the thought of the city of blood, Nineveh, where King Pugnacity lives, must have scared the living daylights out of Jonah. No wonder that Jonah, as soon as he's given the assignment to go to that city, refuses and flees. What would have been his business in this ungodly metropolis, he, the pious Jew Jonah, son of Amittai. And yet there are reasons to consider the fact that Jonah with his flight was not only and solely after saving his life. For why should he of all things flee across the sea, the cover of the underworld, and even – as we saw[177] – in the winter or the rainy season with a big risk of ending up in a roaring storm? Later in the story it also appears that he doesn't want to stay alive no matter how (Jonah 4:8-9). This means that he must have had other motives at least. And because the writer of the book leaves us in the dark about this at the moment, we'll have to wait whether we'll be able to find out in the course of the story what Jonah could have moved to flee.

Towards Tarsis. As we already saw[178] it's not immediately clear which place is meant with Tarsis. The Targum, the old Aramaic translation of the Tanakh coming from the synagogues in the land of Israel, leaves aside where Jonah wanted to flee to and translates: "to flee across the sea."[179] Flavius Josephus thinks that here Tartessos in Spain isn't meant, but Tarsis in Cilicia.[180] The rabbis however generally seem to think of Spain yet.[181] On the other hand there is this mention of Tarsis in Ezekiel 27:12 and 1 Kings 10:22, which leads one to think of a city in Asia Minor or in the Balkans. But looking for a univocal location of the Tarsis mentioned here is of little importance and could perhaps stand in the way of understanding the story. Probably the name of this place has evoked both associations with the first readers of the Book of Jonah.[182] In the first place we could think of a city on the coast of Cilicia, which tried, with varying success, to throw off the

Persian shackles. In the second place we could also think of Tartessos, a city on the Atlantic coast of Spain at the Guadalquivir estuary. This was the Phoenicians' most western trading post at the far westerly end of the then known world.[183] There the Atlantic began, which surrounded the earth according to the view at that time.[184] So this place Tartessos was situated at the end of the earth. Anyway, Jonah's flight was a flight to the free world of the remote coastlands (Genesis 10:4-5) in the hope to be able to escape his assignment.

Away from the face of Adonai. The common idea in those days was that each of the gods had his own jurisdiction. Very often the divine service was linked up to the area or the land of that deity (see e.g. 2 Kings 5:17; 17:26). Only when the people which worshipped that deity extended its territory, the jurisdiction of the deity concerned was enlarged as well (cf. Judges 11:24). In Israel we see a breakthrough of this thought in divine territories. Israel's God fashions the sea and the dry land (Jonah 1:9) and therefore the entire world is his jurisdiction. But this doesn't mean yet that the entire world is his dominion of revelation. Where could one expect to come into direct contact with God? Where is his face, his *panim*? Where does He turn to man to form a community with him?

For the first time in the Torah we come across the face of Adonai in the Paradise story. It's characteristic that the man and his wife hide from it, after they have ignored God's command (Genesis 3:8). Kain too turns away from the face of Adonai after the murder of Abel (Genesis 4:14, 16). In both cases the breaking of the contact with God is the consequence of a wrong choice, a wrong action. So dwelling before the face of God – being face to face with Him – has everything to do with being in the right relationship with Him. Especially in a situation of exile such a complete relationship doesn't seem possible. That's why we only come across the face of God in the stories of Israel's journey through the wilderness. After the exodus from Egypt "God's face" accompanies Israel towards Canaan (Exodus 33:14). Israel was not liberated from Egypt by an angel or a seraph, but by God's face, i.e. by the direct contact with His people (Deuteronomy 4:37). After that, God's face travelled along with Israel to the land of Canaan and we could say: it has established itself there together with Israel. Is it then any wonder that we regularly come across Adonai's face in connection with Jerusalem and the Temple?

ANNOTATIONS TO JONAH 1

The Temple in Jerusalem is the very place where the perfect meeting with God is realized and where it can be expected that He will reveal His word (see e.g. Isaiah 6:1-5). The pilgrims go up to Jerusalem to appear before God's face (Psalm 42:3). They turn their faces to Jerusalem, indeed their faces travel to Jerusalem to be able to meet God face to face (Deuteronomy 5:4; see also Luke 9:51-53). And so the Temple is the only place where during certain parts of the liturgy God's Name – written with four letters and replaced here with the word *Adonai* (the LORD) – may be pronounced over the assembled pilgrims who represent the people of Israel before God. Such an intense encounter with God is not possible outside the land of Israel (cf. 1 Samuel 26:19-20). For instance it's remarkable that the prophet Ezekiel never says that in Babel he received the revelation "from before the face of Adonai". The destruction of Jerusalem however, is described by Ezekiel as a turning away of God's face (Ezekiel 7:22) and the exile as the hiding of His face (Ezekiel 39:23-24). When God brings about a reversal in the fate of Israel (Ezekiel 39:25) and causes them to live again in their land (Ezekiel 39:26), it says: "And I shall no longer hide my face from them" (Ezekiel 39:29). In Babel Ezekiel is far removed from God's face (cf. Psalm 137), but in his visions of the new temple Adonai's face plays an important part again (Ezekiel 41:22; 43:24; 44:3; 46:3, 9).

So we can see that already in the Tanakh the Temple in Jerusalem and the face of Adonai are closely connected. In the Talmud the words 'before His face' are also a designation for 'in the Tabernacle'.[185] In the Midrash this intense contact with God – that is when his Name is pronounced – is connected with his revelation and takes place in the Temple.[186] So we should interpret the expression 'before the face of Adonai' in the Book of Jonah also as the place where God makes contact with his people personally and intensely by means of the sacrificial service and as the place where He reveals Himself to Israel and especially to the prophets by means of his commands. And this is completely in keeping with the early rabbinical tradition that Jonah received his assignment in the Temple during The Feast of Tabernacles, Sukkoth.[187] This 'away from the face of Adonai' in our verse means very clearly that Jonah, in order to break off further contact with Adonai, ran away from the Temple in Jerusalem in an attempt to withdraw from the assignment revealed to him.

And he goes down. The journey of the Israelites to the tabernacle and later to Jerusalem is described in the Tanakh with the verb *alah*, which means 'to go up' or 'to ascend' (among other things in 1 Samuel 1:7; 1 Kings 12:28; 2 Kings 19:14; 23:2; Isaiah 2:3). This links up with the idea put into words in the later rabbinical literature that the Temple in Jerusalem lies on the highest mountain in the centre of the earth[188] (see also picture 4.1). Once more I'd like to point out the old midrash that Jonah received his assignment from God in the Temple in Jerusalem during Sukkoth. Entirely in line with the above mentioned 'away from the face of Adonai', Jonah's descent should be understood as a descent from Jerusalem to Jafo. His descent is a descent from the centre of Judaism, away from the centre of the world, towards the extreme ends of the earth.

There is yet another aspect to this descent of Jonah's. In a lot of Bible stories a person's descent is not always meant as a geographical one. It's often an indication of moral decay or the abandonment of the tradition. For instance this verb is used in Genesis 38:1 for Judah, when he turns his back on his family and starts a family of his own, which is evil in the eyes of Adonai. The verb 'to descend' is also used if and when one ends up in a situation of exile. Meaning this, we repeatedly come across this verb in the Genesis stories of Jacob and his twelve sons. The journey to Egypt is described in this story as a descent[a] and is in agreement with the descent into the Sheol (Genesis 44:29, 31). Unfortunately the verb 'to descent' is completely lost in translation in many renderings.

Here, in Jonah 1:3, we come across a descent in the context of a man with a calling who runs away from his designation. The verb appears four times in the Book of Jonah, twice in this verse, once in 1:5 and finally once again in 2:7. It's remarkable that till Jonah 2:7 it's always said of Jonah that he descends, but nowhere that he ascends. And at least once – in Jonah 1:6 – there had been the opportunity to do so, when Jonah had to climb up out of the hold of the ship to its deck. In the Jonah story we should also take into account the link between the verb 'to descend', the getting into exile and the descent into the Sheol, such as we came across before in the stories about Jacob and his

---

[a] Genesis 37:25; 39:1; 42:2, 3, 38; 43:4, 5, 15, 20; 44:21, 23, 26a, 26b; 45:9, 13; 46:3, 4.

sons. In section 5.2 I stated that Jonah 2, the Psalm of Jonah, can be seen against the background of the Babylonian exile. So here we see the vision the writer of the Book of Jonah had on the history of Israel/Judah of the days of Jeroboam II. It was one slow but sure descent into the absolute low of the exile. Only in the midst of the Sheol of Babylon an upward movement could be discerned (Jonah 2:7b).

Jafo. Already early in Antiquity Jafo was a seaport on the Eastern coast of the Mediterranean. As early as the 12th century BC it was a settlement of the Sea Peoples from Greece to which the Philistines belonged as well.[189] In later centuries Jafo was an important seaport for Israel (2 Chronicles 2:16; Ezra 3:7), but it was never a part of Israel's territory[190] (cf. Joshua 19:46). Only during the rule of Jonathan Maccabee (161-143 BC) it was conquered by the Jews (1 Maccabees 10:75-76). However, in the Persian time it was supervised by the Phoenician seaport Sidon.[191]

The choice of the writer of the Book of Jonah for Jafo as the place from which Jonah sailed doesn't quite speak for itself. It's true, seen from Jerusalem Jafo was the nearest seaport, but a departure via the Phoenician seaport Sidon wouldn't have been strange too, the more so if we consider the fact that the historical Jonah came from the northern village of Gath-ha-Chefer, that was just as far from Sidon as from Jafo. This means that the mention of Jafo could perhaps be meant to call up more associations than only an association with just a seaport. We remember the already discussed linguistic relation between the words *Jafo* and *Jafet*, Noah's third son, who, in the list of peoples of Genesis 10, is the ancestor of the northern peoples to which also the Greeks belonged.[192] Moreover, Jafo was the place where the Greek hero Perseus saved his beloved Andromeda from the power of a seamonster, a common belief in those days. In the Persian days even the trade from and to the land of Israel was done for the greater part with and by the Greeks via the port of Jafo.[193] For the first readers of the Book of Jonah in the days of the Persian rule Jafo was by all odds the gate to the free world of the west, where especially the Greeks kept trying to withdraw from the Persian influence.

A ship. Israel never was a seafaring nation and never had a fleet of some importance, neither for trading nor for war purposes. That's why King Solomon hired Phoenician ships and sailors for transports across the sea (1 Kings 5:1-9; 9:26-27; 10:22). Only once a king of Israel tried to build up a fleet of traders, the so-called Tarsis ships. That was King Jehosaphat of Judah (868-847 BC). But that fleet perished immediately after it had left the harbour (1 Kings 22:49-50).

Going to Tarsis. These 'Ships of Tarsis' (Isaiah 2:16; 23:1, 14; 60:9; Psalm 48:8) were purpose-built ships for the long haul trade,[194] comparable with the East Indiamen. Since the Phoenicians had found the course to the west and had carefully kept it a secret,[195] one may think here of a Phoenician ship. However, even ships which didn't sail to Tarsis, but for instance towards Ofir, situated on the coast of the Red Sea, could be called 'ships of Tarsis' (1 Kings 22:49).

The fare thereof. In Hebrew *sêcharah*. This word comes from the verb *sachar*, which means 'to work for a wage' or 'to hire oneself out as a field hand'. The word *sêcharah* means *'her* wages': of the ship. So Jonah hires ship ànd crew. The rabbis don't understand *sêcharah* as 'fare', but as the rent for ship ànd crew. A midrash tells us that Jonah pays the price of the entire cargo.[196] The rest of the story doesn't mention the presence of other passengers whatsoever. And so we'll see that Jonah is treated by the crew with all the respect due to a client. As the one who chartered the ship, Jonah is, as it were, the employer of the crew. Such a course of events, when a ship sailed for a client, wasn't unusual in antiquity.[197]

With them. With the crew, in the service of Jonah.

Towards Tarsis. In the Tanakh (1 Kings 10:22) and in the later rabbinical tradition we can read that a voyage to Spain (Tarsessos) and back could last three years. A Jew who didn't come back within this period, lost the right of usufruct of his land.[198] So Jonah prepares for a long stay abroad. However, the irony of the story is that Jonah will already be back after three days!

Jonah 1:4

> And Adonai throws a wind, a (very) big one, towards the sea. And (then) occurs a storm, a (very) big one, in the sea and the ship reckons to be wrecked.

Throws. A well-aimed throw. The same verb is used when Saul throws his spear to David (1 Samuel 18:11; 20:33; see also Ezekiel 32:4). In Jonah 1:5, 12 and 15 this verb is used again.

Annotations to Jonah 1

A wind, a (very) big one. The Midrash tells us that this wind was aimed only against the ship in which Jonah sailed. Other ships weren't troubled by it. Just like the wind on Sinai (1 Kings 19:11), which was only observed by Elijah, and the storm which killed Job's children (Job 1:19), which was directed to that house only.[199]

The word 'wind' (Hebrew: *ru'ach*) is often translated with 'spirit' or 'breath'. In the Bible this word is used for the first time in the first verses of the Torah. The *ru'ach* (spirit) of God was hovering over the waters. After the heading of the Creation story in Genesis 1 the 'brooding' of the *ru'ach* (the spirit) of God over the waters was His first action of involvement with the creation. The expression 'spirit of God' expresses His influence on the world. As such the image of the *ru'ach*, the wind, the breath is a profound image: we can't see the wind and we can't see God either, but we do and can see both their effects on the world. I remember that Jonah's flight was an attempt to evade contact with God and His revelation.[200] Here we can see that indeed Jonah has evaded God's area of revelation, but not his jurisdiction. It's remarkable that at sea He doesn't speak to Jonah anywhere, while His active presence is no less 'big'.

The sea. I already wrote about the meaning of the sea in the language of images of Tanakh in section 5.2. The sea as the face of the abyss – read also: the Sheol, the suppression by the enemies of Israel, the exile – is an extremely risky escape route for Jonah, but at the same time the only possibility to evade the word of Adonai. In a midrash Rabbi Eliezer makes Jonah say to himself: "See here, I want to escape from His presence to a place where His glory isn't proclaimed. If I will ascend to the Heavens, it is written thereof: 'And His glory is above the heavens' (Psalm 113:4). If I'll ascend above the earth (it is written thereof): 'The whole earth is full of his glory' (Isaiah 6:3). See here, I'll escape to the sea, to a place where His glory isn't proclaimed."[201] The irony of the story is that it will be just Jonah who will shortly proclaim God's glory at sea (Jonah 1:9) and who will – in spite of himself – push out the frontiers of God's domain of revelation temporarily till the lid of the Sheol. Could this be the lesson Jonah had to learn and could this be the message the writer of the Book of Jonah wanted to confront his fellow Jews with, that is to say, that Israel should proclaim Adonai to the nations of the world if they ask for it?

And the ship reckons to be wrecked. The point is that 'reckons' is the intensive form of the verb which does not only mean 'to think' or 'to intend', but which can also mean 'to reckon', 'to attribute to', 'to estimate' and 'to take into account'.[202] I've chosen 'to reckon' because of the alliteration with 'wrecked'. That's also the case in Hebrew between *chishêvah* ('reckons') and *lêhishaveir* ('to be broken'). Why is this ship depicted as a thinking being?

Depicting so-called lifeless things as animated beings occurs regularly in the eastern way of thought and narrative. In the Tanakh we come across: A land that sins (Ezekiel 14:13), chariots in a dead sleep (Psalm76:7), mourning roads (Lamentations 1:4). In the apocryphal book Judith we read about a bed that feels ashamed (Judith 9:3). Even today we can still read this usage in the words of rabbis. Within the scope of the attempts to preserve the synagogue of Zwolle Rabbi J.S. Jacobs wrote that this synagogue "will show the pews, empty pews, which cry because they are not occupied, and the walls which shout, because they can hardly hear the prayer of the Jews, because it reverberates only in Treblinka, Bergen-Belsen, Sobibor ..."

But there is something more going on. In a way the entire creation is seen as animated. That's not a matter of animism, but of perception of and respect for the earthly reality: Who jumps with joy, sees even the mountains jump with joy. And something special is the matter with ships. The Bible considers them to belong to the living world.[a] The Midrash considers them to be included in God's blessing to Abraham (Genesis 12:; 18:18).[203]

Jonah 1:5

> And afraid are the mariners and they cry out, (every) man to his god, and they throw the tools that (are) in the ship into the sea to lighten itself of them. And Jonah has gone down into the sides of the ship and he has lain down and is fast asleep.

And afraid are. The Hebrew verb *jara*, usually translated with 'to fear', does not only mean 'to be afraid of'. That's not even the most

---

[a] Psalm 104:25-26; Proverbs 30:19; Revelations 8:9; see also Proverbs 31:14.

important meaning of the verb. In the first place it means 'to respect', an aspect anyway also present in the English verb 'to fear'. So the mariners are not only afraid of the storm, but they also respect the storm as an act of the gods. They not only want to save their lives, no, they also want to restore a good relationship with the world of the gods. So we should pay attention to the fact that these sailors, in the eyes of the writer of the Book of Jonah, are more altruistic and religious than many – even today perhaps – would be prepared to believe.

The mariners. In Hebrew: *malachim*. Besides, not a word is said here about other passengers than Jonah.[204] The word *malachim* comes from the verb *malach*, which means 'to salt'. So we could somewhat graphically translate *malachim* with 'salt-men'. Undoubtedly this description has something to do with the salty smell of the sailors. For real landlubbers this was certainly a designation with a negative connotation. This must have been the case in Israel as well, because seagoing didn't have a favourable reputation, as we already saw before.[205] So Jonah found himself in suspicious company.

(Every) man to his god. Every people, every country, every trade even, had its own god or gods in those days. The Midrash says that there were representatives of the seventy peoples of the world on board.[206] So all the gods of the world were worshipped (cf. Micah 4:5). So the ship has become a world in a nutshell.[207] If and when Jonah (Israel) fails in his (its) assignment, it's not only Jonah (Israel) in danger but also the entire world! Which attitude to life is asked of Jonah, the Israelite, to save the world?

And they throw the tools ... into the sea. It is possible that jettisoning the cargo was not only meant to lighten the ship. Making a sacrifice to the angered gods of the sea could have motivated this action in those days.

To lighten itself of them. Clearly it's not about making the ship lighter. The sailors lighten themselves. The storm is not so much directed towards the ship but to its crew.[208] What else can they do than throwing overboard their possessions showing their gods that they mean well?

And Jonah has gone down. The story has a remarkable composition, because chronologically Jonah's descent into the ship happens before the storm hits the ship. Chronologically the order of the verses in Jonah 1 should be: 1-3, 5b, 4-5a, 6. However, there are various reasons why the writer could have preferred the present order. For instance the story becomes more exciting by it. Action and reaction follow directly: flight – storm, sleep – call. Now Jonah's sleep contrasts much more with the violence of the storm and with the sailors' fear already known with the readers. Also the captain's appeal in the next verse is introduced more directly by it. Anyway this figure of speech, a so-called *nachholende Erzählung*, occurs more often in the Book of Jonah.[209] As it were the story makes a new start again.

Has gone down. For the third time Jonah's descent is mentioned. One could say: Jonah descends time and again, now also in relation to the representatives of the peoples of the world.[210]

The sides of the ship. The Hebrew word for 'ship' comes from the verb 'to cover'. So it's a ship with decks and a hold. Not much is known about the construction of a Tarsis ship. The number of pictures of cargo ships from that time is smaller than that of warships. The pictures show ships with upper and lower decks suitable for soldiers and oarsmen (see pictures 6.1 and 6.2). The fact that the words 'sides' or 'flanks' are mentioned – in Hebrew a dualis is used – could suppose that Jonah had descended into the lower deck and had come to the bow of the ship, the place where both sides meet to form the bow or stern, perhaps even the keel. Descending deeper into the ship is simply not possible.

Fast asleep. The Hebrew word is in the so-called niphal-form which can be understood passively: "He is overcome by sleep," but also reflexively: "He allowed himself to be overcome by sleep". In the second case it's a conscious effort of Jonah himself. It's the same kind of sleep God caused the man Adam to be overcome by, before He made of him man and woman (Genesis 2:21). "Jonah slept and snored," so the translation of the Septuagint (2nd century BC) goes. The images and terms used here make one think very much of death:[211]

- Jonah descends into the ship (the world in a nutshell),
- he lies down in the lowest part (the grave, the Sheol),
- and is overcome by sleep (resembling the sleep of the dead).

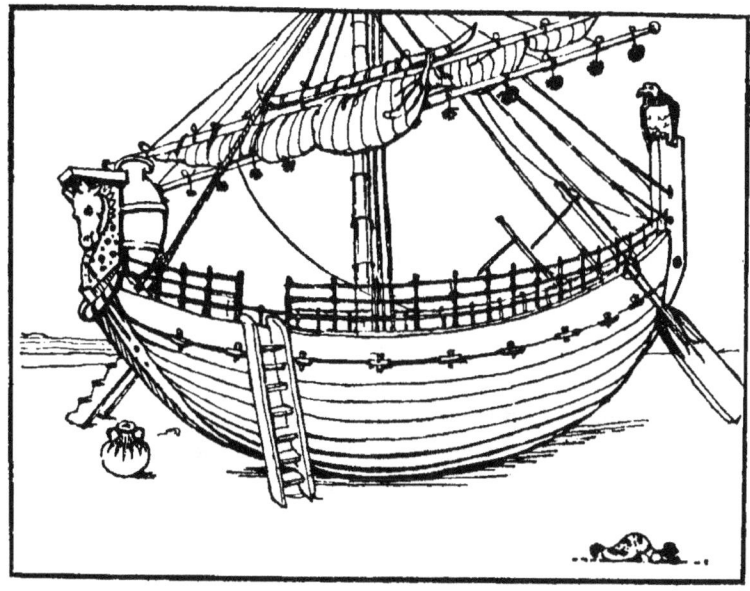

Picture 6.1 *Phoenician cargo ship (ca. 1700 BC).*

Picture 6.2 *Phoenician warship (ca. 700 BC).*

The verbal form used here *wajeiradam* can be understood as an active form of falling asleep. Jonah has all his actions, from his flight to his deep sleep, done *deliberately*. It can be concluded from this that Jonah doesn't flee from Adonai out of laziness or fear, but because he has a fundamental difference of opinion with the Holy One, blessed be He. Jonah wants to make it impossible for God to speak to the Ninevites via his prophet. Why so excessively recalcitrant? And why doesn't God dismiss him as a worthless prophet? And why doesn't He allow Jonah to sleep on quietly?

Jonah 1:6

> And (then) comes to him the master of the rigging and he says to him: "What('s the matter) with you, who is so fast asleep! Rise up, call to your god, perhaps he will change his mind – that god – about us and not we shall perish.

The rigging. In Hebrew: *hachoveil*. The word comes from *chèvel*, which means 'hawser' or 'a ship's rope'. Here it designates the crew of the ship. But it must be said that this word seemed to have a negative connotation as well when used for people, comparable with the word 'rif-raff', or 'scum' or 'rabble', just as in Dutch the word 'tuig' can be used for the rigging as well as for rif-raff.[212] When later the sailors appear to behave positively they are no longer called 'rigging' but 'men' (Jonah 1:10 and 16). Obviously the writer of the Book of Jonah refers in this way to certain expectations, which could have existed with a big part of his audience with regards to sailors. But in the course of the story he shakes up those expectations considerably and turns them upside down eventually. Such a reversal of fixed opinions about certain groups of people occurs in the Bible more often.[a]

Rise up, and call. The same words as in God's order to Jonah: "Rise up ... and call" (Jonah 1:2). But could Jonah call to God as he hasn't even turned into the road to Nineveh to obey and fulfil God's order with regards to this city?

---

[a] An Egyptian princess appears to be able to save the Hebrew boy Moses (Exodus 2:6-7). The Moabitic woman Ruth appears to be able to become the ancestress of King David (Ruth 4:17).

ANNOTATIONS TO JONAH 1

To your god. It doesn't say: 'to Adonai'. The shipmaster, does not yet know the name of Jonah's God and so won't be able to mention it.

Perhaps he will change his mind ... about us. The shipmaster finds the same connection between prayer and mercy that many believers make: If you pray to God intensively enough, He will be merciful to you. But the story doesn't make this connection. In the first place all this crying out doesn't make the storm abate. In the second place Jonah doesn't seem to comply with the call of the shipmaster anywhere in the following. It's as if Jonah realizes that there's no point in all that calling and praying to God. When man has jeopardized the relation with God by his own actions, something else is needed than piety of words. Something must be done. The mariners too begin to realize that other measures should be taken. But what measures, if you don't know which god you're dealing with?

Jonah 1:7

> And they say, (each) man to his fellow: "Let us go and let us cast lots and we may know for whose cause this evil, this one, (is) upon us." And they cast lots and (then) falls the lot on Jonah.

Cast lots. The storyteller leaves Jonah and the shipmaster behind in the hold. Without any change the story continues on deck, where clearly the terrified crew has abandoned praying. Other measures should be taken. The perpetrator of all this calamity should be found. For disasters don't occur just like that. Sometimes, when the cause can't be found, disasters should be attributed to the arbitrariness, the tyranny or even – but of course nobody dare say this out loud – to the sadism of one or more gods or demons. Then one can only try to placate the gods and spirits with prayers and sacrifices. But the cause of the disasters is mostly and usually the misconduct of the people. And this needn't at all be the collective guilt of an entire community as was the case with Sodom and Gomorra (Genesis 18:16-33) or with Nineveh. Also by one single individual both a blessing and a curse can be called down on the entire community (a blessing: Genesis 12:3; 18:18; a curse: Joshua 7:1-15; 2 Samuel 24:1-17). If it isn't obvious who causes the calamity, either because the perpetrator doesn't report himself, or

Annotations to Jonah 1

because he isn't aware of his action, the community has only one means left to discover the cause: casting the lots.

In Israel the lots were cast in various situations. That was for instance the case when the land was to be divided between the tribes and family clans (Numbers 26:52-56). At Yom Kippur, the Day of Atonement, the scapegoat was marked out by the lot for Azazel (Leviticus 16:8-10). Also in the Temple certain priestly duties were divided among the priests by means of the lot (Luke 1:9). However, the lots were not cast all the time. Clearly casting the lots was a ritual act in Israel, about which we read in Proverbs 16:33: "The lot is cast into the lap; but the whole disposing thereof is of the LORD." In other words: casting the lots is not a matter in itself, but should be subjected to the rules and laws of Adonai. So casting the lots as a game (playing at dice) didn't occur in Israel, anyway.

Casting the lots is about taking decisions people can not, will not or may not take mutually. When drawing lots all those involved have equal chances, so afterwards no dissension need arise about the outcome. In this way the use of lots could prevent conflicts and political strife, not only after the event but also before. One should understand the use of the lots in this sense when people are designated for special functions such as king (1 Samuel 10:20-21), as the one who makes the incense offering (Luke 1:9) or as apostle (Acts 1:26). In the Talmud we read an illustrative story about this: "Initially it was like this: Everyone who wanted to do so could clean the altar of the ashes. However, when there were many, they used to run up the slope and he who was first to be at four cubits (from the altar) got the right to clean it. Now it happened once that two [men] reached the decisive point at the same time and one of them pushed the other aside so that he fell and broke his leg. When the court saw that it carried a great risk with it, it ruled that the right to clean the altar should only be appointed by casting the lots." [213]

How the lots should be cast was undoubtedly subjected to strict rules. These were handed down by tradition. If mistakes were made, then the outcome would be invalid. Not much is known about the exact procedures. But we do know that each person or party had its own dice when casting them (see for instance Leviticus 16:8). When it was about people the name of that man or woman was probably written on it. So it was as if one was cast personally. How the outcome was established, is not known in all cases. Sometimes was the one whose stone hit the ground first the one indicated.[214]

In our case with Jonah it was about finding the culprit or the perpetrator. There are two comparable cases in Tanakh, both illustrative for the Jonah story. That's in the first place the story of Achan after the debacle at Ai (Joshua 7:13-18) who's pointed out by the lot, and in the second place the case of Jonathan who's pointed out after the silence of Adonai in the fight against the Philistines (1 Samuel 14:36-45). I'll return to it at the next verse. Anyway, we can ask ourselves how it would be possible to cast the lots in a ship in a violent gale, and by reason of that to take an important decision. Not only an actual event but the liturgical background of the Purim festival seems to have been decisive for the matter.[215]

For whose cause. This word is a compound of the Hebrew words *bê* (by), *shè* (the one), *lê* (to, towards) and *mi* (who). It's an Aramaism, an expression derived from Aramaic, which doesn't occur in Hebrew originally.[216] Some translations of the Bible still use here the word 'guilt' or 'fault',[217] which is wrong because of two reasons. In the first place guilt is out of the question in Hebrew: It's still to be proved! The question is who this storm is about, or who this storm is pointed at. In the second place it's not a matter of course that 'for whose cause?' means one of the people on board. Just as well it could mean "for whose god?"

Jonah 1:8

> And they say to him: "Tell, we pray, to us for whose cause this evil (is) upon us. What (is) your mission and where are you going to? What is your country and of what people are you?"

Tell, we pray, to us. 'Tell' is from the same Hebrew verb from which the word *haggadah* comes. It's usually translated with 'to tell', or 'bring forward', 'make known'.

Now that the lot had fallen to Jonah and he is suspected to be the cause of the calamity, we could ask ourselves why the sailors had not thrown Jonah overboard at once. Undoubtedly the reason is that being pointed at by the lot was not sufficient enough to declare someone guilty. A confession is always needed. In the two comparable

Annotations to Jonah 1

Tanakh stories about Achan and Jonathan (Joshua 7:13-18; 1 Samuel 14:36-45) we come across exactly that course of events. A confession is asked from Achan as well from Jonathan before the punishment can be executed (Joshua 7:19; 1 Samuel 14:43). In the Talmud we find the following commentary on the story of Achan:[218]

> When the Holy One, blessed be He, said to Joshua: "Israel has sinned," said Joshua: "Master of the Universe, who has committed that sin?" God answered: "Am I an informer? Go and cast the lots."

Here the Talmud indicates clearly that finding a culprit is a matter of the community itself. During this process one can't appeal to God directly. When other means fail one could – if the worst comes to the worst – resort to the lots. And the Talmud continues:

> Then Joshua went and cast the lot, and the lot fell on Achan, who said to him: "Joshua, do you want to point me out by the lot? You and the priest Eleazar are both the greatest ones of this time ... "

In other words: You should know better!

> "... and if I should throw de lot between both of you, it would always fall on one of you."

What Achan really wants to say is: The lot always falls on someone, that's the way it is, and that's why it has fallen on me! But the story continues:

> "Then Joshua answered: "I beg you, don't disparage the lot, because once the land of Israel will be divided by the lot ..."

In other words: If you undermine the authority of the lot, you'll provoke strife between the tribes of Israel about the territory and you'll endanger the peace in Israel. Joshua continues in this Talmud story:

Annotations to Jonah 1

"Because it is written: 'But the land shall be divided by lot' (Numbers 26:55). Do confess!" Rabina[a] said: "Joshua convinced Achan with the words: 'We only want you to confess and nothing else. Aye, confess and you'll be relieved.'" Then Achan answered Joshua and said: "It's true, I have sinned against Adonai, the God of Israel."

In this Talmud story we can clearly see how the judicial process will be embarrassed when the suspect refuses to confess. The question is whether judgement could be passed when the suspect sticks to his refusal, which is clearly shown in the continuation of the Jonah story.

For whose cause. The words "For whose cause the evil, this (here), (is) about us" are not found in some Hebrew manuscript and in many manuscripts of the Septuagint as well. Perhaps it's a question of a glosse, a later explanatory insertion to the "for whose cause" in verse 7.[219] I've already said that the sailors could also have meant: "Which god is behind all this?"[220]

This evil. The pagan idea is that misconduct evokes retaliation as the answer of the gods (see for instance Acts 28:3-4). However, in Jewish-biblical thought it is generally the misconduct itself which brings disasters. In this sense is the story of Achan at Jericho illustrative. Jericho was the first city in the land of Canaan conquered by Israel. So the loot of Jericho is a "firstling-loot". The firstlings always come to Adonai. Giving up the firstlings to Him implies the recognition that everything in this world is God's and that Israel should use all his possessions in accordance with His will. The part of the loot Achan kept back for himself wasn't just a form of theft. It was an infringement of the fundamental relation between God and Israel. That's why Achan had to be stoned: Not because God had to be avenged by means of a life, but because the *conduct* personified by Achan must be expelled from Israel. When people break off the right relation with God by their headstrong choices, they become "god-less" and go – seen from the Bible – from bad to worse. The question after the origin of evil should not be answered with a theology about God, but with teachings which lead man to live a just life.

---

[a] Babylonian rabbi ca. 450 CE.

Your mission, your country, that people. The Hebrew word for 'mission' can also mean: 'business', 'profession', 'trade', 'function', 'task', 'assignment', 'mission', or 'calling'. In the case of 'trade' it can be taken as an economic activity.[221] But the questions of the sailors after all these facts undoubtedly have an aim behind it. Beyond Israel in those days it was a very usual thing that each people, each country, each trade had its own deity. What the sailors especially were interested in was which god was behind the storm.

Jonah 1:9

> And he says to them: "A Hebrew (man) (am) I, and Adonai, God of the heavens, I fear (Him), who makes the sea and the dry land."

A Hebrew. From the verb 'to step over', 'to cross' or 'to cross over'. So the word *Hebrew* could mean something like 'passer-by', 'transient', 'rambler' or even 'Bedouin'. Sometimes it's also translated as 'someone coming from the other side',[222] which stresses the fundamentally other position of Israel (or the Israelite) in the pagan world of Antiquity. It's rather remarkable that the word 'a Hebrew (man)' as the designation of an Israelite is only used by gentiles, or to make oneself known to the gentiles.[a] That's also the case here in Jonah 1:9. The word is connected with the name of Abraham's forefather Eber, whose name in the lists of the generations in Genesis 10 and 11 is followed by an extra remark (Genesis 10:21; see also Genesis 10:24-25; 11:14-17).

A Hebrew (man)(am) I. Although the lot fell on Jonah, his answer doesn't look like a confession of guilt at all. It looks more like the proud answer of someone who knows he isn't accountable to his fellow man in a matter between him and God. He only tells them the name of his people and mentions further the Name of the God within whose jurisdiction he falls. Only later in the story it becomes clear that he has also told the sailors to be in conflict with his God (see Jonah 1:10b and 12b). But Jonah keeps mum towards the sailors about the

---

[a] See e.g. Genesis 14:13; 39:14, 17; 40:15; 41:12; 43:32; Exodus 2:7; 3:18; 5:3; 1 Samuel 4:6.

nature and contents of his controversy with the Holy One, blessed be His Name.

Adonai. The LORD. Here the Name of the God of Israel is proclaimed to the sailors, the representatives of the seventy nations of the world.[223] As we saw in Section 2.5, the text of Jonah 1:9-10a is the centre of the story in Jonah 1:4-16. This announcement of the Name of the God of Israel to the nations – with them "fearing God" as a result – is the meaning of Jonah's stay on board, the meaning of Israel's stay in the world, evidently. Anyway, I'd like to observe that this announcement to the men is one they asked for themselves and so this doesn't look like mission in the traditional Christian sense of the word.

God of the heavens. This expression and its sequel 'who makes the sea and the dry land' form variations adapted to the situation of the standard phrasing 'who made the heavens and the earth', sometimes completed with 'the sea and all that is in it'.[a] The God of Israel is proclaimed here – in the continuation of Genesis 1 – as the God under whose jurisdiction not only Jonah falls, but the entire creation as well. Therefore this wording serves to distinguish clearly between the God of Israel and the other gods. Generally their jurisdiction is represented as something more restricted.[224]

I fear. Not so much 'being afraid of' than 'to respect' or 'to honour'. Just as the sailors feared in Jonah 1:5.[225] The term does not only accentuate the distance between God and man. 'Fearing God' is chiefly an attitude to life which shows that one accepts God's jurisdiction over the world and especially over one's own life. The God Jonah makes known to the representatives of the nations of the world, is in the first place a God who should be feared, respected in his say, his authority over life. In fact, this 'confession' of Jonah is not only the centre of the story of the storm at sea. It's also a turning point in Jonah's action. For the first time in the story he breaks his silence. He didn't answer the call of the master (Jonah 1:6). Now he does. What's more, after his flight 'away from the face of Adonai' Jonah expresses here for the first time his acknowledgement of God's jurisdiction over

---

a   See e.g. Exodus 20:11; 31:17; 2 Kings 10:15; Isaiah 37:16; 42:5; 44:25; 45:12-13, 18; 51:13; Jeremiah 10:12; 32:17; 51:15; 2 Chronicles 2:12; Nehemiah 9:6; Psalms 95:5; 102:26; 115:15; 121:2; 124:8; 134:3; 136:5-6; 146:6; Proverbs 3:19.

the creation and over Jonah himself. How will the sailors react on this 'confession' obtained with so much difficulty, that isn't really a confession but an acknowledgement?

Who makes. From the verb *asah* which is commonly translated with 'to make'. In the context of the making of the creation by God it can get the sound of 'making something out of nothing'. This meaning however, is doubtful. Rather *asah* is making from something that is already available. So new things can come into being from existing materials, but existing things can also change into other forms by it. With the words 'Who makes' we needn't think of 'making something out of nothing'.

Jonah 1:10

> And (then) fear the men a fear (very) big and they say to him: "What (is) this (now that) you have made?" For (now) know the men that away from the face of Adonai he (is) fleeing, for he has told (it) to them.

The men. First they were called 'sailors' or 'rigging', but from now on they are called 'men'. The suspicious strangers appear to be receptive to the knowledge and fear of Adonai. The reader of the Book of Jonah should, whether he wants it or not, begin to see them as 'men', that is as respectable human beings.

A fear (very) big. If the sailors feared for the storm and for their gods with a 'normal fear' (Jonah 1:5), now – once they know they're dealing with the God of heaven and earth – they experience mortal fear.

What (is) this (now that) you have made. This expression needn't be a question for more information as such. It can also be seen as a cry of horror. It's the same 'question' God asks Eve in Genesis 3:13. In this way the Jonah story is strongly connected with the story of the first sin. The essence of the creation is at stake if Jonah refuses to fulfil his assignment. In the following Jonah seems indeed to come to realize his disobedience.

For he has told (it) to them. Verse 10 confirms what we stated in the previous verse: Indeed Jonah confesses his flight from Adonai, but the reason of that flight remains wrapped in mystery.[226] So this shouldn't be seen as a 'real' confession.

Jonah 1:11

> And they say to him: "What shall we do to you so that calm may be the sea unto us, for the sea (is) going and storming.

What shall we do to you. Jonah is the only man on board who is acquainted with Adonai, God of the heavens. So he should also be the only man who can say how to allay the anger of this God. The result is that now Jonah is 'suspect' and 'judge' at the same time. After all, he is the only one who knows what he has done wrong and according to which law he should be sentenced. This lends the continuation of the story a double bottom.

Jonah 1:12

> And he says to them: "Take me up and throw me into the sea, and calm will be the sea unto you, for knowing (am) I, that for my sake this storm, this big one, (is) upon you."

And throw me into the sea. Evidently Jonah knows he's guilty of death and that for two reasons. In the first place he didn't fulfil God's assignment. In the second place he jeopardized the lives of these men, the representatives of the seventy nations of the world. He'd put the existence of the ship, the world in miniature,[227] on the line because of his unwillingness.

Now we could wonder, why Jonah condemns himself so radically without trying to come to terms with God. Why doesn't he convert? Why doesn't he confess his guilt and doesn't he promise God to fulfil his assignment yet? I'd like to point at the problematic nature of 'seer and prophet', discussed in section 4.4. Jonah wants to be a seer and not a prophet. In this respect he behaves consequently. The judgement of the culprit should be unconditional, whether it concerns Nineveh or Jonah himself. Jonah judges himself as a seer. But the narrators have something remarkable up their sleeves for him yet.

Annotations to Jonah 1

And calm will be the sea unto you. Although Jonah considers himself the seer he also wants to be for Nineveh, for the men he'll be a prophet – perhaps without realizing it. His judgement on behalf of Adonai has a conditional content for the men in the ship: if they execute this sentence with regard to Jonah – and in doing so become the executors of the justice of Jonah's God – they will be saved. So Jonah, the seer, is made a prophet by God, against his wish.

For knowing (am) I that for my sake. What Jonah does know, is formulated by the Talmud:[228] "A false prophet is he who prophesizes something he hasn't learned (from God) and he hasn't been assigned to do. His execution is done by men. But *who withhold his prophecy* or despises the words of the prophet, ànd the prophet who breaks his own words, (he) will be executed by heaven. Because it is written: '... that whosoever will not hearken unto My words which he shall speak in My name, *I will require it of him.*' (Deuteronomy 18:18 ff.)." And the commentary on this reads:[229] "Who withholds his prophecy: for instance Jonah, the son of Amitai." Jonah knows that God demands an explanation of him by wind and storm.

Jonah 1:13

> And hard row the men to turn around to the dry (land), and not (at all) they can (do it), for the sea (is) going and storming against them.

And ... row the men. From the verb 'to break through' or 'to plough through' (the waves). The idea is that the oars plough through the waves.

Why don't the men throw Jonah overboard yet? Do they consider Jonah's self-condemnation all too radical, because they still don't know what exactly he has done? Are they afraid of the consequences when the financier of the voyage, the man who chartered the ship,[230] is going to be jettisoned? Don't they trust Jonah and do they look on his solution as the ultimate attempt to escape from his God? In other words: are they rowing desperately to dry land to deliver Jonah at his God on land, so that He should decide then and there what to do with Jonah? Or is it of great importance to the narrator of the Book of Jonah to sympathetically present the representatives of the nations of the word? In verse 14 we'll be further informed.

ANNOTATIONS TO JONAH 1

To turn around to dry land. From the Hebrew verb with meanings like 'to return', 'to turn around' or 'to convert'. The Hebrew word *têshuvah* ('conversion') is also derived from this verb. In those days the ships sailed as much as possible in sight of the coast, so that it was possible to row ashore in an emergency.

And not (at all) they could (do it). This is strange: The storm blows them away from the coast, actually. And that means that this storm wasn't meant by God to fetch Jonah back! Jonah's radical self-condemnation is not only an impulse of himself, just like that. This shows that Jonah's judgement is God's judgement as well. Jonah should be jettisoned! The conflict between Jonah and God is so fundamental that there's no way back for Jonah than through the Sheol (Jonah 2:3). We should bear in mind that in a story like this it's not about a historical person who should be sentenced to death, because he's done something wrong. In the first place Jonah is the personification of a certain religious attitude. What should disappear from the ship – this world in miniature – is the religious mentality of which Jonah is the exponent. Not the man Jonah should be cast into the Sheol, but his unwillingness to participate in God's intentions with the world.

Jonah 1:14

> And (then) they call to Adonai and they say: "Oh, Adonai, not (at all) let us perish for the soul of this man (here), and not (at all) give upon us blood (that is) innocent, for You, Adonai, according to your wish You do."

Oh, Adonai. The master of the crew has called up Jonah to pray to his god (Jonah 1:6) without mentioning His Name. By Jonah's testimony this unknown God becomes known to the sailors by His Name (compare Exodus 3:13-14 and 6:1-2). And so they no longer turn to God (*eilohim*), but to the LORD (*Adonai*).

For the soul of this man (here). The word *nèfesh* is often translated by 'soul'. It comes from the verb 'to breath'. Therefore *nèfesh* also means 'breath' or 'breath of life' and alludes to being alive or being animated. That's why the translation 'life' occurs as well. Yet the word *nèfesh* has a wider meaning. It relates to the entire personality, to that which makes man who he is, which drives him and what inspires him to his actions. A modern translation of someone's *nèfesh* could be someone's 'identity'. That's why we can also translate the word *nèfesh* with 'inspiration' or 'way of life'. Here I've chosen for 'soul', because I think that this word contains most of all nuances of the word *nèfesh*. It's about a person's entirety.[231]

Blood (that is) innocent. A legal term. So it's about the execution of a sentence. When the sailors speak about innocent blood, it needn't mean that they consider him to be not guilty. Maybe the question for the men could be whether a death sentence was allowed to be pronounced and executed. Although the lot fell on Jonah and the God who has probably caused the storm is known by now, Jonah still hasn't confessed a crime committed by him after all. So the men run the big risk to commit a miscarriage of justice by executing Jonah's judgement right away. And an erroneously executed death sentence makes the witnesses and the executors guilty of death. So the essence of this prayer is: "Please, don't take us for murderers who act out of self-interest or carelessness, but please, Adonai, do take the responsibility for this execution upon Yourself." You see, how could they know whether Jonah's God will accept their execution of the sentence with gratitude?

According to Your wish. Often translated with "as it pleases You". However, it's not about 'wishing' in the sense of wanting to do something arbitrarily. It's about wanting to do something motivated and for the greater good.

Jonah 1:15

> And up they take Jonah and they throw him towards the sea. And silent becomes the sea, from its raging.

And they throw him. A delightful midrash shows that even now the men did their utmost and tried to keep Jonah alive. It is told:[232] "They (the men) took him up (and lowered him) into the sea to the back of his knees and the storm calmed down. They pulled him up to the deck and the sea raged again to them. They threw him (into the sea) to his navel and the storm calmed down. Again they pulled him up and again the sea raged to them. They threw him (once more into the sea) up to his neck and the storm calmed down. Once more they pulled him up in their midst. And once more the sea raged to them. And finally when they threw him into the sea completely the sea immediately calmed down, as is written: 'And up they take Jonah and they throw him towards the sea. And silent becomes the sea, from its raging' (Jonah 1:15)."

And silent becomes the sea, from its raging. The sentence on the seer from Israel who didn't want to be a prophet, has been executed. But because of this the ship of the world is saved. Adonai's reality is never simple, unambiguous or straightforward. As He produces order from chaos and light from darkness, so He will be able to bring about the salvation of the world from Jonah's disobedience.

Jonah 1:16

> And (then) fear the men a fear (very) big with regards to Adonai and they sacrifice a sacrifice to Adonai and they promise promises.

A fear (very) big with regards to Adonai. If the writer of the Book of Jonah hadn't included this verse in the story it would never have struck anyone. Does he want to point out to his fellow-Jews the fact that the nations become God fearing should be seen as a positive consequence of Israel's stay in the diaspora, that perhaps it's even going to be its major sense? The large-scale joining of proselytes, which after the Babylonian exile made Judaism grow into the larger community of the later Roman empire, hasn't been unwelcome, without a doubt, to the writer of the Book of Jonah.

And they sacrifice a sacrifice to Adonai. Whether this action means their conversion to Judaism, can't be said with certainty, because there was already a possibility for non-Jews to have sacrifices made. The form of the verb, however, points into the direction of an own sacrifice. And where else could this sacrifice to Adonai be made than in the Temple in Jerusalem, the place where the story in Jonah 1:1 had begun as well?[233] Is it in the light of Isaiah 56:6-7 by any chance that the stay of Jonah/Israel in the ship of the world resulted in the act of making a sacrifice by these representatives of the world population?^a

---

a   Isaiah 56:6-7a reads: "Also the sons of the stranger, that join themselves to the LORD, to serve him, and to love the name of the LORD, to be his servants, every one that keeps the sabbath from polluting it, and takes hold of my covenant; even them will I bring to my holy mountain, and make them joyful in my house of prayer: their burnt offerings and their sacrifices *shall be* accepted upon my altar; for my house shall be called a house of prayer for all people."

7 Out of the belly of Sheol
Annotations to Jonah 2:1-11 (1:17-2:10)

Jonah 2:1 (1:17)

> And (then) prepares Adonai a fish, a big (one), to swallow up Jonah. And it occurs: Jonah inside the fish, three days and three nights.

And (then) prepares Adonai a fish, a big (one). The verb used here could mean 'to set aside' in the sense of 'to order'.[234] In that case it's usually translated with "Adonai appointed a fish" (NKJV). But the meaning 'to set aside' is possible in the sense of 'to dispose of', 'to hold at the disposal of', 'to keep in stock', or 'to be designed for'. This second meaning is reflected in a midrash that says that God created this fish towards the evening of the sixth day of the Creation.[235] So from the first week He had this fish at His disposal, a fish destined especially to save Jonah.

A fish, a big (one). Before we'll go on reading in Jonah 2 it's important to think again about the meaning of the big fish that swallows Jonah. It so happens that the tragedy of the Book of Jonah is that with most people it's only known because of this one motive of the fish, which is often depicted as a whale. The natural history interpretation of the story causes questions like: 'What kind of fish was it? Which fish has a gullet big enough to swallow a human?' etc. But these and such questions are entirely irrelevant when reading the Book of Jonah. They'll even interfere with the attempt to come to a good understanding of the meaning of the story. The only significant question here is: 'Why does the writer of the Book of Jonah speak about a big fish in this verse? To be able to answer this question we'll have to consider the function of Jonah 2:1-11 within the scope of the entire book.

In section 4.5.b we saw that Jonah 2 could be read as a Pesach story. Especially remarkable is the relation between the Psalm of Jonah and the song of Moses and Miriam at the Red Sea (Exodus 15:1-21). Both songs are songs of liberation from exile. In the case of Moses and Miriam it was about liberation from the Egyptian exile, but in section 5.2 we saw that the Psalm of Jonah should be read as a song about liberation from the Babylonian exile. The imagery of Jonah 2 fits in entirely with the imagery the Tanakh uses when speaking about exile and submissiveness to nations hostile to Israel. Besides the big sea animals in this language have the meaning of the superpowers which threatened Israel generally: Assyria, Egypt and Babylonia especially. Anyway, in some other Tanakh stories animals represent peoples and nations. For example that is the case with animals in Isaiah's vision of the messianic realm of peace in which "the wolf shall dwell with the lamb."[a] Also in Daniel's vision of the four beasts and of the ram and the goat, animals symbolize the great empires (see Daniel 7 and 8). Now it's remarkable that in the first of both visions all four animals came up from the sea (Daniel 7:2-3). How should we explain the big fish in Jonah in this respect?

It goes without saying to think, in the first place, of the image used in Jeremiah 51:34 for Nebuchadnezzar, the king of Babel, who exiled the Jews.[236] The image Jeremiah uses (Hebrew: *tanin*), means 'dragon from the sea' or 'sea monster'. Obviously this image has a very negative sound which lacks in the designation 'big fish' in the Jonah story. In this respect it's remarkable that in rabbinic literature this big fish isn't compared anywhere with the Leviathan (Job 3:8; 41:1; Psalm 74:14; 104:26), which serves as an image of Assyria and Babylonia in the Tanakh as well (Isaiah 27:1). On the other hand the midrash distinguishes clearly between the big fish of Jonah and the primeval monster, the Leviathan: during Jonah's three days journey through the Sheol, the big fish encounters the Leviathan. However, Jonah knows how to chase away the monster by going to stand up in the open mouth of the big fish and showing the Leviathan the sign of the circumcision. It's so frightened by this that it flees away a distance of two days.[237] On account of this it's not the most obvious conclusion to take the big fish of Jonah as an image of Babylonia.

Now it's not surprising that the big fish couldn't be interpreted in this sense very easily. After all it doesn't only swallow Jonah, but the fish also vomits him out again (Jonah 2:11). And this can't be said of Babylon with regards to the Jews. It could be said however of the Persian empire, which – after having conquered Babylon – allowed the

---

[a] Compare the animals in Isaiah 11:6-8 with the peoples and nations in the following verses 9-10.

Jews to return to Jerusalem.[238] If the big fish in the Book of Jonah should be interpreted as a symbol of a superpower – and the imagery of the Tanakh strongly suggests this thought – then it's obvious to think of the Persian empire. After all, it's the only superpower that is approached positively in Tanakh on a regular basis. Did the writer of Jonah want to say that the Persian empire should be seen as a means for God to save Israel from a possible fall in the Babylonian exile? Within this frame I'd like to mention the next link of images in the Book of Jonah itself.

A remarkable link can be noticed between Nineveh, the big fish and the Kikayon (the 'miracle tree') in Jonah 4. For Nineveh and the big fish we find the following similarities:

- both are described as being 'big' (Jonah 1:2; 2:1; 3:2 and 3);
- in both cases the expression 'three days' plays a part (Jonah 2:1; 3:3);
- in the frame of the Book of Jonah both can be interpreted as a designation for the Persian empire;[239]
- finally and remarkably the cuneiform symbol for Nineveh is a fish in a house.[240]

Even the big fish and the Kikayon have some aspects in common:

- both are 'disposed of' by Adonai (Jonah 1:17; 4:6);
- in both cases the night motive plays a part (Jonah 2:1; 4:10).

And finally, the story itself establishes a parallelism between Nineveh and the Kikayon:

- through the burning of God's anger against Nineveh and the burning to Jonah because of the Kikayon (Jonah 4:9);
- in God's answer to Jonah: 'You have pity on the Kikayon ..., and not at all I'll have pity on Nineveh?' (Jonah 4:10-11).

Now in the Book of Jonah the following image of the Persian empire arises. Initially Nineveh represents the threatening aspect. The big fish is the kind, saving aspect. The Kikayon is the perishable aspect of the Persian empire God uses to try and make it clear to Jonah that Israel's attitude with regard to this empire shouldn't aim at its fall, but at improving its morale and at enjoying its protection. Moreover it's not only about their own profit the Jews could have of the Persian empire and through which they could define their attitude in the first place. It's also about their compassion with the fate of its inhabitants. From the situation in which the Book of Jonah was written – Israel under the Persian empire – Jonah 2:1-11 can be seen as a retrospect of the liberation from the Babylonian exile, a liberation in which the Persians have played a prominent part. This retrospect also determines the contents of the psalm Jonah is going to pray later.

Finally we should consider for a while the associations called up by the motive of the big fish with the myths of the peoples and especially those from Greek mythology.[241] As well as similarities there are obvious differences between the big fish of Jonah and the sea monsters which occur in similar myths and legends. These sea monsters are almost always a threat to the principal character of the story. Therefore they should be fought against and, if possible, be killed. In certain versions of the myths of the Greek heroes Heracles and Perseus they enter the jaws of the sea monster to kill it from within.[242] As well as the similarity we also find here the great contrast with the Jonah story. The big fish isn't a threat to Jonah, but his rescue. Couldn't this be the irony of the story, that Jonah is fetched back from the free Greek world with the help of a literary motive that seemed to be derived from that same free Greek world, but which is used here as an image of its greatest adversary, the Persian empire? The orientation on the Greek world, which must have been firm among the anti-Persia orientated Jews, is ironically ridiculed by this. That's why the big fish is much more than a literary motive only. It's an element in a political-religious argument that next to a choice of position in an internal Jewish discussion also stands for a strategy of cooperation with the Persian government.

Three days and three nights. Why this exact determination of time? It wouldn't have struck any reader if this whole mention from 'and it happens' to 'nights' had not occurred in the text. The expression 'three days and three nights' we meet in 1 Samuel 30:12 in exactly the same way. There a young Egyptian is found in the field and when they gave him something to eat "his strength came back to him; for he had eaten no bread nor drunk water for three days and three nights"

(NKJV) so the text reads. The text shows a clear indication of what is meant with this expression: the period of three days and three nights makes up the no-man's-land between life and death in time. Also in Esther 4:16 the time span plays a part in a matter of life and death. The idea existed that when a human body didn't show any sign of life during three days an three nights, its soul won't return to it.[243] In ancient Judaism the custom existed to visit the grave of a deceased person after three days and check whether he or she was dead indeed.[244] After these three days there was no hope of a comeback to life.[a] In the New Testament this fact determines the period of three days Jesus was in the grave (Matthew 27:63-64; Acts 10:40). The evangelist Matthew links this time span explicitly to Jonah's stay in the fish (Matthew 12:40). With regard to Jonah we could say therefore that his return from the fish and from the Sheol (Jonah 2:11) should be seen as a form of resurrection from the death. A true motive of Pesach!

Jonah 2:2 (2:1)

> And (then) prays Jonah to Adonai, his God, from inside the fish.

And (then) prays. In the Bible it's not exceptional that a story is interrupted by a prayer in the form of a song or psalm.[b] Such a song could be meant as a commentary on the earlier told story, or as a kind of summary (of it). It's also possible that the song already existed and that the writers of the Bible story found it suitable to insert it into their story. A clear example of this is the song that is sung in 2 Samuel 22 following on the story of David, because this song is almost literally equal to Psalm 18. Now it's quite possible that when the psalms were collected Psalm 18 was taken from 2 Samuel 22. But the opposite is more probable. Another example is the song of Elisabeth in Luke 1:46-55.[c, 245] It's an adaptation of Hanna's song in 1 Samuel 2:1-10.

---

[a] See e.g. Luke 24:21 and the mention of 'four days' in John 11:17.
[b] Exodus 15:1-21; Deuteronomy 32:1-43; Judges 5:1-31; 1 Samuel 2:1-10; 2 Samuel 1:17-21; 3:33-34; 22:1-51; 23:1-7; Isaiah 38:9-22; 1 Chronicles 16:7-36; 17:16-27; 29:10-19; Judith 16:1-17; Tobit 13:1-8; 1 Maccabees 1:26-28, 36-40; 2:7-14; 3:2-9, 45; Luke 1:46-55, 67-79; 2:39-52.
[c] As argued elsewhere, this is not the song of Mary, but of Elisabeth (see endnote).

However, there's a third possibility. The Psalm of Jonah could have been an existing song, that inspired the writer to the story of Jonah and he included the song in his story as well. Then the story is, as it were, written around the song as an attempt to actualize it, a very probable course of events at the coming about of the Book of Jonah. The Psalm of Jonah is a song which describes the liberation from the Babylonian exile and which thanks God for it. It could have come into being in Babylon itself in anticipation of deliverance. This prospect for the Jews living in Babylon is expressed by Deutero-Isaiah in Isaiah 40:1 ff., "Comfort ye, comfort ye, My people." More than likely even the Psalm of Jonah was one of the songs the returning Jews had sung during their journey from Babylon to Jerusalem. The fact is that the literal movement of the psalm is from the Sheol (the exile) to the sacrificial service in the Temple. It's quite possible that the song continued playing a part in the liturgy of the Temple, as a sacrificial song to commemorate the return from exile. It's been one of the many songs which next to the 150 psalms from the Book of Psalms circulated in Israel. If the writer of the Book of Jonah had used the song to compose his story around, he'd wanted to make it clear that the tenor of his story was all about Israel's return from exile. Does Jonah in his story serve as a model for those fellow Jews who after the exile wanted to reclaim Israel's national independence from the Persians? Or has it only been the author's intention to argue that not only Israel should be delivered from exile, but also the nations of the world from the exile in which they've detained themselves? Anyhow, Jonah's assignment to go to Nineveh – into the opposite direction – is in line with Israel's deliverance.

Jonah 2:3 (2:2)

> And he says: "I call because of the affliction to me to Adonai and He answers me. Out of the belly of Sheol I shout for help, You hear my voice.

Because of the affliction. From the Hebrew verb *tsarar* with the meanings 'to tie', 'to bind up', 'to be distressed', etc. In Hebrew this verb calls up associations with the Hebrew name of Egypt, *Mitsra'im*, the land of oppression and distress, although both words aren't related etymologically.

Out of the belly. This word is usually translated with 'belly' or 'lap'. However, it comes from the verb 'to bear' and so it could also be translated with 'womb'. At first sight a strange combination: womb and Sheol. But in the oriental or eastern way of thought at that time and in biblical thought as well, life and death were in line permanently. Death is not only the inevitable end of biological life (Genesis 3:19), but it's also often the situation from which new life arises (see e.g. 2 Chronicles 13:21; Ezekiel 37:1-14).

The belly of Sheol. One of the three hell-gates, through which one could descend into the 'belly of Sheol' – that is to say into the bowels of the underworld – is the sea off Tarsis, according to the Talmud.[246] In ancient times one was under the impression that there were layers or floors in the underworld (compare Isaiah 14:15; Ezekiel 32:23). The same goes for the heavens (compare 1 Kings 8:27; 2 Corinthians 12:2). The belly of Sheol was supposed to be one of the deeper layers of the underworld. Jonah however, will only reach the deepest layer in Jonah 2:7.

Jonah 2:4 (2:3)

> And You cast me into the deep in the heart of the seas and the floods surround me. All Your wrecking billows and Your waves: over me they pass.

And you cast me. If we compare this expression with the text in Jonah 1:15, we could – at first sight – find a remarkable difference. Here the text says that God throws Jonah into the sea, there the men of the ship did so. However, this is an apparent opposite. The men executed the sentence which Jonah – as God's representative – had pronounced on himself. So they acted indirectly on behalf of the God of Israel. And if people execute a decision of God, then – in a meditation about it – the executors could be missed out. This phenomenon could regularly be found in Tanakh, in rabbinical literature and in Jewish worship.

When God saves Israel from Egypt, Israel itself is really understood to set off. When at the shore of the Red Sea the Egyptians charge at Israel and Moses addresses Israel that God will fight for them and so they should be silent (Exodus 14:9, 13-14), God calls him to order with the words: "Why do you [Moses] cry to me? Do tell the children of Israel to go forward!" In the midrash we read Rabbi Elieser's comments: "The Holy One, blessed be He, said to Moses: 'Moses, my children are in distress, the sea is a barrier and the enemy pursues them, and you are there praying long prayers! Why do you cry to Me?'"[247] The meaning of this story is to explain clearly that God will only be able to rescue Israel if it cooperates (compare Jeremiah 15:19). This thought is so obvious in Tanakh that often it isn't put in words in stories and songs of the exodus.

In the Talmud too we can read such a representation of things. In an argument on the fact that God is quite different from men, one states that indeed God cursed Noah's son Canaan but didn't kill him subsequently.[248] Here the Talmud refers to the curse in Genesis 9:25, which, however, was pronounced by Noah! Here too we notice how God's actions and those of men are closely tied together. The same relation between God's and men's actions can be noticed in the Jewish practice of prayer. When a Jew prays for recovery, he doesn't assume that God interferes directly in the course of a disease. Faith healing only by the power of prayer isn't known in Judaism. A prayer for recovery is a prayer to God whether He will *let* us recover, whether He wants to give the doctors a clear insight and allows them to diagnose correctly in time and to establish the correct therapy.[249] In this case God's action always involves man's action. One could say: If God has hands, they should be ours.

This idea can also be found in the liturgy of Judaism. The blessing on bread: "Blessed are You, Adonai, our God, King of the World, who brings forth bread from the earth" is a good example of this. God is praised and thanked for something that has involved a lot of human labour, while all is presented as God's work. All this should make us very careful when the Bible speaks about God doing something. Often – and perhaps always – acting *people* are meant without being mentioned specifically. At least that's the case here in the Psalm of Jonah.

In the heart of the seas. At high sea, the shore is no longer visible. This is unknown territory, both in surface as in depth. In section 5.2 we saw that in Tanakh the sea often represents the point of assembly of all anti-Jewish and anti-divine powers in the world. Why did Jonah have to end up there of all places? Why couldn't he be set ashore to go to Nineveh yet. If we keep an eye on the associations with the violent and bellicose Assur (Assyria), called up by the name of Nineveh,[250] we see that the 'seas' and 'Nineveh' are identical in this respect. Both are indications of what goes against the God of Israel, the creator of heaven and earth. Obviously Jonah has to experience personally what it means to be in this moral sphere of death of anti-divine forces. But it's also possible to return to Adonai from this realm of death, a possibility not only for Jonah, but even for Nineveh. Will Jonah understand now which fate he has to proclaim to Nineveh?

Over me they pass. Derived from the same Hebrew verb as the word 'Hebrew'.

Jonah 2:5 (2:4)

> And I, I say: "I am driven away from before Your eyes. Yet I will go on and look to the temple of Your holiness.

I am driven away from before Your eyes. This is being exiled from the land of the living. This needn't mean the bodily death (compare Isaiah 55:3; Ezekiel 3:20-21; 18:32; 33:13, 19). Remarkably this exile is ascribed to God, as it was indeed Jonah himself who ran away from before Adonai's face (Jonah 1:3). But here it's also true what we saw in Jonah 2:4, namely that the actions of God and those of man are in line: God drives away who runs away from Him and He liberates who returns to Him. So it's often man himself who executes God's actions (compare Jeremiah 15:19).

To the temple. Some scholars think that 'to look to the temple' cannot be linked up with the story of Jonah.[251] To my mind they employ too limited a frame of exegesis in that case. In the first place we saw in section 4.1 that the Book of Jonah is one of those parts of Tanakh in which the then biblical world view comes to the fore powerfully. In this world view the temple in Jerusalem is the centre of the world, so it's not surprising that Jonah turns his eyes from the outermost fields of the creation towards that centre.

In the second place – and this fits in exactly with this – we saw in the commentary on Jonah 1:1 ff., that Jonah received his assignment of God in the temple in Jerusalem. The Book of Jonah needn't tell us this explicitly, because for every Jew from the 5th or 6th century BC this was just a matter of course. Only in the later Midrash this fact is stated explicitly.[252]

In the third place the mention of the temple fits in well with the Jonah story. In Tanakh the going up to Jerusalem and its temple is always the sign of the restoration of the relation between man and God (see for instance Psalm 43). The temple is the palace of God where He reveals Himself to his prophets (see for instance Isaiah 6:1-4). Although the heavens are God's dwelling (Psalm2:4), He is especially present in his temple in Jerusalem where He receives the sacrifices and prayers (see for instance Psalm 66:13-15). The temple is therefore the place where God dwells (Psalm 5:8; 9:12 etc.). That's also the reason why prayers are said with one's face turned to Jerusalem (1 Kings 8:48-49; Psalm 28:2; 134:2; 138:2; Daniel 6:11). Even today the wall towards Jerusalem in a Jewish house is marked and all synagogues are oriented towards the city where once the temple stood.

Was Jonah's crying out in Jonah 2:3 a first attempt to come into contact with God again, it's only here that we find a sign which says that Jonah wishes to restore his relation with God completely. That's possible only now: judgement and punishment have been executed. Jonah has submitted to it. So his transgression has been forgiven. And only then restoration of relation and reconciliation can be considered.

Your holiness. From the verb 'to be holy' which perhaps should better be rendered with 'to set apart', 'to put something to a special use'. One of the most important aspects of the temple service was the sanctification of the Name of God. That sanctification consisted of the special treatment this Name – that consisted of four letters – was treated with. This Name was not pronounced aloud, except during two parts of the liturgy of the temple:[253]

- the daily blessing of the people by the priest with the blessing of Aaron (Numbers 6:24-26);
- the confession of sins on the Day of Atonement pronounced by the high priest in the Holy of Holiest (Leviticus 16).

For the Jews in exile it must have been one of the saddest matters that the Name could no longer resound across the people. After all, that was the climax of Israel's contact with God in the temple in Jerusalem.

Jonah 2:6 (2:5)

> (They) encompass me, the waters, (even) to (my) soul, the depth surrounds me, the weeds are wrapped about my head.

To (my) soul. The translation of the Hebrew word *nèfesh* causes a lot of problems. It means 'throat' originally. So one could translate: "The waters seized me by the throat." Derived from 'throat' are the meanings 'breath', 'breath of life', 'life' and 'soul'. So another translation could be: "The waters take my breath away"; "The waters are after my life"; "The waters surround me up to my soul." But all these translations do not quite cover the meaning of the Hebrew word *nèfesh*. For it has also the sound of 'person', that which makes man to what he is: his identity. Because Hebrew thought is directed towards action and therefore someone's motives, his way of life, and his actions define his identity. That explains the translation 'soul'. Also the word 'inspiration' could be used here, a word which fits in closely with the meaning 'breath'.

However we should realize that in Hebrew-biblical thought someone's life, his motives or inspiration and his way of life form an entirety. Inspiration should be transformed into a way of life and it is this way of life which determines whether man lives in the biblical sense. In that sense we come across the word *nèfesh* in the story of the Creation: When man let himself be inspired by God ("to breathe air into"), he becomes a living being (Genesis 2:7). And how could one better be inspired by God than by studying and practising his assignments and instructions on how to live? Only then one really lives in the sense of Torah (Deuteronomy 33:11-20). So it's more than only Jonah's (or Israel's) biological life which is surrounded by the waters. Jonah's attitude to life is submitted to the test of the waters. It's the sense of Israel's existence which in the precariousness of the exile happens to be at stake.

Weeds. This word only occurs in Tanakh in the Hebrew expression *jam suf*, usually translated with "the Red Sea" (Exodus 15:4). The Hebrew word *suf* means: 'sea-weed'. The word clearly refers to Exodus 15, the story of the passage through the Red Sea. In section 4.5.b I showed the relation between the Psalm of Jonah and the song Moses

Annotations to Jonah 2

and Miriam sung that passage. Both songs are songs about the liberation from the exile.

Jonah 2:7 (2:6)

> To the foundations of the mountains I go down, the earth with her bars blocking my (access) to the world. And (then) You causes my life to go up from corruption, Adonai, my God.

To the foundations. Usually translated with 'foundations, bottoms'. The word comes from the verb 'to cut off', the reason why it can also mean 'the final end'. The image one had of the world in those days (see picture 4.1), was an image in which the mountains stood on the bottom of the sea, far below the surface of the earth. They were the pillars of the earth. This image makes one think of a construction of a house filled with water on which the earth lies like a kind of roof. The sequel of this verse can be interpreted in the same way: "The earth with her bars blocking my (access) to the world."
The word *bêrichèiha* ('her bars') is often translated with 'bolts' or 'bars', because in those days doors were usually locked by means of a bar. But also a difficult pierceable construction of a roof can be well thought of here.

I go down. The same verb as in Jonah 1:3 and 5 when Jonah descends. Jonah's behaviour up till now was dominated by the descend from Jerusalem, the centre of the world,[254] to the now reached deepest point of the Sheol. The way back can only begin here.

Her bars. See above at *To the foundations*.

To the world. The idea *olam* includes both world and time. This can't be reproduced in English. It's often translated rather one-sidedly with 'eternity'. So the thought of something like 'the hereafter' is improper in this case. The *olam* in the sense of 'time' means in fact the time we live in, the time of our ancestors and the time of our children's children. In this case the word 'time' may be replaced by 'world'. Here I chose 'world', but I'd like to add that this shouldn't be understood as timeless. Therefore a better translation would be 'world without end', which is already frequently used in English liturgy.[255]

And (then) you cause ... to go up. From the verb *alah*, used for Israel's going up or ascending to Jerusalem and the temple. This link with the temple happens again in the next verse (Jonah 2:8). Probably nothing else has been awaited more eagerly by lots of Jews than being able "to go up" again to Jerusalem to again attend the service of the temple. And then that moment came when the Persian king Kores (Cyrus) carried out God's liberation and allowed the people to return (Ezra 1:1 ff).

Jonah 2:8 (2:7)

> When faints in me my soul: Adonai I remember and (then) goes to You my prayer, to the temple of Your holiness.

Jonah 2:9 (2:8)

> They who observe worthless vanities: their kindness they forsake.

They who observe. From the verb *'shamar'* with the meanings 'to keep', 'to observe', 'to protect', 'to retain', 'to watch', 'to regard' etc. This verb is also used with regards to keeping or observing God's instructions or laws. in this song of Jonah serving idols is meant (see the following).

Worthless vanities. At first sight a rather vague expression. In fact it's a pleonasm, because both words can be translated with 'vanity' as well as with 'worthlessness'. So we could also write 'vanities of worthlessness'. The Hebrew expression is so vague that for translators it's open to various interpretations respectively. This becomes obvious as soon as we are going to compare various translations of this verse:

- They who observe *lying vanities* forsake their own mercy (King James Version, KJV).
- Those who worship *worthless idols* forfeit the mercy that could be theirs (New English Translation Bible, NET Bible).
- Those who hold on to *worthless idols* abandon their loyalty [to you] (God's Word Translation, GWT).

As can be seen, the KJV is a verbal text, as far as one could speak of a literal translation. the NET Bible and the GWT are more specific in their interpretation of the various terms. The Hebrew words *havlei-*

shaw are translated with 'worthless idols'. This looks rather arbitrarily, but on second thoughts it's not. The word *havlei* is a form of the word *hèvel*, a word that elsewhere in Tanakh is an indication for the idols of the nations. "They are a vanity, a work of delusion", we read in Jeremiah's sermon about God and the idols (Jeremiah 10:15). Earlier in that sermon he speaks unambiguously: "For the customs of the peoples are vanity; for it is but a tree which one cutteth out of the forest" (Jeremiah 10: 3a, KJV).

Elsewhere in Tanakh this same word *hèvel* has become a kind of standard expression for foreign gods.[a] But also in other texts from which the context of idolatry is not immediately clear, this word should be explained as a designation of idolatry (e.g. in Psalm 31:7, "I hate them that regard lying vanities"). This now does not only make an interpretation possible in terms of idols, but even probable. After all, here in Jonah 2:9 it's all about "to observe" or "to maintain". But two questions do appear with this verse in the song of Jonah:

- What's the link between this verse and the Jonah narrative in its entirety?
- What's the meaning of this verse as part of the Psalm of Jonah?

Before answering those questions, we'll first look at the next word.

Their kindness. The Hebrew word *chasdam* is a form of the word *chèsed*. It's not only translated with 'mercy' but also with 'kindness', 'benevolence', 'love', 'loyalty', faithfulness', 'friendship' and the like. By and large *chèsed* is about being well-disposed and the translation 'benevolence' isn't so bad afterall. Here in Jonah 2:9 (English 2:8) the GWT writes: "Their loyalty [to you]". Obviously the translators considered this to be an indication of God. And that hasn't occurred on a random basis. For instance in Psalm 144:2 the psalmist calls God *chasdi* ('my mercy' or 'my benevolence'). In some other psalms too the word *chèsed* is a designation for God (Psalm 32:10; 101:1).[b] And further we

---

[a] The English Standard Version (ESV) uses various translations. For instance in Deuteronomy 32:21 "idols"; in 1 Kings 16:13, 26 "idols"; in Jeremiah 2:5 "worthless(ness)"; 14:22 "false gods"; 16:19 "worthless things"; 51:18 "worthless".

[b] See the KJV for the rendering with 'mercy'.

come across this word as one of God's qualities (Psalm 5:8; 6:5; 13:6; etc.). If we can explain the words 'worthless vanities' as idols – as we saw above – then we can certainly explain 'their mercy' as a designation for the God of Israel.

They forsake. Now we have reached the point where the two above questions can be answered. The first question was: What's the link between this verse and the Jonah narrative in its entirety? The answer to that question can be brief and to the point: "Nothing!" There's really no way whatsoever that shows us what the link could be between Jonah 2:9 and the rest of the Jonah narrative. This verse cannot allude to Jonah himself. His argument with God and his flight for God in Jonah 1 cannot be described as 'worthless vanities', let alone that Jonah would "observe" them. Besides if we consider these "worthless things" as a designation for idols then there is no link at all with Jonah's behaviour in Jonah 1 given his proud "confession of faith" in Jonah 1:9.

At the same time it should be observed that the whole verse is in the plural. This opens (up) the possibility that it refers to the men of the ship Jonah found himself with, or to the Ninevites Jonah still had to go to. But that too isn't a matter of course. At first the men of the ship do worship their idols yet, but afterwards convert to the God of Jonah instead of leaving Him. The Ninevites don't worship any idols at all in Jonah 3 and they too convert to God. Therefore there is only one explanation for this verse, namely that it ended up in this way together with the whole song (Jonah 2:3-10) in the Book of Jonah. And so we'll have to answer the second question: What's the meaning of this verse as part of the song of Jonah?

Commenting on Jonah 2:2 under: *And then he prays* I suggested the possibility that the Psalm of Jonah once belonged to the songs the returning exiles had sung during their journey from Babylon to Jerusalem. That background reflects Jonah 2:9 crystal-clear. It's beyond doubt that many Jews during their stay in Babylon had become estranged from their ancestors' way of life. Living in their pagan surroundings they would have assimilated probably, taking over customs from the native population, and some even went to participate in Babylonian religious practices. Those who went farthest in this, participated in the pagan cult and so "worshipped lying vanities". They are the people who'd left "their benevolence." Meant here are those who'd stayed behind, renounced Judaism and merged into their pagan surroundings. The returning exiles have called on their assimilated fellow Jews for the last time in the vague, somewhat covert wordings of this verse, to go up with them to Jerusalem, the city of the one God: That they should leave the worthless vanities and observe their kindness! If not, the Sheol will swallow them for ever and ever.

Jonah 2:10 (2:9)

> And I: with a voice of thanksgiving I will sacrifice to You. What I have promised I shall fulfil: salvation [is] of Adonai.

And I: with a voice of thanksgiving I will sacrifice to You. The peace offering (Leviticus 3:1-17) could have three subtle distinctions:

- A vow-offering (*nèder* – Leviticus 7:16; 22:18-23);
- A voluntary-offering (*nêdavah* – Leviticus 7:16; 22: 29-30);
- A thanks-offering (*todah* – Leviticus 7:12-15; 22:29-30).

All these offerings were made according to the same ritual. After the ritual slaughter the animal was divided between God, the priests and the person who made the sacrifice. The blood was for God. It was poured out at the base of the altar. The fat too and some internal organs were for God and were burned at the altar. The breastpiece and the right shank were for the priests. What was left was for the person who'd made the offering, who then laid on a sacrificial meal with it with family and friends. In the case of a thanks-offering the meat of the sacrificial animal must be eaten entirely on the day of the sacrifice. Nothing should be left to the next morning (Leviticus 7:15). Both the giving of the offering and the sacrificial meal were accompanied by songs and prayers. If the assumption is correct that the song of Jonah was sung by the returning exiles on their way to the land of Israel and Jerusalem then it was probably also sung during the thanks-offering which must have been the pinnacle of the return of every returned Jew.

Jonah 2:11 (2:10)

> And (then) says Adonai to the fish and it vomits (out) Jonah upon the dry land.

Jonah is back to square one again. Did he learn something from this episode?

8   Who knows He turns around

Annotations to Jonah 3:1-10

Jonah 3:1

> And it occurs – a word of Adonai – to Jonah the second time, to say:

Jonah 3:2

> "Rise up, go to Nineveh, that city, the big one, and call against her the calling that I word to you."

Nineveh. In the first place the name of this city evokes historical associations with the Assyrian empire.[256] But 'Nineveh' as a designation for the Persian empire is much more important yet for the Jonah narrative.[257]

That city, the big one. The city – and especially the big city – is not always well thought-of in Tanakh. In this context it's quite remarkable that the first city in the Torah was built by the first murderer of men Kain (Genesis 4:17-18). This characterizes the city as a place of violence and as a way of life which makes itself mighty by bloodshed. And the second city in Torah happens to be Nineveh! Together with three other cities it was located in Assur and built by the mighty (Hebrew *gibor*) Nimrod (Genesis 10:11). There too we come across the expression 'the big city' (Genesis 10:12) which – according to the rabbis – refers to Nineveh.[258]

The next city in Torah is Babel (Genesis 11:4). That too is a story that tells us that a big city always tends to resist God and his plans with the world, or worse even: to proclaim itself divine. This really means that the city hinders man to fulfil his divine assignment (see also: Genesis 11:4b). After Babel we come at Ur of the Chaldeans, the city Abram had to leave, because he couldn't find his life fulfilment there (Genesis 11:28, 31). And this seemingly being not enough, we end up – reading the Torah – at Sodom and Gomorrah (Genesis 13:10; 19:1-29).

It seems that de stories of Genesis have reached their rock bottom with the destruction of Sodom and Gomorrah and so have come to a certain conclusion. After this event the theme of the city in Genesis doesn't come up any longer in that specific way. However, it's yet remarkable that during the conquest of the land of Kanaan by the Israelites the first conquest was the capture and the destruction of a city: Jericho (Joshua 5:13 ff.). And when eventually the Lord chooses to live in a city in the land of Israel, the name of that city ought to be Jerusalem, that is 'City of Peace', a name as an eternal assignment for its inhabitants. In that respect Jerusalem is the opposite for all powerful and big capitals of the world. But in the long run this assignment of being a city of peace is not only intended for Jerusalem, but also for all other cities of the world. Jonah the seer should learn to cooperate as a prophet to turn de city of blood, Nineveh, into a city of peace.

Jonah 3:3

> And up rises Jonah, and he goes to Nineveh according to the word of Adonai. And Nineveh is a city, (very) big, before God with a going of three days.

Is. The Hebrew verb used here is in the perfect tense, which is usually interpreted as the past tense 'was'. Some commentators conclude that Nineveh didn't exist any longer in the time of the writing of the Book of Jonah. However, the perfect tense can express a permanent situation as well. And in that case it's not about a city that once existed and which disappeared once and for all, but about all Ninevehs of all places and of all ages, which are always "big" for God and which always threaten His kingship of the world: Nineveh, Babylon, Persepolis, Antioch, Rome, Berlin, etc.

A city (very) big for God. This expression occurs only here in Tanakh. It's the superlative and can be translated with 'extremely big'.[a] A bible writer will not quickly be inclined that something in the world "is big for God". When in Genesis 11 people say to each other: "Come, let us build ourselves a city and a tower with its top in the

---

[a] Somewhat cognate expressions are found in Genesis 10:9; Isaiah 14:13; Psalms 36:7; 80:11.

heavens" (11:4), then, some time later, the writer continues very ironically: "And the LORD came down to see the city and the tower, which the children of man had built" (11:15). Clearly that big city and that big tower were so small that the LORD had to come down to inspect them. And so this expression "big for God" only occurs here in Jonah and nowhere else in Tanakh. Clearly it's about *the* capital of an empire, *the* centre of power. This is confirmed by the legendary dimensions of the city.

With a going of three days. In fact it reads: "a walk/going of three days". In section 5.1 we saw that the historical Nineveh had a circumference of about 13 kilometres, that is "a walk of three hours" for someone who walks at a normal pace. So the meaning of the expression "three days" should be found elsewhere. I remember saying of Jonah 2:1: *Three days and three nights*. It's the time span which marks the definitive verge of life and death. In this respect the words 'life' and 'death' shouln't be taken purely biological, but in the spirit of Deuteronomy 30:11-20, as designations for a life in accordance with God's intentions and a life which runs counter to God's intentions. For God Nineveh is a city of the dead which should be resurrected by Jonah.

Jonah 3:4

> And (then) begins Jonah to go into the city by going a day, (only) one, and he calls and says: "Yet forty (times) a day and Nineveh shall be overthrown."

By going a day, (only) one. Without any doubt this expression is meant to be in sharp contrast to the 'going of three days' in the last verse. It alludes to the minimal way in which Jonah carries out his assignment. It's true, Jonah went to Nineveh, probably not because of his own conviction, but perhaps he'd realized that there's no getting away from God. Jonah's rescue from the Sheol has not changed his thoughts on Nineveh. The difference of opinion between God and Jonah enters its second episode. Within the scope of wider historical exegesis we could argue that here the writer of the Book of Jonah addresses his fellow Jews who after the Babylonian exile ran the risk of making the same mistake as did many of their ancestors before the

Yet forty (times) a day and Nineveh shall be overthrown. This message is very short indeed, not to say incomplete. God's words in Jonah 1:2 "for up comes their evil to My face" aren't mentioned at all. Even the God of heaven and earth isn't mentioned, let alone that his Name is proclaimed. The Ninevites aren't offered any way out too. Jonah's proclamation is the unconditional message of a seer[259] for whom the fall of the evil city is a matter-of-course.

Here a curious tension is revealed in the story, which brings us back to the problem of the motives underlying Jonah's behaviour.[260] First Jonah flees to Tarshish to avoid prophesying against Nineveh. But now, forced by God with storm and fish, he goes, but he hardly carries out his assignment. It looks very much as if he wants to leave the Ninevites in ignorance about God's intention to destroy the city and, if he has no choice, to leave them uninformed about which God it is who will decide their fate. But why? Does Jonah realize perhaps that if the Ninevites convert, God won't execute his judgement? And why does he want to prevent that? Does he take the view that the evil of Nineveh is so big that it can't escape unpunished by any conversion at all? Or is he anxious about the prestige of prophesy which could lose out if the proclaimed fall won't happen?

In this last direction the problem of Jonah's motives is solved by the rabbis.[261] Before now Jonah had – supposedly – prophesied against Jerusalem, but after the inhabitants had converted and the fall was cancelled, they called him a false prophet. It could have been the same in the case of Nineveh, but worse even! If the Ninevites convert, and the destruction keeps off, then not only Jonah's name as a prophet is at stake but even the Name of God whose word Jonah speaks. Just like Moses in Numbers 14:15-16 Jonah is concerned about God's Name among the nations of the world. Just because he's concerned about the sanctification of the Name, he tries to prevent from proclaiming a prophecy which won't come true and so will ridicule the Name in the eyes of the nations of the world.

This rabbinical explanation fits in with the problem of a seer who doesn't want to be a prophet.[262] The question that could be asked, following this explanation, whether Jonah was perhaps more anxious about the sanctification of the Name than God Himself. And one could also wonder if Jonah really thought that the sanctification of the Name was served more with the destruction than with the conversion of Nineveh. After all he could have worded his proclamation of judgement in a conditional way. Anyhow, at this moment the story doesn't supply us with clear indications about Jonah's motives. That's why I'll return to this problem later.

Forty (times) a day. When the number forty turns up in a bible story, it's not always a positive sign. Because the first time it occurs is in the story of the big flood when it's pouring with rain for forty days and forty nights on the earth (Genesis 7:4, 12, 17; 8:6). Another important series of stories in which the number forty plays an important part, is the one of the journey of the Israelites through the wilderness. This journey comes after a stay of 400 years in Egypt (Genesis 15:13), the land that's called *Mitsrajim* in Hebrew, which could be explained as 'land of oppression'. Forty years does the journey take from Egypt to Canaan.[a] The prophet Elijah too, lived in the wilderness for forty days when he had to flee from queen Jezebel who persecuted those who served the God of Israel (1 Kings 18:4, 13; 19:8).

These examples show that a period of forty days or forty years quite often closes a period of injustice, oppression or persecution. But at the same time there is another side to a period of forty days or years. It's not only a period of evil coming to an end, but it can also be a preparation to a new, a better situation. The world is washed clean of the moral evil by the great flood. And then a new beginning can be made: a new world appears from the waters. The forty years of Israel's stay in the wilderness does not only close a period of slavery, but they also prepare Israel for a new existence as a free people in the land of Canaan. And Elijah too, had to learn to overcome his fear of Jezebel in the wilderness in a period of forty days. After that he gets a new assignment which in the end will lead to the fall of the house of Ahab and Jezebel.

Therefore forty days or forty years is a period of transition especially, meant as a preparation for a new existence. That's why such a period often has the character of a training or probationary period. Israel's forty years in the wilderness are a school for the people pre-

---

[a] Exodus 16:35; Numbers 14:33-34; 32:13; Deuteronomy 2:7; 8:2, 4; 29:5; Joshua 5:6.

eminently. Israel should learn to live according to God's rules. And tests with their ups and downs simply belong to that learning process.[263] When a test fails, a new learning process follows, a new attempt to live in harmony with God. Elijah too, has to learn in the wilderness that God isn't a God characterized by violent means like wind, earthquakes and fire, although He had to use them sometimes, but that He is a God of "the sound of a low whisper" (1 Kings 19:11-12. ESV), as He was also heard by Adam and Eve in the Garden of Eden: "And they heard the sound of the LORD God walking in the garden in the cool of the day" (Genesis 3:8. ESV). In the end His aim is a heavenly world without violence. Even a prophet had to learn that again and again. In that same line lies also the liturgical period of 1 Ellul to 10 Tishri, as a preparatory period of forty days for the Day of Atonement, in which a change of life in the form of conversion and penance is practised.[264]

Such being the case, I'd like to mention yet another remarkable aspect of the number forty. Three kings reigned Israel and Judah for forty years:

- David (2 Samuel 5:4; 1 Kings 2:11; 1 Chronicles 29:27);
- Solomon (1 Kings 11:42; 2 Chronicles 9:30);
- Jehoash (2 Kings 12:1; 2 Chronicles 24:1).

These three kings are all described in the books of Samuel and Kings, in spite of their mistakes and imperfections, as just and wise kings who devoted themselves to the construction and restoration of the temple in Jerusalem.[a] Whether all three of them really, that is historically, ruled for forty years exactly, is neither here nor there. The writers of the books of Samuel and Kings mention 'forty years' to say: if you want to know to be a just king, watch David, Solomon and Jehoash. You can learn that from them. Here too 'forty' refers to the duration of a school, a training in kingship. This is perhaps the same

---

[a] The later book 2 Chronicles gives in 2 Chronicles 24 a wholly deviant story about the last phase of the life of Jehoash. Remarkable is for instance the positive appreciation in 2 Kings 12:21 "And they buried him with his fathers in the city of David"(ESV), as opposed to the disapproval in 2 Chronicles 24:25 "and they buried him in the city of David, but they did not bury him in the tombs of the kings."(ESV).

reason why – in the biblical-Jewish tradition – these forty years constitute a man's life span. Each life ought to be a school from beginning to end. And learning means: finding the ways which lead to God's kingship of this world. It's exactly such a period of forty days granted to Nineveh to learn to live an new life.

Be overthrown. In Hebrew: *nèhpachet*. We meet this form also at the overthrow or destruction of Sodom and Gomorrah (Genesis 19:21, 25, 29). This verb is linked so much with the fate of these two cities that it's used almost always when and where that fate is remembered.[a] So there isn't any doubt that – in the eyes of the writer – Jonah with regard to Nineveh had had the fate of Sodom and Gomorrah in mind. But once more this story has a double bottom here.[265] For the Hebrew verb here is in the niphal-form and can be understood as a passive form ('is overturned') but also as a reflexive verb form ('turns over'). In that last case the sentence gets quite another meaning. Or – as the rabbis teach us – the word *nèhpachet* can in addition to 'turning over' as destruction also mean 'a turning over' as a change of conviction.[266, b] So God uses the seer Jonah in this way – against Jonah's wish – for a prophetic end.

Jonah 3:5

> And (then) trust the men of Nineveh in God. And they call a fast and put on sackcloth from their biggest (ones) and to their smallest (ones).

And (then) the men trust. From the same verb as the word 'amen.' This verb is often translated with 'to believe', but given the associations this calls up in Christianity with endorsing certain persuasions, I consider this translation less suitable. It's better to think of a complex of meanings which involves 'to trust', 'to entrust', 'to consider reliable', and which is cognate to the complex of meanings 'to be faithful to', 'to be reliable', 'to be just'. Hence the translation "the men trust in

---

[a] Deuteronomy 29:23; Isaiah 13:19; Jeremiah 20:16; 49:18; 50:40; Amos 4:11; Lamentations 4:6.
[b] The verb concerned is also used in that second meaning in other places in Tanakh, as in: Exodus 14:5; 1 Samuel 10:6; Isaiah 63:10; Psalm 30:12.

God". In other words: They were certain that God would react positively to their conversion.

In God. From here to Jonah 3:10 God is consistently called 'God' (Hebrew: *eilohim*), and the use of His Name of four letters (rendered with *Adonai* or 'the LORD') is avoided. So the Ninevites convert to a for them nameless God. This is not surprising considering the fact that Jonah hasn't mentioned the Name in his argument (Jonah 3:4). Besides, as we saw before, the designation *eilohim* means especially "God as creator and judge of the world".[267] Contrary to the distress of the mariners, owing to Jonah's behaviour, the distress of Nineveh is the consequence of her own evil. So the Ninevites can't convert to the LORD (*Adonai*) who would save them from an anxious position which they themselves can't be blamed for. They should convert to God (*Eilohim*) who holds them responsible for their way of life and their actions. No reference at all is found in the story to a possible idolatry of the Ninevites. Seen from a biblical perspective, the gentiles won't be punished either for idolatry. But they will for treading on morality, ethics and justice.[268] A bad society comes under the judgement of *Eilohim*, even if they don't know Him as *Adonai*.

Here another, important feature of the story can be seen. One needn't know the God of Israel as such to be able yet to be a good human. Non-Jews, who, in any way, will come to live as the Holy One, blessed be He, wants them to do, live as if "before His face." Even when they know little or nothing of the biblical-Jewish tradition. I'd like to mention that in Jonah's discussion with God in Jonah 4, God doesn't call upon Jonah anywhere to enter Nineveh once more to make known God's Name to the Ninevites. It's sufficient that they'll go back on their evil ways and that they'll reinstate morality, ethics and justice in their society. They will certainly be allowed to know Him further, also as the God of the Name, *but it's not necessary!*

And they call a fast, and put on sackcloth. These are the usual customs at mourning and penance. The idea in those days was that there wasn't a big distance between mourning and penance. An unconverted human, someone who hasn't undergone yet the cleansing of penance, is a dead soul, even if he or she is alive and kicking biologically.[a]

---

[a]   Compare for instance Lukas 15:24 with 32.

From their biggest (ones) and to their smallest (ones). Here probably we shouldn't translate 'from the adults to the small children', but 'from the high priest to the tanner'. Because in verse 7 the word 'big' is also used for highplaced people.

Jonah 3:6

> And (then) comes the word to the king of Nineveh. And he rises up from his throne and he makes pass his robe from over him. And he covers (himself with) sackcloth, and he sits on the dust.

The king of Nineveh. A non-historical title.[269]

His robe. From the verb with the basic meaning 'to glorify (oneself)'. Clothing and social functions often go together, not only nowadays, but also in the ancient Near East, and certainly in the case of dignitaries. This however, is not only the case with them. The priests' garments in ancient Israel were of the utmost importance (see Exodus 28 e.g.). Even the prophets were recognized by their coats (2 Kings 1:8; Zechariah 13:4). When a king takes off his coat, it's an official act that amounts to the laying down (temporarily) of his function.

Jonah 3:7

> And he causes (it) to be cried out, and to be said through Nineveh by the decree of the king and his big ones, saying: "The humans and the beasts, the cattle and the sheep, not (at all) they taste anything, not (at all) they feed, and the waters they shall not drink.

By the decree. This word with the meaning of 'command' happens only here in the Hebrew of Tanakh. In the Aramaic parts of Tanakh however, it occurs more often (Ezra 6:3 ff.; Daniel 3:10, 29). It has probably been derived from the same verb as the verb 'to taste', that's used later in this verse.[270] That's why it could also be translated with: 'after the taste of the king'.

The king and his big ones. An expression indicating the situation of the government in the Persian empire.[271] Also in other Bible stories which describe the situation of the Persian court or are described after the model of this court, these 'big ones' are mentioned (Esther 1:3, 14;

Daniel 3:2; 6:5). Haman was such a great one and after his fall he's succeeded as such by Mordechai (Esther 3:1; 8:2). Daniel and a cousin of Tobit held a similar position as well (Daniel 2:49; 5:29; 6:2; Tobit 1:21-22). In these stories written in or after the Persian time, the Assyrian and Babylonian courts are described after the Persian model.

The humans and the beasts, the cattle and the sheep. In the covenant God made with Noah animals are included expressly (Genesis 9:10). But they too appear to come under the regulations of the Sinai covenant. So animals can be sentenced because they are legally liable.[a] Another consequence is that the sabbatical peace is also meant for animals,[b] as well as the social services.[c] And then it's a matter of course that animals are also part of mourning and penance. Anyway, this also happened outside Israel.[272]

Not at all they taste. This and the following verbs are all in the so-called imperfect tense.[273] This 'command' is not in the imperative, nor in the subjunctive mood but in the simple present. It looks more as if the course of events in the city is described, than that the population is forced to do something. In accordance with good biblical custom the legislation fits in with the existing practice either to legitimize this or to bend it into a more desirable direction. After all the practice of fasting is already described in Jonah 3:5. Here it's only specified further what should be understood by that fasting, and it's widened to the animals of the city.

Jonah 3:8

> And they cover themselves (with) sackcloth, the humans and the beasts, and they call to God with force. And they turn around, (each) man from his path of evil and from the violence that (is) in (the palm of) their hands.

---

[a] Genesis 3:14; Exodus 6:7; 19:13; 21:28, 29, 32; Leviticus 20:15-16; Joshua 7:24; Jeremiah 7:20; 21:6.
[b] Exodus 20:10; 23:12; Deuteronomy 5:14.
[c] Leviticus 25:6-7. Compare also Deuteronomy 24:5 with Leviticus 19:9 and 23:22.

And they cover themselves. The imperfect tense of the verbs in this verse also allow a translation in the simple past. Then it should read: "and they covered ... and they called ... and they turned around ..." The king's command should have ended at the end of the last verse, while here the situation in the city should be described. But given the following verse, in which the king continued with his command, this verse too should be considered a part of that command. Even the covering with sackcloth has already been described in the verses 5 and 6. The only addition here is that the practice of conversion involves the animals as well.

And they call. From here the king's command adds actions to the practice of conversion, which haven't been mentioned yet. There's a climax approaching. It all began with fasting which can be done without influencing social life too much. Next came the sackcloth and mourning garments, which unsettled the social relations – visible in the people's attires[274] – radically. Now the calling to God is added which causes quite another way of contact with each other. And finally one turns one's back on evil and violence. And that is of course what it's all about in the end – witness Jonah 1:2.

And they turn around. From the same verb used in Jonah 1:13 (see there).

The violence. Hebrew: *hèchamas*. This word is in the story of the Flood a closer specification of the word 'evil' (*ra'ah*) (Genesis 6: 11 and 13). So it's about the same quality of evil of the generation of before the Flood and is comparable with the evil of Sodom.[275] The word *chamas* is never used for idolatry. It's especially about social injustice based on the use of violence. The rabbis describe a general rule according to which God only takes immediate action in the life of nations when they commit this kind of sin. *Chamas*, social violence and social oppression, is destructive for a just social order and goes against God's wish that people should experience life and welfare in a just society. Then He intervenes in order to maintain his creation, something He wouldn't do if the sin would only consist of idolatry or immoral but nonviolent behaviour.[276]

That is in the palm of their hands. For instance stolen goods: Each time one touches it, it's again 'the violence that is in your hands'.[277]

Jonah 3:9

> Who knows He turns around and He repents – this God – and (then) He turns around from the burning of his anger, and not we shall perish."

Who knows He turns around. It is written: "And I will make them joyful in My house of prayer" (Isaiah 56:7). It isn't written: Your house of prayer." It is written: My house of prayer." It follows that God has His own house of prayer. What does He pray? Rabbi Zutra bar Tobia answered in the name of Rab: "[He prays:] May it be My will, that My mercy keeps My wrath in check. That My mercy rules My sense of justice. That I shall treat My children after My mercy and not after the strict justice." So the Talmud says.[278]

Jonah 3:10

> And (then) sees this God their works, for they turn around from their path of evil. And (then) repents this God of the evil which He has worded to do to them and not (at all) He does (it).

And (then) sees this God their works. 'Their works' is from the same verb that earlier was rendered with 'to bring about' (e.g. in Jonah 1:9). The Talmud comments on this expression:[279] "On a fast day the elder of the community speaks penetrating words: 'Brothers, of the inhabitants of Nineveh it is not written: God saw their sackcloth and their fast. It is written: God sees their works, for they turn around from their path of evil. Then it says: "Rend your hearts and not your garments" (Joel 2:13).'"

And not (at all) He does (it). The biblical-Jewish tradition does not only assume God's just jurisdiction of evil, but also His inclination to forgive the malignant one who converts. In the Midrash we read:[280] "Three things can annul a decree of God: Prayer, practicing mercy and remorse."

9 And I, wouldn´t I have pity on Nineveh?
Annotations to Jonah 4:1-11

Jonah 4:1

> And it causes evil to Jonah, an evil, (very) big, and it burns in him.

And it causes evil to Jonah. Sodom and Gomorra have been "overthrown" without mercy.[281] Many other judgements were proclaimed by earlier seer-prophets on behalf of God without the possibility to avert this through remorse and conversion. Recall the stories of Samuel and Saul, Nathan and David, Elijah and Ahab (section 4.4). By not overthrowing Nineveh, God Himself injures Jonah's authority as a seer-prophet (compare Deuteronomy 18:21-22 and Jeremiah 28:6-9). He even injures his own Name as a reliable God, and does so even in the eyes of the nations of the world.

The traditional Jewish idea is that here the real ground for Jonah's attempted escape could lie. For isn't the sanctification of God's Name the higher aim of the creation? And isn't it Israel's aim – as expressed in the Eighteen Benedictions (also called the Amidah) on Rosh Hashanah and Yom Kippur – that all creatures should be filled with reverence for God? Who seeks the sanctification of God's Name can't stand vicious and mocking remarks about Him, not even by a villain from Nineveh. And now – so Jonah thinks – God harms his own Name in the eye of the world.[282] But what Jonah doesn't see is that God rather harms a certain view on prophecy. Jonah shouldn't aim at the execution of the severe judgement, the law of Medes and Persians, which can't be changed even by the king of kings once it is promulgated. No, Jonah should aim at the reversal of Nineveh's inclination, after which grace and mercy will follow. Because how else can God's Name be made big in this world than by patience, kind-heartedness, pity and by forgiving those renouncing their evil?

Jonah 4:2

> And he prays to Adonai and he says: "Oh, Adonai, was not this my word when I was on my soil? Because of that I hurried to flee towards Tarsis. For I know that You (are) a God, gracious and compassionate, slowly (becoming) angry and abundant in kindness, repenting of this evil.

This my word. This term can also mean 'my line of thought' and even 'my action'. Jonah's line of thought in the previous verse also occurs in the Midrash as follows.[283] Before Jonah was sent to Nineveh, he'd once been sent to Jerusalem to tell her inhabitants about their impending judgement. But when the inhabitants of the city converted and the judgement wasn't executed, some fools among them began to call Jonah a false prophet. Now that Jonah again receives such an assignation, he ponders: "I know that the nations are inclined to convert, and they will do so. Then the fury of the Holy One, praised be He, will be aimed at Israel, because it didn't convert on the word of the prophets. And bad enough as it is, Israel will call me a false prophet and so will the nations."

A God gracious etc. Five qualities of God are mentioned here. It's an anthology from the thirteen qualities mentioned in Exodus 34:6-7 (compare also Exodus 32: 12-14). Here I'd like to point at a peculiar triangle in Tanakh. Exodus 34 belongs to the part *Ki Tisa* (Exodus 30-11 – 34:35), that is read from the Torah in the synagogue in the month of Adar. The accompanying reading from the Prophets (*haftarah*) is the part 1 Kings 18:1-39 from the Eliah stories.[284] Who compares Exodus 34 with this and the other Eliah stories will find many thematic similarities. In section 3.3 we already saw many similarities between Jonah 4 and the Eliah stories. The links between Jonah 4, Exodus 34 and the Eliah stories form a triplet or triangle of stories:

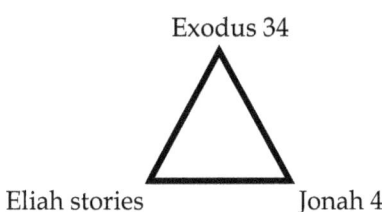

Besides, the here in Jonah mentioned anthology from Exodus 34:6-7 is the same as the one mentioned in Joel 2:13. There it refers to God's attitude towards Israel. From this Exodus and Joel background we may conclude that in Jonah 4 the issue is not God's forgiveness in itself. With regards to Israel, in the time the Book of Jonah was being written, His forgiveness had become a matter of course. So the issue of the Book of Jonah is the question of God's forgiveness with respect to the nations. Therefore it's remarkable that in the anthology of God's qualities the second half of Exodus 34:7 is lacking: "But He by no means leaves the guilty unpunished, responding to the transgression of fathers by dealing with children and children's children, to the third and fourth generation."[a] However, the mention of God's justice here in Jonah 4:2, is unnecessary. He would certainly have turned over Nineveh, if it hadn't converted. But will He be forgiving as well, if Nineveh does convert? Here in Jonah 4 it's stated explicitly that God's forgiveness, if the nations convert, applies even to the worst of the nations of the world. Obviously this is something Jonah doesn't approve of.

Jonah 4:3

> And now, Adonai, take please my soul from me, for good is my death over my life."

For good (is) my death. We could wonder if this isn't a somewhat exaggerated reaction of Jonah's, who yet in Jonah 2 praised God because He'd lifted his life from doom. However, this expression in the story isn't meant merely as a psychological analysis of Jonah's emotional situation. We'd rather see in these words of Jonah's an obvious reference to Eliah's who wanted to be allowed to die during his escape from Queen Jezebel (1 Kings 19:4). Both prophets had taken the view that their performance had failed. And a failed prophet has no reason to exist any longer. According to Elijah Israel's disobedience was the cause of that failure (1 Kings 19:10 and 14). Jonah however

---

[a] Exodus 20:5 adds: "of those who reject me." If they don't – in other words, if they renounce the iniquity of their fathers – they'll again fall under God's forgiveness (Exodus 20:6).

thinks that God Himself has made him a failed prophet. Hasn't he therefore yet more reason than Elijah to choose death over life?

Furthermore the story here calls forth strong associations with the paradise stories in Genesis 2 and 3. Words like 'good' and 'evil', 'life' and 'death' play an important part there. Adam and Eve forfeited the good creation by their disobedience. Jonah runs the risk to be lost for the repair of the creation, a repair aimed at by God with his attempts to save Nineveh from evil and destruction. Jonah the seer condemns himself to death for the second time on the basis of his own severe idea of justice and asks God to execute his judgement.[285] However, the consequence of the story is that now as well the judgement of the seer Jonah is doomed to fail: God is merciful, also for Jonah.

Jonah 4:4

> And (then) says Adonai: "Is it good (that) it burns to you?"

Is it good. This is the first time in the Book of Jonah that Adonai addresses Jonah directly. Unlike Jonah who has flown into a rage about God's mercy, it appears that the Holy One, praised be He, has not flown into a rage about Jonah's unbending idea of justice. God doesn't judge, but asks for fairness. The continuation of the story consists of one long, patient attempt of Adonai's to win over Jonah to His mercy towards the evil Nineveh.

Jonah 4:5

> And (then) leaves Jonah out of the city, and he sits down on the east side of the city and he makes for himself there a tabernacle. And he sits under it in the shadow till he sees what occurs to the city.

And (then) leaves Jonah out of the city. Who reads a story like this in a historic- chronological way, will stumble on some difficulties in this verse. One could wonder: Does Jonah only now leave the city, now that he's seen that Nineveh has converted, and now that he's had his first "conversation" with God? Or does this verse refer to something that already happened before?

Many exegetes are convinced that this verse was taken from its original place between Jonah 3:4 and 5. However, I've showed in section 2.5 that this verse fits completely in the step-by-step construction of Jonah 4. Besides in section 4.5.d we saw that the *sukkah* or tabernacle mentioned in this verse contains an obvious reference to the Feast of Tabernacles, which in this place forms the liturgical background of the story of Jonah. It would sooner be harmful than conducive to the argument the writer is developing as well in Jonah 3 and 4, if Jonah 4:5 was "put back" between Jonah 3:4 and 5. There the enormous effect of Jonah's sermon would only postpone and delay, while here in Jonah 4:4-6 the theme of the gourd would happened out of the blue. So only one conclusion is possible: the place of this verse is here, and nowhere else! And even if it hadn't been in a specimen copy of the Book of Jonah, yet the writer has put it here to a better effect and determinedly.

On the east side. The east is where the Garden of Eden is (Genesis 2:8). What better place could Jonah find to sit down? But it's also the perfect place to watch (from) what's going to happen to the city at dawn.[286]

Tabernacle. The same word as in the Feast of Tabernacles (*Sukkoth*). As mentioned before, the Feast of Tabernacles is the liturgical background of this verse in Jonah 4 (section 4.5.d). This festival is celebrated at the end of the summer from 15 to 22 *Tishri* (September/October). It's a feast with a twofold original meaning. For one thing the end of the harvest is celebrated. So in the older parts of the Torah it's called the 'Feast of ingathering' as well (Exodus 23:16; 34:22). At this festival the crop from the threshing floor and the presses – the grain, the oil and the wine – was placed before Adonai (Deuteronomy16:13). On the other hand the Feast of Tabernacles reminds one of Israel's journey through the wilderness, when the people had to live in tents and huts for forty years (Leviticus 23:43). So it isn't the festival of the liberation like Pesach (Passover), but the festival of the liberty in which one hasn't got any other masters above one than only God and in which one trusts entirely on His protection. Through the roof of the tabernacle people can watch the heavens and God can as it were look directly into the tabernacle. So the tabernacle teaches (us) that there isn't a barrier between God and man.[287] In line with this lies the fact that the dedication of the Temple of Solomon took place during the Feast of Tabernacles (1 Kings 8:1-5; 2 Chronicles 7:8-20). This is pre-eminently the feast of Israel's freedom under God's kingship, a freedom and a kingship in which – according to the later prophesy – all nations are allowed to participate as well by celebrating the Feast of Tabernacles (Zechariah 14:16-19).

Against this background the image of the *sukkah*, the tabernacle, plays an obvious part. If there's one image that represents the image of a free Israel, ruled only by God, it should be the tabernacle. A clear sign of Jonah's instinct of freedom. Jonah leaves Nineveh to celebrate his freedom and watch the fall of the city from the shadow of his tabernacle. And in doing so he is in the Persian time the model for those people in Israel who want to back out of the Persian empire and to precipitate the fall of it for the sake of Israel's freedom.

Jonah 4:6

> And (then) prepares Adonai God a Kikayon and it comes up over Jonah to make it occur a shadow over his head to draw him away from his anger. And (then) rejoices Jonah about the Kikayon (with) a joy, (very) big.

Adonai God. The only time this combination of designations for God is used in the Book of Jonah. Note that in this combination – as elsewhere in Tanakh – *Adonai* is always mentioned first.[288] The Name He bears as God of the covenant precedes the designation for God as the creator and the judge of the world. In Jonah 4 He's only called – till this verse – *Adonai*, but now the designation *Eilohim* ('God') is added. In the following verses even He is only called *Eilohim* (Jonah 4:7-9). Undoubtedly the writers of the Book of Jonah have wanted to make it clear that the LORD (*Adonai*) with his mercy and forgiveness doesn't act from impotence, but from the clear choice *not* to use his power to destroy Nineveh. He'd certainly been able to do otherwise, but He doesn't, and this he is – as God (*Eilohim*), as creator and judge of the world – going to make clear to Jonah from now on.

A Kikayon. This kind of tree appears only here in Tanakh. This Kikayon is probably the Ricinus Communis, a bushlike kind of tree, fastgrowing with big shady leaves.[289] In Greek and in Koptic this plant is called *Kiki*, hence the probable relation with *Kikayon*.[290]

However, more important than the question after the kind of tree is the question why God disposes this Kikayon for Jonah. The first reason the text mentions: "To make it occur a shadow over his head." But that reason doesn't really solve the question, because in the previous verse Jonah had already built a tabernacle in which shadow he'd sat down. The second reason the text mentions: "To draw him away from his anger." That gives more clues. Jonah celebrates his Feast of Tabernacles, the festival of freedom. But Nineveh still exists, so it isn't an undivided joy for Jonah to celebrate this festival with. He sits in his *sukkah*, his tabernacle, but for him it's not a real festival, because he's angry. And that when the Feast of Tabernacles is a festival of joy, pre-eminently![291] If Jonah can't muster up joy, God Himself will help him to celebrate the festival as it should be done. But at the same time, the Holy One, blessed be He, has something else in mind. That's why we have to follow up the Kikayon in the rest of the story.

And (then) Jonah rejoices. This sudden reversal in Jonah's state of mind can be declared in one way only. Jonah, who after his angry argument with God (Jonah 4:2-4) has stubbornly left the city to watch whether it still would be swept from the face of the earth, is now suddenly "blessed" by God with a shady tree. For Jonah this can't mean anything else than that God tries to approach him again. Is God trying to return to Jonah and his ideas about Nineveh? Does God realize on further consideration that Jonah – perhaps – could be right? Jonah can't but understand the appearance of the Kikayon in this way!

To draw him away. Hebrew: *lêhatsil*. In the sense of 'to withdraw from captivity or need' this verb can also mean 'to save' or 'to liberate'. In Hebrew there is a clear alliteration with the word *tseil* (shadow), although both words derive from different roots.

A joy (very) big. Only now, when it looks as if God is going to agree with him yet, Jonah celebrates his Feast of Tabernacles in the right mood. After the more serious festivals like Rosh Hashanah (Jewish New Year) and Yom Kippur (Day of Atonement), which fall in the first half of the month of Tishri, Sukkoth (Feast of Tabernacles) is in the second half of that month pre-eminently a festival of joy. The theme of joy occurs regularly in the Bible already, when the Feast of Tabernacles is mentioned (Leviticus 23:40; Deuteronomy 16:14-15; 2 Chronicles 7:10; Nehemiah 8:18). The same is the case in later writings like the pseudepigraphic *Book of Jubilees*, in which the Feast of Tabernacles and joy are inextricably bound up with each other.[292] Flavius Josephus too, the Jewish historian from the end of the 1st century CE, mentions that Ezra requested the people not to shed tears of emotion during the Feast of Tabernacles, because it was a festival during which one wasn't allowed to cry, indeed it was even forbidden![293] This theme occurs in the Midrash as well:[294]

> "Three times joy is mentioned with reference to the festival [of the Feast of Tabernacles]: 'You shall rejoice in your feast' (Deuteronomy 16:14); 'So that you will be altogether joyful' (Deuteronomy 16:15); 'And you shall rejoice before the LORD, your God, seven days' (Leviticus 23:40). However, one won't be able to find even one mention of joy with regards to Pesach (Passover). Why? Because on Pesach one can't know yet the result of one's harvest. And there's but one mention of joy with regards to Shavuoth (Feast of Weeks): 'Then you shall keep the Feast of Weeks […], and you shall rejoice' (Deuteronomy 16:10-11). Why? Because the crops [have then been harvested] and collected […]. But with regards to Sukkoth, when the crop and fruits from the trees had been stocked up [and atonement for one's sins had been brought about at Yom Kippur], joy is mentioned three times."

The climax of the joy of Sukkoth occurs even on the day after the feast: Simchat Torah or Rejoicing of the Law. This day – on which the reading of the Torah is ended at Deuteronomy 33 and is begun again at Genesis 1 – has even the word 'joy' in its name. Whether this day was already celebrated as such in the Persian time, is not clear, but initiatives could already have existed even then.

The joy with which Jonah will be able now to celebrate the Feast of Tabernacles is probably not only caused by the fact that God – by making the Kikayon grow for Jonah – seems to have converted to Jonah's ideas. There's another aspect involved for Jonah: that he can still expect the destruction of Nineveh (Persia) and thus the definitive liberation of Israel. Does that make his joy to a 'joy (very) big'?

Jonah 4:7

> And (then) prepares this God a worm when comes up the twilight the (next) morning. And it strikes the Kikayon and it withers.

A Worm. A worm is an unclean animal, usually connected with death and decay (Exodus 16:20; Deuteronomy 28:39; Isaiah 14:11; 66:24).

When comes up the twilight the (next) morning. This moment of the day is the very right moment for the destruction of Nineveh. Sodom and Gomorrah have been destroyed at dawn (Genesis 19:15, 23-24). The same goes for the fall of Jericho (Joshua 6:15). In both stories and in this Jonah story as well the word *hashachar* ('dawn') is used. So this should be Jonah's moment of "truth". Now it'll indeed turn out whether God has chosen his side or not.

And it strikes the Kikayon and it withers. However, instead of Nineveh God destroys the Kikayon. Nowhere in the Book of Jonah it's clearer than here that the Kikayon is a symbol of Nineveh. The parallel Nineveh-Kikayon (in Hebrew there is a certain alliteration: Ni-Neveh – Ki-Ka-jon) is once more underlined by Adonai Himself in his final speech (see Jonah 4:10-11).[295] So the image of the worm means in fact: God is certainly able to destroy – as Jonah wishes – Nineveh, but He doesn't use His power! He is the God who has used the Kikayon (Nineveh-Persia) for its shadow over Jonah's (Israël's) head. And He's also the God who'll decide when and where this situation should end. As long as Adonai is concerned about Nineveh, so long Jonah shouldn't want to conquer high-handedly this city with both his tabernacle and all his freedom. It's an argument completely in line with the books of Ezra and Nehemiah with their favourable attitude towards the Persian empire.

Jonah 4:8

> And it occurs when up rises the sun. And (then) prepares God a wind from the east, a piercing (one). And (then) strikes the sun on the head of Jonah and he becomes faint and he requests his soul to die and he says: "Good (is) my death over my life."

A wind from the east, a piercing (one). When the east wind is mentioned, the so-called Sirocco or Chamsin could be thought of,[296] from the wilderness, notorious for its scorching heat (see e.g. Genesis 41:6, 23, 27; Ezekiel 17:10; 19:12). That's why this wind can be a symbol of vanity and uselessness, and of the feebleness it causes (Job 15:2). It can be part of the fate of the wicked person (Job 27:21). Besides, the east wind or the scorching wind is often a symbol of the heat of the wrath of God, either towards Israel or towards the nations.[a] Here in Jonah 4:8 the word *ru'ach* is used for 'wind', which is often translated with 'spirit' or – if it's about the *ru'ach* of Adonai, with 'holy spirit'. So one could also translate with: "And God prepared the spirit from the east, piercing." And indeed, one could consider here the spirit of God as shown in a verse like Hosea 13:15, where the scorching wind, which will hit Efraim, is called "the east wind, the wind (or *ru'ach*) from Adonai, from the wilderness."

This east wind, sent by God, is not only a destructive force. Sometimes, when used against Israel's enemies, it's also a saving force. For it is the east wind that at sea causes the ships from Tarsis and Tyrus to break up into pieces and to wreck (Ezekiel 27:26; Psalm 48:8). This is (also) an image that is of importance to the Jonah story. It reminds us of the big wind in Jonah 1 which almost wrecks the ship in which Jonah sails and which prevents the oarsmen to take it ashore (Jonah 1:4, 13). It was an offshore wind[297] and so it must have been an east wind off the coast of the land of Israel! Furthermore we see that this big wind forced Jonah to go through the reedy waters of the realm of the dead (the Sheol), and once more we end up at the story of Israel's exodus from Egypt.[298] And incidentally, in Exodus 14:21 it's the east wind that blows a path for Israel through the waters of the Sea of Reeds (Red Sea), that is a way through the violence of the nations. But that wind will irrevocably turn against Israel and against Jonah if they only want to be delivered for the sake of themselves.

And (then) strikes the sun. During the heat of the day – especially when an east wind is blowing – there is a very real danger of a sunstroke. Such a sunstroke can result in death or apparent death (2 Kings 4:18-20; Judit 8:2-3). One of the comforting images used to

---

a   Exodus 10:13; Isaiah 27:8; Jeremiah 4:11; 18:17; Habakkuk 1:9; Psalm 11:6.

describe Israel's return from exile is that "the sun shall not strike" those who will return (Isaiah 49:10; Psalm 121:6).

He requests his soul. It's remarkable that Jonah in Jonah 4:3 asks Adonai to be allowed to die, when here he asks his own soul or breath of life to be allowed to die. This alludes to the fact that, anyway, he's understood that God won't allow him this "favour." Trying to return the responsibility for one's own life to God is a human habit as old as mankind. Already Adam reproached God that He'd given him such a badly performing wife (Genesis 3:12). Elijah too wished to give God back the responsibility for his life and his task as a prophet with an appeal to the shortcomings of his ancestors (1Koningen 19:4).[299] So Jonah has now reached the point that he understands that this God wouldn't allow this to happen. As in Jonah 1:12 when God wasn't there to give Him back the responsibility, Jonah now accepts the responsibility for his own life. But] what motivates him?

To die. The wish to die is confirmed by Jonah once more and explicitly so with the words: "Good (is) my death over my life." Now that it has become quite clear that God won't meet this longing, the question should be asked after the motives on the basis of which Jonah came to this longing and this saying. It could be that he'd once more withdraw from his task by running away, not across the sea – the lid on the realm of the dead (the Sheol) – as in Jonah 1:3, but into death straight away. He has, however, no clear assignment left to fulfil as in Jonah 1:1-2. It's also possible that he's realized having acted in the wrong way, and now condemns himself to death! Such self-condemnations and the execution of the sentence, occur a couple of times in Tanakh (2 Samuel 17:23; 1 Kings 16:18).[a] Jonah has already once condemned himself before (in Jonah 1:12). Here it would have been the second time for him to do so. But it's doubtful yet, because he's performed his assignment and apart from his anger about the rescue of Nineveh he hasn't done much blameworthy. What other motive can be involved yet?

---

[a] Judas' suicide (Matthew 27:5) can be considered as such too.

Annotations to Jonah 4

Jonah 4:9

> And (then) says God to Jonah: "Is it good that it burns to you because of the Kikayon?" And he says: "It is good that it burns to me towards my death."

That it burns to you because of the Kikayon. Here we find the answer to the question we asked in the previous verse. It doesn't 'burn' to Jonah because of the insight that his ideas would be wrong, but it burns to him because of the Kikayon. His longing for death only originates from self-pity now. That's the sad fate of anyone who watches himself fail because of an improper concept of the social, political and religious reality and who doesn't manage to turn around to a better insight. The fact remains that apparently Jonah doesn't want to accept any responsibility yet for Nineveh and for the world. Not Jonah is responsible for the fate of the Kikayon, the fate of Nineveh and the fate of the world, but the Kikayon, Nineveh and the world are responsible for the fate of Jonah, or so he seems to think. When God explains very clearly that Jonah, in doing so, puts His creation upside down, he pines away with self-pity. And it's as if the author puts the words "It is good that it burns to me towards my death" in his mouth with a hidden meaning: This Jonah, he'd better die! But even now God's patience with Jonah isn't at its end, yet.

Jonah 4:10

> And (then) says Adonai: "You, you have pity on the Kikayon for which not (at all) you have laboured, and (which) not (at all) you have caused to become big, which (like) a son of the night it has occured, and (like) a son of the night it has perished.

You have pity. The same Hebrew verb occurs also in other places in Tanakh. A quick comparison of the mentioned texts shows that many translations are possible.[a] Generally speaking it appears that it always

---

[a] Genesis 45:11; Deuteronomy 7:16; 13:8; 19:13, 21; 25:12; 1 Samuel 24:11; Isaiah 13:18; Jeremiah 13:14; 21:7; Ezekiel 5:11; 7:4; 8:18; 9:5, 10; 16:5; 20:17; 24:14; Joel 2:17; Psalm 72:13.

means something like "to sympathize with distress and care." Sometimes God refuses to sympathize with distress (Jeremiah 13:14). But also a refusal to sympathize assumes the possibility to sympathize indeed.

Jonah 4:11

> And I, (would)n't I have pity on Nineveh, that city, the big one, in which (there are) more than sixscore thousand humans that do not know (what is) between their right hand and their left hand, and (also) beasts, (very) many?"

Sixscore thousand. For 'twelve' the text literally reads 'two and ten'. When the author of the Book of Jonah want to show somewhere how the fate of Israel and Nineveh are interwoven, then it should be here: the size of the city is described with a multiple of twelve, the number of the tribes of Israel. Concern for the fates of Israel and Nineveh should go hand in hand. In the days of Jonah it's the concern for the fate of the Persian empire, as I argued before repeatedly. But not only Ninevites live in Nineveh, and not only Persians in the Persian empire.

Humans. Here only the singular 'human' is used in fact, derived from the verbal stem A-D-M with the etymon "to be red" or "to become red". The word *admati* in Jonah 4:2, 'my soil' has also been derived from this verbal stem. The connection between 'red' and 'soil' refers to the reddish colour of the soil in the land of Israel. So in Hebrew man lives on the soil. Remarkably the word *adam* is used here and not the word *ish* ('man'), indicating a direct link with the stories of the creation and paradise. In God's eye the population of Nineveh is a symbol of all humankind.

Between their right hand and their left hand. The right side is according to Ecclesiastes 10:2 the side of a wise man, but a fool's heart (is) at his left (KJV). God is at man's right hand to stand by him (Isaiah 41:13; 45:1; 63:12; Psalm 16:8; 73:23; 109:31; 110:5). The place at God's right hand is the place of honour (Psalm 110:5).[a] That's why the right-

---

[a] See also Mark 10:37, 40; 12:36; 14:62; 16:19; Matthew 20:21, 23; 22:44; 26:64; Luke 20:42; Acts 2:34.

eous ones are on God's right hand (see e.g. Matthew 25:32-33). The left hand conversely is often linked with foolishness and evil. It's remarkable that being left-handed is described as a disability in Judges 3: That's why the non-righteous ones are on God's left hand (see e.g. Matthew 25:32, 41). This means that we could translate this with: "People who don't know the difference between good and evil." But how could they know this when the only person who can teach them is only interested in his own fate? What fate lies ahead of Israel and the world when God's prophets are more concerned about themselves and about being in the right with their sermons than about their assignment in that world?

And (also) beasts, (very) many. And if you won't do it because of the people, well do it because of the innocent cattle!

10 What shall we do to you?
Updating the Book of Jonah

In this last chapter I'll discuss a number of questions dealing with the update of the Book of Jonah in our days. For just like the writer of Jonah who brought the then historical figure of Jonah up to date in his own religious and political surroundings, so we could try to bring the story up to date for our own ends at the beginning of the 21st century. It might be possible in the form of a contemporary story, but it won't be easy. Who should be the central figure? And to which city in which country he or she should be sent and with what message? I won't present such a story here! After all, as modern Westerners who are more used to follow abstract discussions than to read a story as an argument of which we have to decipher the message from among the literary images. Bringing a Bible story today up to date could also be done by describing its tenor and by showing how this tenor could be applied in our own world.

In the first place it must be said that bringing a Bible story up to date – or its message – won't lead to an unambiguous idea or perspective of actions. Bible stories can be brought up to date in all kinds of fields and in all kinds of ways. Let's take the Jonah story for instance. It can be brought up to date in the liturgical field by reading it in the synagogue each year in the afternoon service of Yom Kippur. Or in the church by reading it each year on the Sunday after Yom Kippur. Then our thoughts can be concentrated around the fact that reconciliation with each other and God is not only a matter to pursue for ourselves, but that we're also obliged to offer our fellow men the chance to turn back from an improper way of life – suppose they still have a modicum of morality.

However, there's also the possibility to update the meaning of the Book of Jonah in a social and political field. Then what does it mean that Jonah "is sent to a land of war"? Should we take that pacifistically? Should we set off for the country of our worst enemies and take to the streets calling out peacefully for a change? After all, everyone knows there is a huge chance to be arrested, tortured, locked up or even executed!

Updating the Book of Jonah

If we want to apply the meaning of the Book of Jonah in our own days, we'd better not rely on our superficial impressions of it. We'll have to proceed carefully. In the first place we'll have to research the circumstances in the days of the writer of the Bible book and to try to work out which questions he's trying to find an answer to with his story. Next we'll have to see and gather his answer to those questions from the Bible story. After that an investigation will follow into the circumstances which we live in and according to which they agree and differ with the circumstances of those days. Only then after this comparison has been made, it can be worked out whether Jonah's message is applicable in our time and if so in which respect and in which measure. But there's something else to take into account.

Bible stories were written by Israelites and for Israelites, by Jews and for Jews. With regard to the Book of Jonah it can also be said: By and for Jews in the 5th or the 4th century BC. The book gives Jewish answers to Jewish questions. Who unlinks the Bible story from its Jewish context, runs the risk to derive an unbiblical answer to an unbiblical question. This is what happened in Christianity for ages on end, not only with the stories from the Hebrew Bible, but even with many a story from the Gospels.[300] Therefore Bible stories can only be updated in line with their original meaning if and when they are explained and applied within the entire biblical frame of thought and action. They presuppose an ethical attitude which fits in with the image of man in the Torah.[301] That too belongs to the historical circumstances the Jonah story originated from, and that's exactly what is often lacking in our circumstances of today. After all, Christianity, the most cognate religion with Judaism, has explained the Hebrew Bible already for ages with the help of quite another hermeneutic framework than was and is used in Judaism. This means that for an as reliably possible update of the Book of Jonah, we'll have to include the Torah and the prophets in a way we could learn from the Talmud and the Midrash, the oral Torah of Judaism.

In this book I have shown that the Book of Jonah – in the light of the biblical-Jewish tradition and against the background of its time – can be read as a message to the Jews of the 5th and 4th century BC not to be willing to shake off the Persian empire in which they lived, at the cost of much violence and in favour of the free Greek world, but to assist this empire in improving itself ethically. Which lessons can we derive from it for our situation now? The Persian empire – with all its faults – was an empire which in general relied on political ethics which accepted the defeated nations as they were. It was an empire in which was thought about notions of good and evil. In which defeated nations weren't massacred, but involved in governing the empire. Something could be improved in such an empire! So the message of the Book of Jonah was about a power the defeated nations could have come to an agreement with, and about forms of cooperation by far to be preferred to a permanent situation of rebellion.

Now in the first place an interesting question arises whether to this intent of the Book of Jonah any consequences can be connected with regard to Judaism and the state of Israel nowadays. Therefore I'd like to say that the situation in which the biggest part of the Jewish people has been for ages on end, bears a resemblance to Jonah's stay in Nineveh. From the Babylonian exile (589-538 BC) a big part of the Jews has lived against its wishes in the diaspora. The extent of Judaism in the 1st century CE is even explained from the many non-Jews who, because of their contacts with Jews everywhere in the world, felt attracted by Judaism and converted. So "Jonah in the diaspora" has brought quite a lot of non-Jews to the Torah in all those centuries. After the destruction of Jerusalem by the Romans in the year 70 CE, that process went into quite another direction owing to the rise of Christianity and later of the Islam. Anyway, these two religions are both strongly influenced by the Judaism of the 1st and 7th century respectively. This can be considered an unintended "Jonah-effect." Proselytism, however, almost disappeared since then, because both shoots of the trunk of the so-called Abrahamic religions have, in fact, the conversion of non-Jews to Judaism made almost impossible. Since then Judaism has delivered – in spite of persecution and discrimination – its peaceful and positive contributions to the surrounding cultures along other roads. Those were the roads of philosophy, law, science, literature, art and folklore. For Christianity Judaism has even been the proverbial thorn in the theological flesh for ages: many heretical movements in Christian Europe have been influenced by Judaism. Nowadays a theological change occurs in many churches under the influence of the increased knowledge about Judaism and of the Jewish origin of Christianity.[302] In the end one can say that the Judaism of the diaspora has all the more realized its "Jonah-assignment" and it still continues to do so.

What now is the "part of Jonah" played by the State of Israel and can still play in the world around us. In the first place I'd like to say that Israel is a democratic country where freedoms prevail which are considered of utmost importance. This can't be said of the Arab states surrounding Israel. In a democratic country each individual citizen is equal to the State principally. This is the case in Israel, albeit that the inhabitants of the occupied territories aren't Israeli citizens. The Arabian culture by contrast is a tribal culture in which the position of the citizens is determined by the group to which they belong: the family (high or low), the tribe (big or small, powerful or dependent), the ethnic group (Arabs, Persians, Turkish, etc.) and Islamic movement (Sunnites, Shiites, etc). What's more, the great majority would rather like to see Israel disappear than to live in peace with it. The threat of Islamic inspired terror is continuously present in Israel. Generally the difference in culture with the surrounding states and groups of population is so big that one could wonder whether there is a sufficient ethical basis anno 2018 which can be influenced positively by Israel.[303] Therefore, from Jonah going to Ramallah, Riad, Damascus, Bagdad or Teheran cannot much be expected anno 2018. And it's perfectly understandable that the population of Israel because of its safety dare not give the Palestinian territories full self-rule – however sad the situation is for both parties.

There's another course however, along which the state of Israel fulfils its "part of Jonah" in the world, a course not known by many people, unfortunately. Knowledge and science is shared with the world. When big disasters occur assistance is rendered, but also on a small scale by treatment of Arabian patients in Israeli hospitals. One works together with other countries in agrarian development projects. A treaty is made with Jordan about the mutual water supply and to save the Dead Sea from dehydration. Israel sets a good example to its neighbouring countries of how a democratic state shares its power with its citizens in all fields of society. Corrupt politicians and Israeli extremists who make assaults on Palestinians, are prosecuted and judged. One is receptive to positive peace proposals which acknowledge the state of Israel, which renounce violence against its population and institutions and which offer solutions for safe and permanent borders. Today that is in my opinion the "Jonah-part" played by Israel in the hope that someday a Palestinian or Arabic leader will stand up to lead the Middle East once more on the path of peace. After all, the 2018 Middle East looks more like the historical Nineveh of Assyria – the land of war – than like the symbolic Nineveh of the Persian empire of which something good could be expected rather than something bad. Between the Assyria of the historical prophet Jonah (8th century BC) and the Persia of the literary prophet Jonah (5th century BC) were 300 years. I sincerely hope that by the presence of Israel the pacification and the democratization of the Middle East will keep us waiting less longer.

Finally some thoughts about the "part of Jonah" Christians today could play in the world. In my view there is little sense in considering this without recognizing the Torah as the constitution of the world. Jesus too, his first disciples and the evangelists accepted after all the Torah as their guide in life and their teaching.[304] Within such an attitude a favourable approach of other denominations and nations can certainly be derived from the Book of Jonah. But first we must convince ourselves that the political, social and religious relationships within their societies are based on an ethical attitude susceptible to dialogue and a change for the better. If not, the Book of Jonah has little to offer us. Jonah needn't have gone to the Berlin of Nazi Germany. He would have been murdered in one of the many extermination camps of the Third Reich. And anno 2015 Jonah shouldn't try to go at all to the town of Raqqa of the Islamic State in Syria and Iraq. For the eyes of the world – on video – he would have been beheaded. But to the Persepolis of the 5th century, and to the Rome of the 1st century CE[305] Jonah could have safely made a journey in the hope of finding a public and political morality somewhat susceptible to ethical improvement in the spirit of the Torah. And what about a trip to The Hague, Brussels, Rome, Washington, Moskow, Beijing, Ankara, Brasilia, Pretoria, New Delhi or Canberra? You needn't think of "street corner preaching". There are so many, more modern and certainly not only religious approaches imaginable as a Torah-oriented Christian to contribute to the improvement of the personal, social and political ethics of all our capitals, their nations and societies. That is in my view a possible update of the Book of Jonah today.

Appendix 1 – Word stems and their translation

Table A.1

Translations of words/word stems used twice or more in the Book of Jonah and their frequency in the separate chapters. (Jonah 2a = Jonah 2:1-2 and 11; Jonah 2b = Jonah 2:3-10, both in (the) Hebrew (numeration).

English	Stam	Jona 1	Jona 2 a	Jona 2 b	Jona 3	Jona 4	Totaal
Adonai	H-J-H	11	3	4	2	6	26
Amitai / (to trust)	A-M-N	1			1		2
(to be) Angry / Anger	A-N-P				1	1	2
Beasts	B-H-M				2	1	3
Better / (to be good)	J-T-B					3	3
(to be) Big	G-D-L	6	1		4	4	15
to Burn	Ch-R-H				1	4	5
to Call	Q-R-A	3		1	5		9
to Calm	Sj-Th-Q	2					2
to Cast	N-P-L	2					3
City	---	1			3	4	8
to Come Up / to Go Up	Ng-L-H	1		1		2	4
Country	A-R-Ts	1		1			2
to Cover	K-S-H				2		2
to Cry Out	Z-Ng-Q	1			1		2
Day	J-W-M		1		3		4
to Die / Death	M-W-Th					4	4
to Do / to Make	Ng-S'-H	4			3	1	8
to Dry	J-B-Sj	2	1			1	4
Evil	R-Ng-Ng	3			3	4	10
Face	P-N-H	4					4
to Fear / to be afraid	J-R-A	6					6
Fish	D-G-H		4				4
to Flee	B-R-Ch	2		1		1	4
to Give	N-Th-N	2					2
to Go	H-L-K	4			4		8
to Go Down	J-R-D	3	1				4
to Go (In)To	B-W-A	3		1	1		5
God	A-L-H	4	1	1	6	5	17

APPENDIX 1

English	Stam	Jona 1	Jona 2 a	Jona 2 b	Jona 3	Jona 4	Totaal
(to be) Good	T-W-B					2	2
Head	R-A-Sj		1			2	3
(to be) Holy / Holiness	Q-D-Sj		2				2
Human / (to be red) / blood / soil	A-D-M	1			2	2	5
to Hurry	Q-D-M					3	3
Inside	M-Ng		2				2
Jonah	A-N-H	5	4		3	6	18
Kikayon	---					5	5
(to be) Kind	Ch-S-D		1			1	2
King	M-L-K				2		2
to Know	J-D-Ng	3			1	2	6
to Live	Ch-J-H		1			2	3
Lot	G-R-L	3					3
Man	A-J-Sj	3			1		4
Master	R-B-B	1				3	4
Men	A-N-Sj	4			1		5
Night	L-J-L		1			2	3
Nineveh	---	1			7	1	9
to Occur	H-J-H	2	1	4	2	5	10
to Pass	Ng-B-R	1		1	1		3
Path	D-R-K				2		2
People	Ng-M-M	2					2
to Perish	A-B-D	2			1	1	4
(to have) Pity	Ch-W-S					2	2
to Pray	P-L-L		1	1		1	3
to Prepare	M-N-H		1			3	4
to Promise	N-D-R	2		1			3
to Rejoice / Joy	S'-M-Ch					2	2
to Repent	N-Ch-M				2	1	3
to Rise Up	Q-W-M	3			3		6
Sackcloth	S'-Q-Q				3		3
to Sacrifice	Z-B-Ch	2		1			3
to Say	A-M-R	9	2	1	4	6	22
Sea	J-M	11		1			12
Second time	Sj-N-H				1	1	2
to See	R-A-H				1	1	2
Shadow	Ts-L-L					2	2
Ship	A-N-H	3					3
to Sit	J-Sj-B				1	2	3
to Sleep (deeply)	R-D-M	2					2

APPENDIX 1

English	Stam	Jona 1	Jona 2 a b	Jona 3	Jona 4	Totaal
Son	B-N-H	1			2	3
Soul	N-P-Sj	1	2		2	5
to Storm	S-Ng-R	4				4
to Strike	N-K-H				2	2
Sun	Sj-M-Sj				2	2
to Surround	S-B-B		2			2
to Take Up	N-S'-A	2				2
Tarsis	---	3			1	4
to Tast	T-Ng-M			2		2
to Tell	N-G-D	2	1			3
Temple	---			2		2
This	Z-H	6			1	7
Three	Sj-L-Sj		2	1		3
to Throw	T-W-L	4				4
To	Ng-D-H		1	1	4	6
to Turn around	Sj-W-B	1		4		5
Voice	Q-W-L		2			2
Water	M-J		1	1		2
What / Who(se)	M-H	9		2	1	12
Which / That	A-Sj-R	4	1	3	4	12
Wind	R-W-Ch	1			1	2
to Word	D-B-R	1		5	1	7
to Wreck	Sj-B-R	1	1			2

Appendix 2 – Literary relationship between the chapters

The text of this appendix was translated by the author.

The literary relationship between the different units of the text of the Book of Jonah can be inquired by the mutual use of Hebrew word stems. The Psalm of Jonah will be treated as the separated text unit Jonah 2b (Hebrew numbering 2:3-10) because of its deviating literary character. The framing verses will be pointed to as Jonah 2a (2:1-2 and 11). In the tables the real and the 'in case of independence' expected numbers of common word stems are rendered for every pair of text units. The difference between these two numbers tells us something about the literary relationship between both text units. For more explanation and some critical remarks: see beneath table A.2.4.

Tabel A.2.1
Absolute and relative numbers of word stems for each text unit
(in total 168 word stems are found in the Book of Jonah).

Text units	Numbers of word stems	Relative numbers
Jonah 1	75	45%
Jonah 2a	15	9%
Jonah 2b	60	36%
Jonah 3	60	36%
Jonah 4	70	42%

Tabel A.2.2
Numbers of common word stems of each pair of text units (= x).

Text units	Jonah 1	Jonah 2a	Jonah 2b	Jonah 3	Jonah 4
Jonah 1		6	17	25	24
Jonah 2a	6		4	7	9
Jonah 2b	17	4		9	13
Jonah 3	25	7	9		22
Jonah 4	24	9	13	22	

Appendix 2

Tabel A.2.3

Expected numbers of common word stems of each pair of text units in case of independent use of word stems in each of both text units separately (= y).

Tekst units	Jonah 1	Jonah 2a	Jonah 2b	Jonah 3	Jonah 4
Jonah 1		7	27	27	32
Jonah 2a	7		5	5	6
Jonah 2b	27	5		22	25
Jonah 3	25	5	22		25
Jonah 4	32	6	25	25	

Tabel A.2.4

Differences (z) between real (x) and expected (y) numbers of common word stems of each pair of text units (z = x - y).

Tekst units	Jonah 1	Jonah 2a	Jonah 2b	Jonah 3	Jonah 4
Jonha 1		-1	-10	-2	-8
Jonah 2a	-1		-1	+1	+3
Jonah 2b	-10	-1		-13	-12
Jonah 3	-2	+1	-13		-3
Jonah 4	-8	+3	-12	-3	

Explanation

Suppose that the author of the Book of Jonah could only choose word stems from the 168 word stems that are now actually found in his book, then the following reasoning could be set up: If the use of word stems in one of the text units would be statistically independent of that in another text unit then one might expect for example that about 9% of the 75 word stems that are found in Jonah 1, would be found also in Jonah 2a (= about 7 word stems); contrary one would expect that about 45% of the 15 word stems that are found in Jonah 2a (= likewise about 7 word stems) would be also found in Jonah 1. In this way one could calculate the number of common word stems of each pair of text units in case of statistically independent use of word stems in both units of each pair. The difference (z) between the real number of common word stems (x) and the expected number in case of literary independence (y) is possible an indication for the literary relationship between the several parts of the Book of Jonah. If this difference is strongly negative (–) it indicates a low literary relationship between the two text units. If the difference is strongly positive (+) it indicates a high literary relationship. The results in table A.2.4 show clearly that Jonah 2b (the Psalm of Jonah) deviates strongly from Jonah 1, 3 and 4 with respect to the use of word stems. Furthermore it is remarkable that Jonah 1 and Jonah 4 also show a relatively weak relationship with respect of the use of word stems. Contrary Jonah 2a (the frame of the Psalm) and Jonah 4 show a relatively strong relationship on account of the use of word stems. However, two critical remarks must be made about this line of reasoning and its results.

First of all in the foregoing argument it has been presupposed that the author of the Book of Jonah could have selected the word stems for the individual text units only from the 168 word stems that we can now find in his book. In reality he could have chosen from all word stems which belonged to the Hebrew language of his time. If we presuppose for example that he could have chosen from 500 word stems, then Jonah 1 contains only 15% of all the word stems he had available, and Jonah 2b (the Psalm of Jonah) only 12%. In that case the expected number of common word stems of Jonah 1 and Jonah 2b would have been 15% of 60 or 12% of 75, that is to say 9 word stems instead of the 27 in table A.2.3. The difference between the real and the expected number $(x - y)$ would then have been +8 instead of –10. In this case we'll find a positive literary relationship between all text units of the Book of Jonah with respect to the use of word stems.

A second annotation could be as follows. In the foregoing argument it has been presupposed that all word stems would have had an equal chance to be chosen for use. In reality this isn't true. For example the word stem 'to say' (A-M-R) occurs much more often in stories than the word stem 'to word' (D-B-R). This means that much more artificially statistical methods would be necessary to inquire the literary relationship between Biblical text units with respect to the use of word stems. Nonetheless the numbers in table A.2.4 are remarkable because they seem to sustain the insight obtained along a non-statistical road that the literary relationship between Jonah 2b (the Psalm) and the rest of the Book of Jonah is problematic.

Notes

1. Tanakh. Jewish Publication Society, Philadelphia 2003 - 5764.
2. See also: Cohn, 1969, p. 91.
3. See e.g. Wolff, 1975, p. 61.
4. Cohn, 1969, p. 65, 66.
5. Fretheim, 1977, p. 43. In this comparison only the adjective is involved.
6. Wolff, 1975, p. 34.
7. Cohn, 1969, p. 68, 69. Van der Woude (1978, p. 22) gives an example in Jonah 1:4 translated by me as "reckons to be wrecked."
8. Van der Woude, 1978, p. 42.
9. E. J., Jonah.
10. Cohn, 1969, p. 48, 93, 94; Wolff, 1975, p. 61.
11. De Buck, 1941, p. 173 ff.
12. Magonet, 1976, p. 43.
13. A point of view rejected by Van der Woude, 1978, p. 30.
14. Bickerman (1967, p. 12) thinks that the psalm was already circulating under the name of Jonah. Van der Woude (1978, p. 36) also thinks that the author of the Book of Jonah could not possibly have composed the psalm.
15. Wolff (1975, p. 62) even thinks that one shouldn't burden the Book of Jonah with the exegesis of this psalm!
16. See for instance section 4.5.
17. Fretheim, 1977, p. 79. Elsewhere such structures are called 'ring compositions'; see e.g. Bal a.o., 1984, p. 50.
18. Fretheim, 1977, p. 61.
19. Licht, 1978, p. 19.
20. Ginsberg, 1974, p. 114.
21. Wolff, 1975, p. 36.
22. Fretheim, 1977, p. 72.
23. Maier, 1979, p. 26, additionally mentions the next definitions from the exegetical literature: "Moralische Dichtung, Fabel, lehrende Fabel, historische Mythos, Lehrdichtung, Parabel, Heiligenlegende, Legende, kunstvol ausgebaute Sage, kindlich-gemütvolle märchenhafte Form, Märchen, Seemannsgarn."
24. Hausdorff, 1984, p. 23.
25. bT Megillah 31a.
26. See section 2.5.
27. P.R.E., Ed. Friedlander, p. 65, nt. 2.
28. P.R.E. 10.
29. See Rashi on Genesis 10:12.
30. Weinreb, 1970, p. 165.

31 Weinreb, 1970, p. 132.
32 P.R.E. 10.
33 See e.g. Keller, 1965, p. 331.
34 pT Sukka V 55a; Midrash Psalms 36:7. This tradition is the background of Luke 7:11-17 (see: Riet, 2012, section 6.8.c).
35 Scherman and Zlotowitz, 1978, p. xxiv.
36 Genesis Rabbah XXI 5.
37 P.R.E. 10; Seder Olam XVIII.
38 Scherman and Zlotowitz, 1978, p. xxv.
39 Scherman and Zlotowitz, 1978, p. xxv.
40 Scherman and Zlotowitz, 1978, p. xxvi.
41 Van 't Riet, 2005, p. 43 e.v.
42 E.B. Mac., lemma: Nineveh.
43 B.H.W., lemma: Babylonië en Assyrië.
44 See for the above mentioned data: Maier, 1979, p.23 ff. That one could decide on the historicity of the Book of Jonah by virtue of the fact that this historical lee in the Assyrian power links up with the situation as drawn in the story of Jonah seems to me all too easy. Even in the case the author of the Book of Jonah linked up with this idea, it doesn't alter the fact that he could have written a 'historical novella', looking at his own days long after the historical Jonah.
45 Scene on the "Black Obelisk", London, British Museum.
46 Scene on the "Black Obelisk", London, British Museum.
47 Toynbee, 1961, p. 72.
48 Toynbee, 1961, p. 73, 74.
49 In his book *Jerusalem, the Biography* (London 2011, p. 43) Simon Sebag Montefiore uses, with regard to this historical phenomenon, the beautiful image: "The (Assyrian) empire resembled a shark that could survive only by constant consumption."
50 Toynbee, 1961, p. 76.
51 Toynbee, 1961, p. 77-81.
52 Plastercast, British Museum, London.
53 Contenau, 1979, p. 147.
54 Contenau, 1979, p. 148.
55 Contenau, 1979, p. 150.
56 Contenau, 1979, p. 149. Scholars differ of opinion with regard to the first year of Sargon II's government: 724 BCE according to Contenau, 1979, p. 149; 722 BCE according to B.H.W., lemma: Sargon; 721 BCE according to E.B. Mac, lemma: Mesopotamia and Iraq, History of.
57 Contenau, 1979, p. 151-153.
58 Relief from the palace of Ashurbanipal in Nineveh.
59 Relief from the palace of Ashurbanipal in Nineveh.

60 Toynbee, 1961, p. 82.
61 Rashi on Genesis 10:8.
62 Van 't Riet, 2012, e-book edition, p. 103.
63 Translation: The Complete Jewish Bible (Stern, 1998).
64 Genesis Rabbah XVI 4.
65 Krauss, 1966, Volume II, p. 128.
66 See also: B.H.W., lemma: Duif; E.B. Mic, lemma: Pigeon, domestic.
67 Dittmar, sa, passim.
68 Chorus, 1969, p. 37.
69 bT Berachot 53b; bT Sanhedrin 95a.
70 Genesis Rabba I, 15.2.
71 Song of Songs Rabba II, 14.1.
72 P.R.E. 28.
73 The in my view best opinion in this and cognate discussions about the so-called original and secondary tradition is found in: Vermes, 1983, p. 156, nt. 42.
74 E.J., lemma: Turtle dove.
75 P.R.E., Ed. Friedlander, p. 67, note 10.
76 See also: Baron, 1952, Vol. I, p. 155-158.
77 See e.g. Maier, 1979, p. 27.
78 Mekhilta Exodus 19:2.
79 An exception to this is – perhaps – the in Matthew mentioned group of Pharisees, however this has not been representative for the Pharisees in general, let alone Judaism.
80 See: *Luke the Jew*, Van 't Riet, 2012, p. 18.
81 The following information has been derived from: E.J., lemma: Proselytes, k. 1185-1186.
82 Licht, 1978, p. 121.
83 See section 3.1.
84 bT Sanhedrin 89b.
85 bT Sanhedrin 89a.
86 This section is a further development and addition of the article by Zalman Shazar in *Dor le Dor VII*, nr 1, 1978, p. 1ff.
87 bT Megillah 31a.
88 See section 4.1.
89 jT Sukkah 5:1.
90 bT Megillah 31a.
91 At least in a one-year cycle of readings of the Torah. The Book of Jonah seems indeed to come from circles in which the one-year cycle was used and not a three-year cycle, as the sequel of this section shows.
92 Section 3.2.
93 Casson, 1964, p. 56.

94   Although the authors of the Book of Jonah didn't know the Book of Esther (yet), this link need not be based on coincidence. It's even probable that the Book of Esther was only written when in certain Jewish circles the feast of Purim had already been celebrated for some generations and that throwing the *pur* had played a part in one way or another in the genesis of the Purim feast. In that case Esther is a reflection on or an actualization of an existing, older feast. The Babylonian origin of the names of Mordechai and Esther (B.H.W., lemma: Purim), and the Assyrian-Babylonian origin of the word *pur* seems to indicate that. This also doesn't rule out that in the Book of Esther parallels can be pointed out with the Persian New Year's feast (B.H.W., lemma: Purim). The dating of the Book of Jonah in the Persian era, which I'll go into in section 5.1, fits well in with it.
95   Such an 'addition' is also probable in the case of the tabernacle in Jonah 4:5 in connection with the Feast of Tabernacles (see section 4.5.d).
96   Mishnah Ta'anit 1:1-2.
97   PRE 10; Ginzberg, 1968, Vol. IV, p. 248.
98   PRE 10; Ginzberg, 1968, Vol. VI, p. 350, nt. 31.
99   P.R.E. 46; see also: E.J., lemma: Elul.
100 See e.g.: Wolff, 1975, p. 44, nt. 55; Van der Woude, 1978, p. 56 and p. 132, nt. 20.
101 See section 3.2.
102 See section 4.1.
103 E.B. Mic., lemma: Nineveh.
104 E.J., lemma: Jonah, k. 173.
105 E.J., lemma: Jonah, k. 173.
106 B.H.W., lemma: Ninevé.
107 Ginsberg, 1974, p. 114; Van der Woude, 1978, p. 10.
108 E.J., lemma: Jonah, k. 173.
109 Van der Woude, 1978, p. 23.
110 Wolff, 1975, p. 66.
111 Van der Woude, 1978, p. 24.
112 Wolff, 1975, p. 66.
113 Gesenius, 1962, p. 867.
114 E.J., lemma: Jonah, k. 173.
115 Van der Woude, 1978, p. 57.
116 E.J., lemma: Jonah, k. 173.
117 Van der Woude, 1978, p. 25.
118 E.J., lemma: Jonah, k. 173.
119 See also Herodotus 3:31; Van der Woude, 1978, p. 48.
120 Ginsberg, 1974, p. 114.
121 Cohen, 1960, p. 411.

122 The facts of/in this paragraph have been derived from: E.B.Mac., lemma Iran, History of.
123 The facts of/in this paragraph have been derived from: B.H.W., lemma's: Babylonië en Assyrië; Jojakim; Jojakin; Sedekia.
124 The facts of/in this paragraph have been derived from: E.B.Mac., lemma: Iran, History of.
125 See the previous section.
126 The following paragraph is a further elaboration of what can be found in section 6.4 of my book *Luke the Jew* (e-book edition: Van 't Riet, 2012).
127 Sections 4.1, 4.5 en 5.2.
128 The facts in this section have been derived mainly from: E.B. Mac., lemma: Greco-Persian Wars, and: Iran, History of.
129 Casson, 1964, p. 94.
130 E.J., lemma: Persia.
131 E.J., lemma: Persia.
132 E.J., lemma: Persia.
133 E.J., lemma: Persia.
134 Tcherikover, 1975, p. 40-41.
135 Noth, 1966, p. 310-311.
136 Tcherikover, 1975, p. 41.
137 Tcherikover, 1975, p. 41.
138 E.J., lemma: Coins and currency.
139 B.H.W., lemma: Munten (en gewichten).
140 Tcherikover, 1975, p. 41.
141 Gilbert, 1969, p. 10.
142 E.J., lemma: Persia.
143 See also section 5.1.
144 See also section 3.2.
145 B.H.W., lemma: Jafet(h).
146 E.J., lemma: Greece.
147 B.H.W., lemma: Javan.
148 E.B. Mic., lemma: Tartessus. B.H.W., lemma: Tarsis.
149 Bean, 1966, p. 119; Casson, 1964, p. 105.
150 Wolff, 1975, p. 20 ff.
151 E.B. Mic., lemma: Perseus.
152 Tcherikover, 1975, p. 41; Wolff, 1975, p. 26. E.J., lemma: Jaffa, considers it probable that the roots of this connection can already be found in the 12th century BCE.
153 Wolff, 1975, p. 26.
154 Such arguments can be found with: Cohn, 1969, p. 78 ff.; Wolff, 1975, p. 20 ff.; Maier, 1979, p. 19 ff.
155 E.B. Mac., lemma: Iran, History of.

Notes

156 E.B. Mac., lemma: Iran, History of.
157 See for this expression Section 2.4
158 E.B. Mac., lemma: Cyrus the Great, of Persia.
159 E.B. Mac., lemma: Creco-Persian Wars.
160 See e.g. Lamb, 1961, p. 16.
161 Lamb, 1961, p. 133.
162 E.B. Mac., lemma: Iran, History of.
163 E.B. Mac., lemma: Zoroaster.
164 E.B. Mac., lemma: Iran, History of.
165 E.B. Mac., lemma: Creco-Persian Wars.
166 E.B. Mac., lemma: Iran, History of.
167 Noth, 1966, p. 273.
168 Noth, 1966, p. 275 e.v.
169 E.B. Mac., lemma: Iran, History of.
170 See e.g.: Van 't Riet, 2012, section 1.2.
171 Van der Woude, 1978, p. 16.
172 Van der Woude, 1978, p. 16.
173 Scherman & Zlotowitz, 1978, p. 79. Moreover, see the annotations to Jonah 1:2, lemma: *For*.
174 Genesis Rabbah XVI:4.
175 Rav Awraham Ibn Ezra (1089-1164) observes: "Jonah didn't have to foretell the destruction of Nineveh, but only 'that up comes their evil.'" See: Scherman en Zlotowitz, 1978, p. 80.
176 See section 5.2.
177 Section 4.5.a.
178 Section 5.3.
179 Cohn, 1969, p. 12.
180 Jos. Ant. IX.108.
181 See the annotations to Jonah 2:3 under *Out of the belly of Sheol*.
182 See section 5.3.
183 See e.g. M. Baba Batra III.2.
184 See Psalms 24:2; bT Erubin 22b. Compare also Herodotus' *Histories* II.21, 23; IV.8,36. However Herodotus himself rejects this idea about the ocean.
185 Zuidema, 1986, p. 47.
186 Strack & Billerbeck, 1969, Vol. II, p. 311.
187 See Section 4.5.a.
188 Barnard & Van 't Riet, 1984, p. 107.
189 E.J., lemma: Jaffa.
190 B.H.W., lemma: Jafo, Joppe.
191 E.J., lemma: Jaffa.
192 See sections 3.2 and 5.3.

193 See Section 5.3.
194 Van der Woude, 1978, p. 20.
195 Casson, 1964, p. 92 ff.
196 bT Nedarim 38b. See also: Ginzberg, 1968, Vol. IV, p. 247; Vol. VI, p. 349, footnote 28.
197 Casson, 1964, p. 119-120, 143.
198 M. Baba Bathra III.2.
199 Genesis Rabbah XXIV.4; Leviticus Rabbah XV.1; Ecclesiastes Rabbah 1.6.1; P.R.E. 10. The same image occurs in Mark 4:36-37 and in Acts 2:2.
200 See the annotations to Jonah 1:3 lemma: *Away from the face of Adonai*.
201 P.R.E. 10.
202 Gesenius, 1962; Jastrow, 1982.
203 Genesis Rabbah XXXIX.11.
204 See also the annotations to Jonah 1:3 lemma: *The fare thereof*.
205 See also the annotations to Jonah 1:6 lemma: *The wares that were in the ship*
206 P.R.E. 10.
207 P.R.E., Ed. Friedlander, p. 67, note 10.
208 Cf. the annotations on Jonah 1:12 lemma: And the sea will be calm unto you.
209 See Section 2.4.
210 See also the annotations on Jonah 1:3 lemma: And he goes down.
211 See also: Van der Woude, 1978, p. 23.
212 See also the commentary on Jonah 1:5, lemma: *The mariners*.
213 M. Yoma 2:1-2. Translated from English to: E.J., lemma: Lots.
214 E.J., lemma: Lots.
215 See Section 4.5.a.
216 Van der Woude, 1978, p. 24.
217 E.g. the Bible translation into Dutch of the *Dutch Bible Society* (1951) as well as the *Groot Nieuws Bijbel* ("Great News Bible") published in Dutch in 1983 by the *Dutch Bible Society* and the Dutch *Catholic Bible Foundation*. Even the latest Dutch *New Bible Translation* (2004) contains this error.
218 bT Sanhedrin 43b.
219 Van der Woude, 1978, p. 24.
220 See the commentary on Jonah 1:7, lemma: *For whose cause*.
221 Baron, 1952, Vol. I, p. 9.
222 Poppers, 1984.
223 See the comments on Jonah 1:5, lemma: *Each man to his god*.
224 Id.
225 Id.: *And then they fear*
226 See the comments on Jonah 1:9, lemma: *A Hebrew (man)(am) I*.

227 See the notes on Jonah 1:5, lemma: *Each man to his God.*
228 M. Sanhedrin 10:5.
229 bT Sanhedrin 89a.
230 See the notes on Jonah 1:3, lemma: *The fare thereof.*
231 See the further notes on Jonah 2:6, lemma: *To (my) soul.*
232 P.R.E. 10.
233 See Section 4.5.a.
234 The Septuagint translates 'ordered' ('commanded').
235 P.R.E. 10; Genesis Rabbah 5:5; bT Bechoroth 8a.
236 See also the end of section 5.2.
237 P.R.E. 10.
238 See section 4.2 and 5.2.
239 See section 5.4 and the commentary on Jonah 1:2, lemma: *Nineveh.*
240 E.J., lemma: Nineveh.
241 See section 5.3 and the commentary on Jonah 1:3, lemma: *Jafo.*
242 Wolff, 1975, p. 24.
243 Van der Woude, 1978, p. 33.
244 Safrai, 1976, p. 784.
245 Barnard & Van 't Riet, 1984, p. 50; Van 't Riet, 2009, section 4.6.
246 bT Erubin 19a.
247 Mekilta Beshallach 4.
248 bT Joma 75a.
249 Hausdorff, 1984, p. XI.
250 See section 3.5.
251 Van der Woude, 1978, p. 36.
252 See section 4.5.a and the commentary on Jonah 1:3, at : *Away from the face of Adonai.*
253 Strack & Billerbeck, 1969, Vol. II, p. 311.
254 See the commentary on Jonah 1:3, at: *And down he goes.*
255 In *Reading Torah, the Key to the Gospels* (Van 't Riet, 2012, p. 19-20) I discussed the concept of *olam* more extensive. Buber-Rosenzweig translates in German *Weltzeit*. In my view the aspect of time is stressed a bit too much here.
256 See section 3.5.
257 See section 5.4 and the commentary on Jonah 1:2, lemma: *Nineveh.*
258 Scherman en Zlotowitz, 1978, p. 79.
259 See section 4.4.
260 See also the commentary on Jonah 1:3, lemma: *To flee.*
261 Scherman en Zlotowitz, 1978, p. xxvii ff.
262 See section 4.4.
263 See also: Barnard en Van 't Riet, 1986, p. 120.
264 P.R.E. 10; Ginzberg, 1968, vol VI, p. 350, nt. 31. See also section 4.5.c.

Notes

265 See also the commentary on Jonah 1:2, lemma: *For*, and on Jonah 1:11.
266 bT Sanhedrin 89b. See also: Scherman en Zlotowitz, 1978, p. 121-122; Cohn, 1969, p. 17.
267 See the commentary on Jonah 1:1, lemma: *Adonai*.
268 Ginsberg, 1974, p. 116.
269 See section 5.1.
270 Van der Woude, 1978, p. 48.
271 See section 5.1.
272 The Greek historian Herodotus mentions that the Persian soldiers in the war against the Greeks in about 480 BC at the death of Masistius, the captain of the Persian cavalry, shaved their heads and cut their horses' and their mules' manes. (Herodotus IX 24).
273 See section 1.1.
274 See the comments on Jonah 3:6, lemma: *His garment*.
275 Scherman en Zlotowitz, 1978, p. 81.
276 Scherman en Zlotowitz, 1978, p. 81.
277 Mesorah Jona XXXV.
278 bT Berachot 7a. Rabbi Zutra bar Tobia lived in Babylon around 270 CE. Rab (or Rav) is Rabbi Abba Arikha (who died around 247 CE). He was one of the most authotitative rabbis.
279 M Ta'anit 2:1; bT Ta'anit 16a; Pesikta Kahana 28:3.
280 Genesis Rabba 44.12; Ecclesiastes Rabba 5.6.1.
281 See the commentary on Jonah 3:4, lemma: *Be overthrown*.
282 Scherman en Zlotowitz, 1978, p. xxx-xxxii.
283 P.R.E. 10.
284 This is the High German (Ashkenazi) *haftarah*. The Portuguese one is a bit shorter: 1 Kings 18:20-39.
285 See also the commentary on Jonah 1:12 and 13.
286 See for additional commentary at Jonah 4:7.
287 Hausdorff, 1984, p. 232.
288 See for both designations for God the commentary to Jonah 1:1, lemma: *Adonai*.
289 Van der Woude, 1978, p. 57.
290 E.J., lemma: *Castor-oil plant*.
291 See below: *A joy (very) big*.
292 Goodman, 1973, p. 13.
293 Goodman, 1973, p. 17.
294 Goodman, 1973, p. 43-44.
295 If only because of this it is incomprehensible that some commentaries deny this parallel (see e.g. Cohn, 1969, p.87).
296 Beek, 1969, p. 228; Van der Woude, 1978, p. 58.

NOTES

[297] See the commentary on Jonah 1:13, lemma: *And not (at all) they could (do it)*.
[298] See the commentary on Jonah 2:6, lemma: *Weeds*.
[299] See also the commentary on Jonah 4:3, lemma: *For good (is) my death*.
[300] See for two examples: Van 't Riet, 2012.
[301] See for the image of man in the Torah: Van 't Riet, 2006/2014.
[302] See Chapter 7 of my book "Reading Torah, the Key to the Gospels" (Van 't Riet, 2010).
[303] An exception to this are only the Kurds, probably.
[304] Barnard & Van 't Riet, 1986; Van 't Riet, 2010.
[305] See my explanation of the Acts of the Apostles in particularly Chapter 10 of *Luke the Jew* (Van 't Riet, 2009/2012).

Literature

Abbreviations:

B.H.W. Bijbels-Historisch Woordenboek, Deel 1 t/m 6, B. Reicke, L. Rost (Red.), Utrecht/Antwerpen, 1969.
E.B. Mac. Encyclopaedia Britannica, Macropaedia, 15the edition, Chicago etc., 1979.
E.B. Mic. Idem, Micropaedia.
E.J. Encyclopaedia Judaica, Jeruzalem, 1972.
J.P. The Jewish People in the First Century, S. Safrai, M. Stern (Ed.), Assen/Amsterdam, 1976.
N.I.W. Nieuw Israelietisch Weekblad, Amsterdam.
P.R.E. Pirke de Rabbi Eliezer, Ed. G. Friedlander, New York, 1970.

Dutch Literature

Bal, M., Dijk Hemmes, F. van, Ginneken, G. van, *En Sara in haar tent lachte, Patriarchaat en verzet in bijbelverhalen*, Utrecht, 1984.
Barnard, W.J., Riet, P. van 't, *Lukas de Jood, Een joodse inleiding op het evangelie van Lukas en de Handelingen der Apostelen*, Kampen, 1984.
Barnard, W.J., Riet, P. van 't, *Zonder Tora leest niemand wel, Bouwstenen voor een leeswijze van de evangeliën gebaseerd op Tenach en joodse traditie*, Kampen, 1986.
Beek, M.A., *Wegen en voetsporen van het Oude Testament*, 6e druk, Amsterdam/Driebergen, 1969.
Boon, R., *De joodse wortels van de christelijke eredienst*, Amsterdam, 1973.
Buck, A. de, Psalm 107, Godsdiensthistorisch bezien, *Vox Theologica 12*, nr. 6, Assen, juli 1941, p. 173-181.
Casson, L., *Scheepvaart in de Oudheid*, Utrecht/Antwerpen, 1964.
Chorus, A., *Het denkende dier*, Leiden, 1969.
Contenau, G., *Zo leefden de Babyloniërs en Assyriërs ten tijde van Nebukadnezar*, Baarn, 1979.
Dasberg, I., *Gebeden voor de Verzoendag*, Amsterdam, 1983 (2 delen).
Hausdorff, D., *Jom Jom*, 4e druk, Nederlands-Israëlietisch Kerkgenootschap, 1984.
Jona, Een vertaling om voor te lezen, Amsterdam/Boxtel, 1977.
Lamb, H., *Alexander de Grote*, Antwerpen, 1961.
Naastepad, Th.J.M., *Jona, Verklaring van een Bijbelgedeelte*, Kampen, z.j.
Polak, G.I., Polak, M.S., *Gebeden der Nederlandsche Israëliten voor den Verzoendag*, Amsterdam, 1851.

Poppers, M.M., Tot inkeer komen om te blijven leven, *N.I.W.*, 5 oktober 1984, p. 6.
Rasjie's Pentateuch-Commentaar, Vertaling: A.S. Onderwijzer, Nederlands-Israëlietisch Kerkgenootschap, Amsterdam, 1977.
Reisel, M., *Genesis, Transcriptie, verklaring, vertaling*, Den Haag, 1966.
Riet, P. van 't, *Het mensbeeld van de Tora*, Kampen, 2006.
Riet, P. van 't, *Lukas de Jood*, Zwolle, 3ᵉ Herziene uitgave, Zwolle, 2009.
Riet, P. van 't, *Zonder Tora leest niemand wel*, 2ᵉ Herziene uitgave, Zwolle, 2010.
Riet, P. van 't, Twee sjabbatsverhalen van Lukas de Jood, *Folianti-reeks 31*, Zwolle. 2012.
Tijn, M. van, Nicolai, D., *Belofte en catastrofe, De code van het Oude Testament gebroken*, Bloemendaal, 1977.
Toynbee, A., *Oorlog en Beschaving*, Amsterdam, 1961.
Woude, A.S. van der, *De prediking van het Oude Testament, Jona, Nahum*, Nijkerk, 1978.
Zuidema, W., *Op zoek naar Tora, Verkenningen in de rabbijnse traditie*, Baarn, 1986.

English literature

Baron, S.W., *A social and religious history of the Jews, Vol. I, To the beginning of the christian era*, New York/Philadelphia, 1952.
Bean, G.E., *Aegean Turkey, An archaeological guide*, Londen, 1966.
Bickerman, E., *Four strange books of the Bible*, New York, 1967.
Cohen, M.J., *Pathways through the Bible*, Second Edition, Philadelphia, 1960.
Fretheim, T.E., *The message of Jonah*, Minneapolis, Minnesota, 1977.
Gilbert, M., *Jewish History Atlas*, Londen, 1969.
Ginsberg, H.L., *The five megilloth and Jonah*, Second Edition, Philadelphia, 1974.
Ginzberg, L., *The legends of the Jews, Deel I t/m VII*, Philadelphia, 1968.
Goodman, P., *The Sukkot and Simchat Torah Anthology*, Philadelphia, 1973.
Jastrow, M., *Dictionary of the Targumim, Talmud Babli, Yerushalmi and Midrashic Literature*, New York, 1982.
Licht, J., *Story telling in the Bible*, Jeruzalem, 1978.
Magonet, J., *Form and Meaning, Studies in literary techniques in the Book of Jonah*, Bern/Frankfurt, 1976.
Safrai, S., Home and Family, in: *J.P.*, Sect. I, Vol. II, 1976, p. 728-792.
Scherman, N., Zlotowitz, M., *The twelve prophets: Yonah, A new translation with a commentary anthologized from talmudic and rabbinic sources*, New York, 1978.
Shazar, Z., Jonah : Transition from Seer to Prophet, *Dor le Dor VII*, nr. 1, 1978, p. 1-8.

Tcherikover, V., *Hellenistic Civilization and the Jews*, New York, 1975.
Vermes, G., *Jesus and the World of Judaism*, Londen, 1983.

French literature

Keller, C.A., Jonas, Le portrait d'un prophète, *Theologische Zeitschrift 21*, Basel, 1965, p. 329-340.

German literature

Buber, M., Rosenzweig, F., *Bücher der Kündung*, Keulen, 1958.
Cohn, G.H., *Das Buch Jona im Lichte der biblischen Erzählkunst*, Assen, 1969.
Dittmar, H., *Symbol der Sehnsucht Aller*, Düsseldorf, z.j.
Gesenius, W., *Hebräisches und Aramäisches Handwörterbuch*, 17. Auflage, Berlijn/Göttingen/Heidelberg, 1962.
Krauss, S., *Talmudische Archäologie*, Hildesheim, 1966.
Maier, G., Der Prophet Jona, *Wuppertaler Studienbibel*, Wuppertal, 1979.
Noth, M., *Geschichte Israels*, 6e Auflage, Göttingen, 1966.
Strack, H.L., Billerbeck, P., *Kommentar zum Neuen Testament aus Talmud und Midrasch*, 2. Band, München, 1969.
Weinreb, F., *Das Buch Jonah, Der Sinn des Buches Jonah nach der altjüdischen Überlieferung*, Zürich, 1970.
Wolff, H.W., *Studien zum Jonabuch*, Neukirchen, 1975.

About the author

Dr. S.P. (Peter) van 't Riet (1948) studied mathematics and psychology at the Free University of Amsterdam and wrote his thesis on an educational-psychological subject. He was successively a teacher of mathematics at a school for secundary education, teacher of the didactics of mathematics at the Technical University of Delft, manager at the Teacher Training Centre of Zwolle, director and professor at the Windesheim University of Zwolle.

Since the seventies he has studied the Judaism of the first centuries as well as the Jewish exegesis of the Bible, especially the Jewish character of the New Testament. He published the following titles in Dutch (the first four together with his fellow-author Will J. Barnard):

- Luke, the Jew (1984)
- Reading Tora, the Key to the Gospels (1986)
- As a Dove to the Land of Assur (1988)
- Catching the Coat-tail of a Jewish Man (1989)
- The Gospel from the Study-house of Lazarus (1996)
- Luke, the Jew (2e revised edition, 1997)
- Christianity à la Jesus (2001)
- Luke versus Matthew (2005)
- The Image of Man in the Torah (2006)
- The Philosophy of the Creation-story (2008)
- Luke, the Jew (3e revised edition, 2009)
- Reading Tora, the Key to the Gospels (2e revised edition, 2010)

In 2012 two English translation were published as e-books: *Reading Tora, the Key to the Gospels* and *Luke, the Jew*, in 2014 followed by *The Image of Man in the Tora* and in 2018 by *A Dove to the Land of War*. More information about these and other publications of the author can be found on his website: www.petervantriet.nl.

www.ingramcontent.com/pod-product-compliance
Lightning Source LLC
Chambersburg PA
CBHW070656100426
42735CB00039B/2163